In Love and Anger

IN LOVE
AND ANGER

A View of the 'Sixties

ANDREW SINCLAIR

SINCLAIR-STEVENSON

To the innocent ones,
TIMON and MERLIN,
who will create their world

First published in Great Britain 1994
by Sinclair-Stevenson
an imprint of Reed Consumer Books Ltd
Michelin House, 81 Fulham Road, London SW3 6RB
and Auckland, Melbourne, Singapore and Toronto

A CIP catalogue record for this title
is available from the British Library
ISBN 1 85619 386 1

Phototypeset by Intype, London
Printed and bound in Great Britain
by Mackays of Chatham plc, Chatham, Kent

Contents

Illustrations

Acknowledgements

The author and publishers would like to thank all the writers, publishers and literary representatives who have given permission for reprinting quoted material. In some instances it has been difficult to track down copyright holders and the publishers will be glad to make good any omissions in future editions. Works that have been quoted from are listed below, in alphabetical order of the writer.

Sixty-Eight: The Year of the Barricades by David Caute, by kind permission of Weidenfeld & Nicolson. *Permissive Britain* by Christie Davies, by kind permission of Pitman Publishing. *The Times They Are A Changin'* by Bob Dylan, © 1963, 1964 Warner Brothers Music; copyright renewed © 1991 by Special Writer Music. Lawrence Ferlinghetti: *Starting from San Francisco*, Copyright © 1968 Lawrence Ferlinghetti; *Endless Life*, Copyright © 1978 Lawrence Ferlinghetti. Both reprinted by permission of New Directions Publishing. *Thanks for Coming* by Jim Haynes, by kind permission of Faber & Faber. *God Bless the Child* sung by Billie Holiday, lyrics reproduced by kind permission of Carlin Music Corporation. *Revolution*, words and music by John Lennon and Paul McCartney: © Copyright 1968 by Northern Songs, produced by permission of Music Sales Limited. *Peyote* by Michael McClure, by kind permission of the poet. 'To Whom it May Concern' by Adrian Mitchell, from *Adrian Mitchell's Greatest Hits*, published by Bloodaxe. 'How To Kill Cuba' by Adrian Mitchell, from *For Beauty Douglas: Collected Poems 1953–79*, published by Alison & Busby. *Letter to My Fellow Countrymen* by John Osborne, by kind permission of Faber & Faber. *Party-Goers* by Brian Patten by kind permission of HarperCollins Publishers.

1

THE SOFT ESTABLISHMENT

Men do not become what by nature they are meant to be, but what society makes them. The generous feelings, and high propensities of the soul are, as it were, shrunk up, seared, violently wrenched, and amputated, to fit us for our intercourse with the world, something in the manner that beggars maim and mutilate their children, to make them fit for their future situation in life.

WILLIAM HAZLITT, *Essays*

It was a time between times. It was not a war and not a peace, but a cold war. It was not a recovery and not a recession, but a restoration and a rest. It was not prosperity and not poverty, merely the illfare state. It was not so much the time of clubs or of pubs, more of coffee bars. And so, between the champagne and the warm beer, the grounds collected at the bottom of the cup; from them fortunes might be read. It was not the time of Rolls-Royces or of bicycles, rather of motor scooters. There was a median of things, a meridian and a miasma. Yet it was hardly the golden mean of the ancient Greek philosophers, the correct balance for feeling and action in the midst of extremes. It was the waiting-room at the railway station, the pause over tea and currant buns before the next train came. It was the queue at the post office to pick up the undelivered parcel from persons and points unknown. A dull expectancy pervaded the middle 'fifties. It was a time to see through.

Everything could still be faced without losing too much, even at the ending of an empire. Débutantes danced to the dated music of Tommy Kinsman, and the street gangs dressed exactly like Edwardian gentlemen. The rise of the teddy boys appeared to prove that the lower classes were back to aping their betters. These narrow-trousered dandies who coshed and robbed were as proud of their plumage as any aristocratic Mohock who had terrorized Georgian London. The spiv with his flash and criminal ways was gone, the war of the classes was apparently dying out as secretaries began to dress like ladies and thugs like Brigade of Guards officers. The welfare state seemed to have blunted the worst edges of poverty and inequality, and the Tories were too wise to scrap it for the old class conflict that might destroy their chosen strategy of levelling up rather than breaking down. There were nasty bush wars in Kenya and Malaya and Cyprus, troubles in Iran and Egypt, but really, even Rome had never changed its empire so decently from control to commonwealth with so few skirmishes abroad and so firm a truce at home. In this strange interlude of convalescence from a great war and of patriotic complacency everything seemed to be ticking over all right, as long as nobody looked too far ahead.

I was still wearing blinkers, fresh from national service and only twenty years old, up at Trinity, Cambridge University to read history – a process that I was living, of which I knew nothing.

My father was a Colonial Police officer at a time when the colonies were out of date, and their guardians seemed to be species of Tyrannosaurus Rex with truncheons. I had been a King's Scholar at Eton College, and, although my education had been free because of the munificence of King Henry the Sixth of blessed memory, my provenance was privileged. It did no good that the headmaster had said after I left the room on delivering my last piece to the Essay Society, 'Oh dear, I fear we have George Orwell with us again.' Appearances were all. It was useless to state that I had earned my own school fees since the age of thirteen. I seemed to come from the Establishment. The fact that I had done my national service performing public duties in London for the Coldstream Guards was also a fatal distinction. I had not expected to pass the stringent requirements for that particular military entry, and I had been accepted by the Somaliland Scouts, where I had wished to speak Swahili and play Rimbaud in khaki. I have always plunged recklessly into the future like any highlander, and Somalia might well have proved as destructive to my late adolescence as Belgravia. But, instead, I was supplied with a visa that enabled me to become a writer and take a choice that could be called moral.

Particularly during the late 'fifties and the 'sixties, the state did not interfere much in our private lives, except by imposing national service. And, had it not intervened in my own, I doubt if I would have written much or well. Just as the prospect of death unconscionably clears the mind, so the call-up to commit a political murder marshals the intelligence system – in my case, rather late. I was in Florence that sticky summer of 1956, sharing a flat with two friends at the end of my first year at Cambridge – the last gasp of the tradition of long vacations in Italy that dated from the Grand Tour and the fading tutelage of Bernard Berenson and Harold Acton. A brown envelope arrived, forwarded from my borrowed room in a London flat. I was on the Army Reserve and had been recalled to serve because of a crisis at the Suez Canal, commandeered by a certain Colonel Nasser. I should have reported back to Pirbright Camp ten days earlier. I was officially a deserter.

I went to the consulate, and wrote about it shortly after the occasion, although I am no longer sure that a contemporary account is more accurate than hindsight. There is often too much immediate justification in the record of the now:

> They put us through to England remarkably quickly. I sat on the consular seat behind the consular desk. For the consul was so worried at my worry that he insisted on standing, although he was lame in one leg. Eventually, a familiar blah-blah voice, transmuted by a thousand miles of telephone wire into an intermittent travesty of the right accent, said,
> 'Hello. Regimental Adjutant speaking.'
> 'Lieutenant Sinclair reporting from Florence. I'm sorry I'm late, sir.'
> I found that I was shouting with fear and rage into the receiver. I also found that I was suddenly standing to attention, shaking, as if the lame-legged consul on the wrong side of the desk were the Regimental Adjutant himself, calling up Lt. Sinclair, A.A., for his sins against Standing Orders.
> 'Oh, is that you, Andrew, is that you? Nice to hear from you.'
> 'Yes, it's me. In Florence,' I yelled, wondering what on earth the Adjutant's Christian name was. I had forgotten, after a year's escape from national service to university, that covert discipline through overt familiarity was the

particular fetish of the regiment. That, eating with their hats on, and dying with their boots clean.

'Well, it's nice to hear from you. How's Florence?'

'It's all right,' I shouted. 'But you've called me up. I'm sorry I'm late. I'll be back in twenty-four hours.'

'Oh, please don't bother yourself now,' drawled the voice. 'I mean, it was a bit boring of you not turning up in time, so we called up someone else in your place this morning.'

'You mean I don't have to come home now?'

'Please yourself. That Arno country's rather too dusty this time of year, isn't it? I remember it as really quite unpleasantly warm when we liberated Florence in the last show.'

'You mean you don't want me after all?'

'Not at all, Andrew, not at all. But do in future please leave your right address at Headquarters when you go off jaunting on the continent. It really is a dreadful bore if we want you suddenly. So let us know where you are. And do have a lovely holiday, won't you?'

'Yes, sir . . . um . . . um . . . and thank you. Wish you were here.'

'So do I. But no such luck. I'm missing the grouse as it is. Such a bore. Well, thank you for telephoning. And good-bye.'

'Not at all. Good-bye.'

Relief had made me sit down again. I looked at the lame consul, who stood supported on one good leg and his stick, his bad leg hanging between as stiff as a whole dead man nailed on a tree . . .

If I still include that piece of overwriting, it is because Kenneth Tynan was right about first playwrights and first novelists. They dramatize their small lives and see themselves as Christ or Faust.

So, I had allowed somebody else to serve instead of me – actually a good friend of mine. I had shuffled away from responsibility into holiday. As I had not been reading the newspapers in Italy because I was ignorant of the language and too poor to buy the English press, I did not know what the situation at Suez really was. My crassness at Eton and in the Brigade of Guards had been scarcely dented by reading political philosophy at Cambridge, where I returned at the end of the summer.

As in many moral decisions, there was no immediate decision to be made. Only a small situation ending with a joke. The term was uneventful; quiet flowed the Cam. Then came the revolt in Budapest and the Israeli attack on Egypt, followed by the British and the French ultimatum. All work stopped at the university; fist-fights broke out in the streets; a Tory student even knocked down his supervisor. A friend of mine got drunk listening to the news bulletins, said he was bored with academic November, didn't want to write his weekly essay for the following day, and set off for Hungary from London Airport with ten pounds of penicillin in a package. 'Do what you can to stop me being sent down,' he said off-handedly to me and departed in an undergraduate odour of irresponsible sanctity and heroic unpreparedness, to spend three days wandering around the rubbled city and another three days in the cellar of the British embassy.

I had promised to follow, committed by the affected light-heartedness of my friend. I knew that my own name was top of the list for Reservists, who were to be called up next; I knew that my battalion was ready to move off to Suez at twenty-four hours' notice; I also knew that, by moral and political conviction, I should become a conscientious objector against this nonsensical revival of nineteenth-century gun-boat anti-woggery. Moreover, emotion for the underdog and denial of my own fear made Budapest the antidote to Ismalia. To fight in one war might excuse my refusal to fight in another. Courage might be the best refuge from cowardice.

I collected two casual rowing-men who wanted to go without a fuss, having too much money for the peace of their consciences or for any care about their university degrees. The fourth was a punch-drunk Old Etonian hero-figure, who walked home a hundred miles each holidays, assaulting invisible enemies all the way with rolling shoulders and fists flung out. Two old cars were found, and a quarter of a ton of Red Cross stores.

I interviewed the master of my college, my tutor and
my mother. I told them that my object was to set up a
refugee camp in Austria. I said nothing of going to
Budapest to fight. They told me that, if I went, too many
might follow. I replied correctly that other
undergraduates would only profit by my example to
remain behind. They said I would lose my scholarship,
my state grant and perhaps my place at the university;
they suggested I was seeking a quick emotional thrill
instead of accepting the long-term moral difficulty of
staying put. I replied that I would avoid a court martial,
a bad conscience and the breaking of trust with a friend;
I was making a practical decision and bringing practical
help. Master, tutor and mother were tacitly or explicitly
convinced by my conviction, as I myself was convicted out
of my own mouth.

I had arranged to meet the two cars and the stores in
London, after I had seen my mother for the last time.
Ten minutes before I was due to leave for Cambridge
station to catch the down train, I found a note in my
room, asking me to visit my history supervisor and so-
called moral tutor, Gallagher, in his room. I felt ridiculous
among the piled books in my army boots and government-
surplus flying-jacket.

'I'm going,' I said definitively, selling myself courage.
'It's too late to stop me now.'

'Have a drink,' Gallagher said.

'I can't. I'm going in five minutes.'

'Well, if you've made your mind up,' Gallagher said,
'there's nothing I can say. But I warn you, the last
sacrificial lambs all got killed in Spain. Only the English
poets weren't touched. Heroes are out of date.'

'Perhaps. But I've got to go now.'

'I see. But promise me one thing, will you? Ring me
up, before you leave England.'

'All right. If I can. Good-bye.'

Gallagher nodded his head and scowled. I took the
train to London, drinking tea in the dining-car, hardly
believing that I was implicated in the consequences of my
own professions and actions. I met my mother in the
buffet at the railway hotel in Victoria. She was the
daughter of a South African rancher, and she and I

firmly believed that she was always right. 'You can't go
now,' she said, 'something dreadful has happened in
the family.' She told me what it was. It was the perfect
alibi for cowardice, the strong ethical reason for running
away. 'If you go and get killed,' she said, 'I shall die too.'

If I took her at face-value, or as my mother, which she
was, I did not need to go to Hungary. The road back to
Cambridge was the harder road, hidden victory in
seeming defeat, family before friends. But if I took her
as an emotional woman, who had contradicted her
previous acceptance of my departure because of an
unlucky accident, I could still continue. Yet Suez looked
like being over in a week. America and Russia were
going to put an end to the whole sorry mess. I might not
even be called up [and, in fact, I would not be]. Perhaps
the entire hooha was an emotional pep-pill, as they had
all hinted. Perhaps this was not the occasion, nor I the
man. Perhaps this was another moral crisis which was only
a joke.

'I won't go,' I said. 'I'll go and tell them.'

'I'm sure it's all for the best, darling,' my mother said,
and I felt a guilty ease within me.

I went to meet the others. Four people were there,
loading stores into the two old cars. The hero-figure's
friend had driven down from Cambridge with him to
keep him company.

'I can't come,' I said. And I told them the reason.

'We quite understand,' they said. And they did not,
because it was only a reason, and it was not all the truth.
So I spoke my reason again more convincingly, and again
they said, 'We quite understand.'

'Well, I'd better go then,' said the hero-figure's friend,
gently and gaily, seeing only the simple problem and
the simple answer. 'Perhaps we might get in some winter
sports on the way back. Lucky my passport's in London.'

So I exchanged some boots and army clothes for a
sports jacket and a pair of flannels. And I handed over
some foreign money. And I said, 'I'll come and see you
off at Dover in the morning. I'm so sorry I'm not
coming.' And they looked at me and said, 'We're sorry
too, but we know you can't help it.'

I went to the flat of a friend, and telephoned Gallagher.

'I'm not going now,' I said. I was surprised at the flatness of my own voice, surprised into feeling that I was suffering at not going.

'Good,' Gallagher said. 'How do you feel about it?'

'Not too good.'

'Don't come back for two or three days, then,' Gallagher said. 'I'll fix it all up for you. Go and have a rest. All right?'

'All right. Thank you, sir. Good-bye.'

'Not at all. Good-bye.'

Gallagher had had twenty years' training as a don in not asking obvious questions. But other questioners were waiting for a return. Save Our Souls, Save Our Souls went the Budapest bulletins. But Saviour Sinclair only got as far as Dover the next morning on the workmen's train and a cheap ticket. There, the departure of the four and the two cars was put off for several hours by heavy seas. I talked desultorily. Then, suddenly, I could stand it no longer. For I looked from the pier to where the white cliffs of Dover fell into the sea. They were as white as the myth said. As white as the wings of the gulls flying above them. As white as a feather.

When I returned to Cambridge, I talked little to my friends of the event; and they, in their turn, were careful to respect my silence and my sensibilities. My enemies sneered at me as a half-cock Hemingway; but I put on a face for them and said, 'Hungary is about a hundred miles nearer Dover than Cambridge.' Sometimes, I summed up the whole matter, saying, 'The most courageous thing I ever did was to come back from Dover.' Sometimes, I coined a Gallicism, '*Le courage, c'est paraître un lâche.*' I even went to the lengths of writing an essay on the Twentieth-Century Hero. My theses were that nowadays a man's responsibility to others often made him a man without virtues to himself, and that this century of organization imposed a series of masks and roles on a man, who could only exist behind them as a mere draught.

Yet my acquaintances hurt me most in the first shame-faced week of my return. Loud and filling as double-decker buses in the narrows of Trinity Street, their voices would batter towards me, 'Hullo, thought you were in

Budapest.' While the misinformed understanding of my friends and the misplaced satisfaction of my enemies were tolerable, each time that I saw this immediate surprise at my home-coming, I remembered uneasily the ease of my not-going. My excuse was copper-bottomed; the actual way back seemed to be the moral way forward. Only somewhere in Buda someone had shrapnel in his guts and was dying, and someone else had a bullet in her back and was dead. While I sat in my armchair, practising a twisted grin to convince myself, and singing out of tune,

> 'Yes, we want no messiahs,
> We want no messiahs today . . .'

That was my self-conscious piece at the time about my moral crisis over Suez, when the state put its thumb on me and I tried to stand up to be counted and fell flat on my face. Yet my effort to be honest about the episode was dishonest. My sincerity was my snare. Over-dramatic and hyper-sensitive, soggy with principles and short on analysis, my explanation demonstrated the callow youth I was and thought I was not. Philip Larkin was not too wrong when he bought a copy of my first autobiographical comic novel, *The Breaking of Bumbo*, written while I was still an undergraduate at Cambridge. It was about a young Brigade of Guards officer who tries to lead a mutiny over Suez and is hoist by his own rhetoric and faints on parade and finally is taken into the Establishment. Larkin was to write in a letter: 'Today I bought *The Breaking of Bumbo* by Andrew Sinclair as a Boots' chuck-out – Good God, every "new young" writer I read seems worse than the last. John Braine – there couldn't be anyone worse than him. Oh yes, there could: John Osborne. And now Andrew Sinclair: soft-headed hysterical guardee. Like an upper-class John Wain . . . I've just got to James I's accession to the throne of England. He sounds a terrible *ass*, rather like Andrew Sinclair actually.' In spite of the reaction of the bilious Larkin, the novel was a great success. At the age of twenty-two I found myself second only to William Golding and *The Lord of the Flies* as the best-selling novelist for T. S. Eliot and the other editors at Faber and Faber. I was held to be a part of an odd phenomenon called the Angry Young Men, and I was one of the young among them.

The others seemed to me improbably old, thirty or more. And there was a fundamental difference between us. John Osborne's plays, *Look Back in Anger* and *The Entertainer*, glorified the class war at the kitchen sink and reviled the imperial dream that expired at Suez. Yet in his work and that of Larkin's friend, Kingsley Amis, and John Braine and John Wain, nostalgia bubbled in the pink bottle. Even then, I used to declare a difference of direction. I was trying to kick my way out, they were trying to kick their way in. Their radicalism and socialism were red rungs to be climbed on the way up the social ladder to a high Tory heaven. I was on the slippery Odessa steps down to a failed revolt at the end of the 'sixties, the débâcle of a whole generation, which would prove as ineffective as my own adolescent failure and Bumbo's capers at the last hurrah of Britain's Egyptian adventure.

For the Empire, from which I had come as a wild colonial boy to boarding schools in England, had broken up in 1956 or thereabouts. Its collapse had inverted Marx's declaration: history was now beginning in farce and ending in tragedy. The Duke of York had once marched ten thousand men to the top of a hill and had marched them down again – and children had been mocking him in nursery rhymes ever since. But what about Sir Anthony Eden, our tailor's dummy of a prime minister?

> The grand old Anthony Eden
> Had a hundred thousand men.
> He sailed them to the Suez Canal
> And he sailed them back again.

Satire was the weapon slipped into our hands to assault the Establishment and to incise the last tattoos on the twitching imperial corpse. Philosophically, logical positivism ruled the roost, and we were taught to destroy the meaning of country or glory by asking what they meant. The supreme Wittgenstein was still lecturing with a bleak wit as acute and rare as James Joyce's in *Finnegans Wake* or Samuel Beckett's in *Waiting for Godot,* two other piercing texts of that time. Personally I learned, more from one of Wittgenstein's thrusts than from anyone else, that we should never call ourselves a target: when somebody fired an arrow at us, he was usually aiming at another target – himself.

So, armoured against criticism by logic as well as the egocentric arrogance of the young, I secured a Double First in history by a long grind and dashed off a second novel about contemporary Cambridge, *My Friend Judas,* which proved to be almost as successful as the first one. Written in a private language that teetered between a parody of *The Catcher in the Rye* and *Pilgrim's Progress,* I found myself waved as the red flag of the upper middle classes. Young women wrote to me about fleeing their convent schools to liberty in the Fens, while young men consulted on how to escape national service without a court martial. I appeared to be the apostle of elegant mutiny. But, at Cambridge, I dressed *de rigueur* for the period in old corduroy trousers and thick wool polo-necked sweaters and scuffed black suede shoes, so rarely cleaned that I had to be hoovered before entering any drawingroom, which I hardly ever did. My reaction extended to diet and drink. I used to live on a daily egg, boiled in water I then used for my instant coffee; stale bread and tins of orange segments made up the fare. As for drink, I followed H. L. Mencken's remark about the Democrats, that they quaffed anything which burned and gave thanks to God.

That Spartan streak was not a product of the public school, but of the war. If anything marked my generation, it was the memory of rationing. The regulations of the state about food and black-outs and savings and scrapings were translated into a self-discipline, not into a rebellion. For we had lost our fathers and sometimes our mothers in the last Just War against fascism, the great Satan of the age. We had to grin and bear our own pain, too. At the age of eight, my gashed hand had been sewn up without anaesthetic by a doctor with a large curved needle and the command, 'Don't blub. They need the pain-killers for your fathers at the front.' I did not blub and learned never to show pain again. Such conditioning in childhood made my contemporaries seem rather formidable to the older generation which was ruling us so flabbily.

At our first assault, that generation was to roll over like an old dog to expose its dugs to be tickled by the points of our pen-knives. There was hardly any resistance. Our progress was far too easy for our own good. The 'fifties were waiting for the young Jack the Ripper. We were faced by the literature of gentlemen such as Evelyn Waugh and Henry Green and Graham Greene and Anthony Powell, and of ladies such as Ivy Compton-Burnett and Dame Edith Sitwell and Virginia Woolf. We confronted the artists who had become great in the war and had been paid to describe it, Henry Moore and Graham Sutherland and John Piper. We resisted that hangover from Shakespeare, the efflores-cence of the verse drama of T. S. Eliot and Christopher Fry and Ronald Duncan, and the finale of the boulevard comedy of Noël Coward and Terence Rattigan. In the cinema, we had lost the cutting edge of documentaries and films of the 'forties to the soft social comedies of Ealing Studios: Italian neo-realism had stolen our war horses as they had the four quadrupeds from Byzantium long ago set upon St. Mark's in Venice. The British Broadcasting Corporation had begun to teach a philistine country to become a musical nation over the grand gift of the airwaves. It transmitted spoken poetry for the first time since the miracle plays of the town guilds had reached a whole countryside; it was also to publicize the poems of 'The Movement'. But our inheritance in the arts was small and spotty, nurtured best at the older insti-tutions of learning where I was lucky enough to be at a time when it was easy to strike and tell.

At Cambridge, we were largely unconscious of the growing influence of The Movement, that group of poets centred on St. John's College at Oxford, which was, as John Wain wrote, 'united in homage to Larkin'. The Cambridge poet and literary critic Donald Davie, who wrote in 1952 the important *Purity of Diction in English Verse,* has pointed out that for the last fifty years each new generation of English poets was formed by lively under-graduates at Oxford and picked up its Cambridge recruits 'only afterwards, and incidentally'. The Movement derived from an earlier generation of undergraduates than ours, who had suffered rationing and later conscription during the Second World War, although Larkin himself was found unfit to serve in any command higher than a library opposite a cemetery. As he wrote of his conditioning, in his novel *Jill,* 'At an age when self-importance would have been normal, events cut us ruthlessly down to size.' The rationale of the group was first described by the literary editor of the *Spectator,* J. D. Scott: 'The Movement, as well as being anti-phoney, is anti-wet; sceptical, robust, ironic, prepared to be as uncomfortable as possible.' It did have two great influ-ences from Cambridge: F. R. Leavis and his critical magazine *Scrutiny,* with its call for rigorous analysis and severe anti-romanti-cism; and D. J. Enright, another poet and critic, who would edit a defining Movement anthology, *Poets of the 1950s,* containing poems by himself, Kingsley Amis, Robert Conquest, Donald Davie, Philip Larkin and John Wain. He omitted Thom Gunn, who had been an undergraduate at Trinity, Cambridge, and was held to be another contemporary recruit to The Movement from the Fens. 'I found I was in it before I knew it existed,' Gunn wrote of his joining of the so-called group. 'And I have a certain suspicion that it does *not* exist.'

It did exist, and, as most of its members made their living as critics and lecturers in English literature, the influence and opinions of The Movement – particularly from the pupils of Leavis at Cambridge – would come to dominate the pages of the reviews and small magazines of the 'sixties. The Movement was a consensus with areas of considerable agreement and interaction. As its historian Blake Morrison wrote, it was the most influential trend in England since the Imagists.

In the late 'fifties, however, it was not yet significant. For most of us at Cambridge, philosophy and logical positivism and the meaning of meaning were the fodder of our minds. Satire was

the wooden horse of our future entry into the new media that
were to ingest our lives. At my college there was another trinity
of the Johns rather than the dons; their surnames were Drum-
mond and Tusa and Tydeman. They were all to run programmes
and whole services in the British Broadcasting Corporation, the
leading educator of its age. Somehow they learned as young men
how to tiptoe through the corridors of power from the labyrinths
of the back alleys of Cambridge. I remember being clobbered as
the president of the Cambridge Musical Comedy Society: my
lyrical version of *Trilby* was replaced by some fandango by one of
the Johns and I was removed from office by an ex-Shell Oil
executive called Graeme MacDonald, also to be a power in the
Broadcasting Corporation before a fall from grace. Recalling this
coup, of which I was totally ignorant until I found myself demoted
to press officer after failing to attend a committee meeting to
which I had not been invited, a friend called Bob Wellings told
me that I was absolutely hopeless: 'You resembled a Don Quixote
with battered armour standing in the middle of a ploughed field
waving your sword at your enemies, who are several hedgerows
away.'

This early lesson in how bad I was at committees and at
influencing the right people did not deter me. I seemed to cause
offence pretty well wherever I went. Rereading the self-conscious
recollections of this time, entitled *My Oxford, My Cambridge,* I ran
across a piece by Eleanor Bron, whom I had always admired for
her brilliance as an actress and her beauty. But she did not
admire me. She agreed on the assumptions of Cambridge, but
not on my behaviour to the extraordinary designer, illustrator
and cartoonist Timothy Birdsall, with whom I shared a flat in
the town along with John Bird. Timothy Birdsall, alas, died of
leukaemia, a disease which we were then to ascribe to the overground testing of the atomic bomb. As Bron wrote of her
Cambridge:

> It may all have been ambition but if so it was adulterated
> by a lovely exuberance and a perhaps sneaking desire to

make things good and interesting and if possible enjoyable. There was an assumption, very arrogant, that if you were any good, things would happen. I think it's true too, since Cambridge is on my mind, that we felt able to make this assumption just because we were at Cambridge and not somewhere else. I remember being furious when Andrew Sinclair, back from London having had his first novel picked up by Faber, said very, very kindly to Timothy: 'I put in a good word for you, Timmy.' If Timothy thought about it at all it must have made him laugh but I was outraged – how dare he imagine, I thought, the great condescending oaf, that someone with Timothy's talent needed any spokesman?

I wonder now why we felt so arrogant and self-important, unlike Larkin and his peers, cut down to size by the events of war. Why did we feel we had the right to act out the opinions of our generation, as Eleanor Bron and John Bird and Jonathan Miller and the rest of the cast of *Beyond the Fringe* and *That Was The Week That Was* and *The Establishment* wanted to do? Or as Timothy Birdsall and Marc Boxer did in caricaturing the powers that were, a few decades before *Spitting Image?* Or as the gnomic and refined Michael Frayn did in his surreal sketches for the *Footlights?* Or the Angry Young Men among whom I was a minor Fury? Who chose us, or did we choose ourselves with the divine right of careless youth? Certainly, I was not given to introspection. If a door opened, I walked through it and blacked my eye. I had no sense of myself in time or place or priority, and I don't think my contemporaries had. As Eleanor Bron said, if you were any good, things would happen. The odd thing was, however, that we were generally bourgeois and educated, and things were meant to happen in the late 'fifties to the angry working classes and the popular arts. But briefly, in that time between times, we attacked the old assumptions without putting on the new. We were the heirs of an established past which allowed us to become the predators of the present.

Certainly, the other Angry Young Men had no doubt of their

importance and their right to address or mock the nation. Of the leading protestors, only Kingsley Amis refused to contribute his invective to the essays of the other young writers of the late 'fifties collected in a compendium, *Declaration.* His refusal was short and to the point: 'I hate all this pharisaical twittering about the "state of our civilisation" and I suspect anyone who wants to buttonhole me about "my rôle in society". This book is likely to prove a valuable addition to the cult of Solemn Young Man; I predict a great success for it.'

Amis was right enough. It was an effort to change the image of the Angry Young Men to the Solemn Young Men and to use their publicity to sell a lot of books – and twenty-five thousand copies were sold, in spite of bad reviews which saw in *Declaration* a discordant requiem to a brief phenomenon of protest. What damned the book was its incoherence and its vanity. Except for 'the small personal voice' of Doris Lessing, all the other contributors were expansive in their shrillness and their self-importance. They knew what they were against, but not what they were for. They did not doubt that they were prophets and sages, who had earned their right to play Jeremiah and Ezekiel to their society, although they were still mewling and puking in their experience. They were symptomatic of a brief period of maso-chism within an Establishment which had lost its nerve and almost broken down like the prime minister, Sir Anthony Eden, after the fiasco at Suez, and which appeared to welcome the whips and scorpions of the dissidents.

John Osborne confirmed his talent for scattershot spleen. His targets were obvious – the recent hydrogen-bomb explosion on Christmas Island in the game of nuclear cricket, a proof that the rulers were no longer funny or even dangerous, but murderous. Royalty was the gold filling in the mouth of decay. While the Cross represented values, the Crown represented a substitute for values. The crowds outside St. Peter's in Rome were taking part in a moral system, however detestable, but the mobs in the Mall were only attending 'the last circus of a civilization, that has lost faith in itself'. He had not lost faith in himself, only in doing anything that might change something. He claimed that all art was organized evasion. You responded to Lear or Max Miller – or you did not. 'I can't teach the paralysed to move their limbs. Shakespeare didn't describe symptoms or offer explanations. Neither did Chekhov. Neither do I.' He had hardly met his contemporary iconoclasts such as Kingsley Amis or John Wain or 'any of the rest of those poor unsuccessful freaks'. His hope lay in more pen-pricking. 'It could be an exciting, creative time, so let the scribblers scratch, and let England bleed.'

Also included in *Declaration* was John Wain, another to withdraw from any commitment larger than himself. He walked a tightrope. All he could do was to go on trying to tackle the problems of contemporary life as they confronted him personally; ' "tackle" them by seeking to give them adequate literary expression, rather than "solve" them'. The *enfant terrible* of drama criticism, Kenneth Tynan, was equally solipsistic. Semantic philosophy had taught people to talk sense, but removed value judgements. No longer did the blind lead the blind. The gelded led the drugged. The only solution was self-love. 'Love thy neighbour as thyself' was a maxim stated the wrong way round: you must love yourself first. Even socialism must start as a liberating experience for the individual, a spirit of rapture, a morning exhilaration, before it could be a doctrine to help other people.

The film-maker Lindsay Anderson was equally sceptical about the possibility of action. The sound of the few old socialists singing the 'Red Flag' at the end of the Suez demonstration in Trafalgar Square was 'more of a moan than a song . . . a tired old vision'. People now lived between Matthew Arnold's two worlds, one dead, the other powerless to be born. Jimmy Porter was right in *Look Back in Anger*: there weren't any good, brave causes left, just 'the Brave New-nothing-very-much-thank-you'. The young persons who saw the play saw 'a tremendously forceful expression of their own disgust with contemporary hypocrisies, and at the same time a reflection of their own sense of confusion and lack of focus'. Kingsley Amis was honest in his pamphlet for the Fabian Society, *Socialism and the Intellectuals*, to react against any kind of political idealism, writing that 'the best and most trust-worthy political motive is self-interest. I share a widespread sus-picion of the professional exposer of causes, the do-gooder, the archetypal social worker who knows better than I do what is good for me.' John Wain had equally disavowed all responsibility in the *Twentieth Century* in a piece subtitled *A Young Man Who is not Angry*: he did not want a change in England's class-bound society, because the English people didn't want a classless society. 'Who am I to try to interfere with anything so deep-rooted?'

Yet Anderson finally did not like the 'lingering, irrational, shame-faced humanism' of Amis nor the weak 'liberalism' of Wain. Reactions were all *against*; faiths were all negatives. Toler-ance was the most positive virtue. Nothing had been more ironic than the immediate collapse of 'the liberal Establishment under the first rude shove from the Outsider's elbow' and the neo-Superman doctrine of Colin Wilson, also represented in *Declar-ation* by two of his fellow-thinkers, Bill Hopkins and Stuart Hol-royd. Anderson did, however, still believe in himself fighting and being committed, at the risk of being called irresponsible, self-righteous, extremist and out of date. And those he attacked – Colin Wilson and his friends – had no answer for him other than something even more out of date. They recommended a return to an existentialist religion, hardly the attitude of the rest of the writers of *Declaration*. Colin Wilson, indeed, thought that there might be 'a spirit of the age', which felt the same needs as himself; in an overpraised book of popular philosophy, *The Outsider*, he had sung of those excluded from society. To write a credo might show people that they felt as he did – the Outsider within them all. His vision of the world was as frankly subjective as William Blake's, but he did believe it could illuminate others. He would lead the people back to religion by his continuous doubting and unending questioning.

Declaration had exposed only an abyss between the iconoclastic Left and the neo-religious Right. They all might throw bricks at government and society and each other; but they had few walls or bridges to build. Only Doris Lessing stood outside the fracas and within her experience. She had been a communist sympathizer; even after the Russian attack on Hungary at the time of Suez, she believed in socialism because of the compassion of its faith. Writers should be committed, the responsible interpreters of their age. The times were so dangerous, violent, explosive and precarious that it was a question of life and death for humanity. 'We are all of us made kin with each other and with everything in the world because of the kinship of possible destruction.' She trusted in a great common cause, the abolition of hunger and poverty in the world. To her, Camus and Sartre and Genet and Beckett only felt 'a tired pity for human beings'. While their derisive rejection of propaganda and the Establishment showed vitality in the young British writers, they were sunk inside their parochialism.

Doris Lessing hoped it was a temporary mood of disillusion which made a socialist such as Kingsley Amis state that self-interest was the only authentic political motive. Britain had always fed people into crusading movements. And as for Colin Wilson saying that he was anti-humanist and anti-materialist like all his generation, it was a sign of his invincible British provincialism that he should claim to speak for his generation. 'Outside the very small sub-class of humanity Mr. Wilson belongs to, vast numbers of people are both humanist and materialist.' In fact, the desire of needy communities not to starve, not to remain illiterate, was 'a great and creative force, one which will affect us all'. In spite of Jimmy Porter, there were great causes left, even if a novelist could only talk as an individual to individuals, in a small personal voice. 'There was nothing more arrogant than to demand a perfect cause to identify oneself with.' The answer was a commitment to a just cause.

Conviction was the title of another significant collection of essays, which was produced the following year: a plainsong answer to the incoherent wailing and critical dirge of *Declaration*. There had been responses to John Lehmann's questions, in *London Magazine*, on Commitment, from many writers including Osborne, Wain and Colin Wilson, as well as D. J. Enright, Roy

Fuller, William Golding, Philip Larkin and Stephen Spender. But although these answers had not been self-centred or dismissive, they had only agreed on the writer's *moral* commitment to his material, which need not necessarily be taken from contemporary events.

In *Conviction*, the editor Norman Mackenzie explained why the young lacked causes now in what he called the stalemate state, 'that curious interval in our social history, in which there was no way back to the world which had guttered out into war, yet no clear way forward to a really new society'. He had no trouble in being a committed socialist. Memory and hope blended into a socialist conviction, which was why this belief had become unfashionable among those who had grown up during and since the war. They had no memory of mass unemployment or the Spanish Civil War, and no one had given them much reason to hope with the Cold War and the threat of the hydrogen bomb. Something had happened to paralyse both action and passion. Although much of Britain was still a slum and the Establishment was riddled by snobbery and false values, those who complained, like Sir Orlando Drought in Trollope's novel *The Prime Minister*, that 'everything is dead' in politics, lacked the effort of will to liven everything up. They felt restless or cynical or resigned, and retreated into private worlds. It was because Britain had become a marginal power between two great powers. A demonstration in Trafalgar Square did not persuade the British government to quit Suez or abandon the atom bomb. Only pressure from America or Russia could do that. There was a failure of morals and of caring, but not of dreaming. 'We are full of dreams, but they are dreams of a vanished past, because nostalgia is the opium of the people.' The two parties had converged in their policies. The Tories were the reluctant servants of the welfare society, while the Labour Party had become the pillar of the Establishment. This was the stalemate state, this was a society without convictions.

In the following essays, most of which suggested limited social tinkering, only the Labour politician Peter Shore correctly defined the practice of the future. He saw a managerial revolution taking control from the old Establishment. The functions of business at the highest level were becoming increasingly political while the politician and the civil servant were more involved in the conduct of industry. Business lent government its outstanding personalities. Industrialists became ministers and headed state boards. Senior civil servants and politicians were recruited to serve huge private enterprises. 'The consequential formation of what has been called a "power élite" must be viewed not as a kind of conspiracy, but as a logical consequence of the unification of business with administration and politics.' Shore did not point out that the same process was happening in the totalitarian régimes of eastern Europe, the creation of what Djilas called a 'New Class' of *apparatchiks* in Yugoslavia. Managers were now the revolutionaries, the rulers with a cause.

Against this true and pessimistic vision, the social sage of our age, Raymond Williams, stressed that culture was ordinary and even tried to define it. Every human society had its own shape and purposes and meanings. These were expressed in institutions and arts and learning. A society could only be made by finding common meanings and directions. It would only grow by active debate and amendment, 'under the pressures of experience, contact, and discovery, writing themselves into the land'. Yet a growing society was made and remade in every individual mind. Culture had two meanings – a whole way of life that included the arts and learning, and also the special processes of discovery and creative effort. 'Culture is ordinary, in every society and in every mind.'

Such an unfashionable and sentimental belief in an ordinary culture common to all made Williams view the few scholars and writers known as the Angry Young Men as people making rude noises in a university tea-shop. There was no need to be rude. If that was culture, nobody wanted it, he affirmed. It was, of course, not culture, but merely made culture into a dirty word. If the people shouting in the tea-shop went on insisting that culture was their trivial differences of behaviour or speech or taste, they could not be stopped, but they could be ignored. They were not that important; they could not take culture from where it belonged. They were only self-important. Culture was ordinary, and it was not doomed. There was no Gresham's Law, by which bad culture drove out good. Through education and more state spending on the arts and a redefinition of what the arts were and the spread of them, the apparent division of a common British culture could be remedied, the divide between 'a remote and self-gracious sophistication [and] a doped mass'.

His conviction was countered by Paul Johnson in his essay, 'A Sense of Outrage'. Johnson had been converted to socialism in Paris after watching the beatings inflicted by French policemen in 1968 on protesting students. He was to become the editor of the *New Statesman* and then suffer a conversion to the Right also paralleled by another contributor to *Conviction*, Hugh Thomas, who had discovered socialism previously when he resigned from the Foreign Office because of the government ineptitude over the Suez affair. Johnson alone believed at that time in a radical attack on the class system. It was true, the leaders of the Labour Party and the trades unions had been given their places within the Establishment. They would only attack piecemeal the class structure, which would grow stronger with each assault, as it had since the Second World War. He would abolish the monarchy and the House of Lords, dispossess the corporate bodies which controlled the public schools and Oxford and Cambridge, end the regimental system in the army, disestablish the Church of England, replace the Inns of Court with a central law college, and abolish the Honours List. 'Transforming society is rather like bombing a factory complex . . . You must destroy the whole simultaneously, otherwise the complex will survive.'

There was no more unity in these *Conviction*s than there had been in the previous and various *Declaration*s. From the stalemate state to the managerial revolution to an ordinary culture to the bombing of the class system, all the voices except the last sounded like the moaning of the 'Red Flag', which Lindsay Anderson had heard in Trafalgar Square. Only the ultimate call to action, the total assault on the class system by somebody who would become its supporter, carried conviction from a sense of outrage. But it was piping in the wind. No political party would dare to carry it out. There would have to be a revolution by the dispossessed and the young, and the next decade would see to the containment of that.

Although both *Declaration* and *Conviction* were disappointing in their incoherence, pessimistic in their vision and trivial in their effect, the sense of self-importance in their contributors gave grounds for hope. Only when a change in a society seems possible are collections of essays by dissidents published at all. Nobody wishes to write uselessly. While it may be arrogant to concoct a diatribe, all ears may not be closed to its scream. The sense that the Establishment was groggy at the knees after Suez, and that it had a soft underbelly that could easily be cut open, inspired these declarations and convictions. The wild sling-shots and arrow-points might provoke punctures and a slow collapse. Yet the protestors did not see that they were like the pygmies of the vast rain forest of the Congo. They might occasionally kill an elephant. Starved of protein, they would hack their way inside, and then slowly devour the raw entrails and eat their way out. They would succeed at the feast and engorge themselves. But they would emerge to find there were other elephants always under the green umbrella of the rain forest, which was not and never would be a common and ordinary culture for all, but merely their country and condition of existence.

2

A CRACK-UP

Of course all life is a process of breaking down, but then blows that do the dramatic side of the work – the big sudden blows that come, or seem to come, from outside – the ones you remember and blame things on and, in moments of weakness, tell your friends about, don't show their effect all at once. There is another sort of blow that comes from within – that you don't feel until it's too late to do anything about it, until you realize with finality that in some regard you will never be as good a man again. The first sort of breakage seems to happen quick – the second kind happens almost without your knowing it but is realized suddenly indeed.

Before I go on with this short history, let me make a general observation – the test of a first-rate intelligence is the ability to hold two opposed ideas in the mind at the same time, and still retain the ability to function. One should, for example, be able to see that things are hopeless and yet be determined to make them otherwise. This philosophy fitted on to my early adult life, when I saw the improbable, the implausible, often the 'impossible', come true. Life was something you dominated if you were any good. Life yielded easily to intelligence and effort, or to what proportion could be mustered of both. It seemed a romantic business to be a successful literary man—

F. SCOTT FITZGERALD, *The Crack-Up*

At Cambridge, the unthinking forwardness of the angry satirists largely ignored the two leading influences on the English language, the arts and the administration of our generation: F. R. Leavis in his vehement bunker in Downing College, and the Victorian secret society, the Apostles, based in King's College. The first seemed to us too narrow and vigorous; the second too exclusive and absurd.

Leavis himself was never fashionable, always at war with the faculty. His was an ideology with a narrow canon of approved reading. To be a member of what Leavis called 'a minority culture', one had to be precise in speech and manners, proper in culture and morals, didactic and 'prepared for others to be affronted, or bored, by one's pretensions'. But his followers were truly devotees.

A former disciple of Leavis, the poet and critic Donald Davie could enter imaginatively into the mind of the fanatic and revolutionary, the commissar and the gauleiter. He understood the appeal of having a body of scriptural texts for reference, and of feeling one of a band of embattled brothers, and of seeing ruthlessness and blind obedience as virtues. But as a Cambridge student both before and after the Second World War, Davie himself could never take to the rival psychological security of communism. 'My generation came up to university in the time of the Molotov-Ribbentrop pact; thus there was no excuse for us if we were starry-eyed about the Stalinist left.'

It was Leavis's commitment to literature that made him so attractive a figure to the poet Thom Gunn, to the critic Karl Miller, and even to the economist John Vaizey, who saw Leavis as the representative of Cambridge's main contribution to the tone of intellectual life: a ruthless, forthright intellectual honesty, exemplified by the puritan revolution. This necessity to bare feelings, to analyse motives, to tell the truth at all costs had its danger, particularly in personal relations. 'We literally sat at his feet,' the theatre director Trevor Nunn said, 'because he didn't have any furniture. He stalked around on the coconut matting – sandals, khaki shorts, shirt open to the waist, flaring grey hair . . . He was wicked, magnetic, full of bitterness and bits of asides – "Who was that about? Eliot?" . . . It was like meeting an evangelist – you come out of the crowd and offer yourself. Here was a man who opened the gate and said: "I don't mind where you run." '

The shock of Leavis extended even to the Victorian secret society of the Apostles, who were reforming and renewing their commitment to the old Cambridge tradition. Scrutiny, analysis, and telling the truth wittily had always been part of the meetings of the secret society, but the influence of G. E. Moore and his misinterpreters had made the group a narcissistic sodality that pursued personal fulfilment and gratification. The communist reaction of the 'thirties within the Apostles was replaced by a puritan and rigorous return to the old Apostolic and university values and traditions, allied with a deliberate professionalism in pursuing a career. Heterosexuality replaced homosexuality. The scandals within the society were no longer a question of Lytton Strachey going off with Maynard Keynes's boyfriend, or vice versa. They were of one Apostle taking away another Apostle's wife and marrying her, or of two Apostles sharing a wife and becoming bitter enemies. The years of close male companionship were over. And if E. M. Forster would still read chapters from his unpublished homosexual novel *Maurice* to favoured undergraduates, he was an elegant anachronism of exaggerated modesty in a clandestine group that was changing with the times.

Karl Miller, a favoured pupil of Leavis's at Downing College, was an exemplar of that change. A scholar from the Royal High School at Edinburgh, he became determinedly proletarian in attitude as a reaction against his national service in the Royal Engineers. With his friends, he joined or rejoined the working class, 'dressing in rough textures and dark, dangerous shades, and looking more like displaced persons than spruce mechanics'.

To them, social mobility was yet another name for snobbery. Miller stayed on at Cambridge to do postgraduate work and join the new breed of Apostles before leaving for the Treasury, then for a career in television, and then to serve as perhaps the most influential literary editor of his age. Alternating with or succeeding a fellow Apostle, Ronald Bryden, Miller became the arbiter of the book pages of the *Spectator,* the *New Statesman,* and the *Listener.* He then broke into fresh print as the London editor of the *New York Review of Books,* followed by founding the *London Review of Books,* at the same time as another Apostle, John Gross, who had succeeded him at the *New Statesman,* was editing the established *Times Literary Supplement.*

While editor of the *Times Literary Supplement,* Gross acted in a most un-Apostolic way: he broke a long tradition by making the unknown reviewers sign their reviews. Secrecy no longer seemed good policy. 'Everyone must confess that there is a dangerous temptation, and an unmanly security, an unfair advantage in concealment,' he wrote of his anonymous reviewers. While a highwayman must wear a mask, 'a man that goes about an honest errand does not want it and will disdain to wear it.' Yet Gross continued to wear his mask as an Apostle and finally would go on to help edit the book pages of the *New York Times.* His rival editor Karl Miller would be unexpectedly appointed, despite little academic experience, to one of the three top chairs in the country, as Lord Northcliffe Professor of Modern English at University College, London. It was a triumph of ability over formal qualifications.

John Vaizey had also declared that a significant consequence of Cambridge was a complex network of acquaintance and shared experience without which he would never have escaped the back streets of his birth to rise to professorships in economics, and to the House of Lords. While there was no 'Cambridge Mafia' that was a political or communications group in Britain, the existence of the Apostles made them suspected of being a secret society that favoured its own members and helped to secure them positions of influence. In fact, Vaizey was correct, and only a complex network of wide relationships and shared experience well outside the confines of the college or club could explain the later success of many Cambridge graduates in the fields of communications, politics and academia, and also in scientific areas. For instance, Peter Hall and Trevor Nunn owed nothing to the Apostles, something to F. R. Leavis and much to the theatrical groups at Cambridge, the Marlowe Society in particular. The only reason that the Apostles were considered a conspiracy was that they took an oath of clandestinity in contradiction to the principles of the university which tolerated them. They were not a cabinet, they were not a business, they were not an intelligence service, they were not a masonic lodge. They would always be misunderstood as long as they clung to the unmanly secrecy from which John Gross liberated his literary reviewers.

The other exemplar of Apostolic liberation in the 'fifties was Jonathan Miller, no relation to Karl Miller, although they married two sisters. Jonathan's father was a leading London psychoanalyst, and he studied medicine at Cambridge, although he had a passionate interest in linguistic philosophy, particularly in Wittgenstein and G. E. Moore. It was Miller's satire on Moore and his apples in the revue *Beyond the Fringe* that showed just how much the younger Apostles repudiated the values of the older ones. Jonathan became one of the most brilliant figures of his time, an intuitive diagnostician, superlative in conversation and mimicry, an inventive comedian and an iconoclastic director of theatre and opera, a man of every talent who was a master of all the trades in which he chose to perform, except the cinema. His success owed nothing to his connections. Above all, he represented the professionalism of his generation of Cambridge graduates, whether Apostles or not, who took their place so easily in the performing arts and communications system of their country.

He was the only satirical performer who was also an Apostle. He despised the term 'satirist', and my school-friend Bamber Gascoigne, the author of one of the first Cambridge revues to transfer to London, declared that his like-minded contemporaries thought that they were spear-heading a revolution. 'In our own way we were, in the sense of helping to get rid of what had gone before. But it wasn't a revolution that would lead anywhere. Kerensky's rather than Lenin's.' Although revue performers and comedians were relentlessly thrown up by Oxbridge for the next fifteen years – a case for the Equal Opportunities Commission in Gascoigne's opinion – their opportunity to perform, particularly on television, was the consequence of the more important breed of producers, directors and presenters who also left Oxbridge in the 'fifties for jobs in television, broadcasting and other communications industries. Where they did not know one another, they knew of one another. The list was legion.

The formation, as Raymond Williams observed, moved through; but satire would not change the world, even if some of us thought briefly that it could. When John Bird and Peter Cook imitated the two Harolds, the prime ministers Macmillan and Wilson, they seemed to be resurrecting the power of satire and Jonathan Swift from the grave of history. But as it happened, they were not piping a 'Lillibulero', a little tune that mocked King James the Second off his throne, or a 'Yankee Doodle Dandy' that lost King George the Third some American colonies. They did not actually chop off the heads of prime ministers or even make them forgo an election. In a curious way, their lampoons were affectionate; they changed the personalities of statesmen into frail human beings.

As it was the first time for some years that a living prime minister had been imitated on the stage, Peter Cook reckoned that his skit of Macmillan had a great deal of weight attached to it. 'There are many people in this country today who are far worse off than yourself,' Cook said in a faded, avuncular way. 'And it is the policy of the Conservative Party to see that this position is maintained.' He stood beside a globe as Charlie Chaplin had when playing Hitler in the film of *The Great Dictator.* Afterwards, Hugh Carleton Greene, the brother of Graham and then the Director-General of the British Broadcasting Corporation, decided to revive the political cabaret of Germany in the first years of the Nazi régime by soliciting some of these

Cambridge performers to join the medium of the people in a television revue, *That Was The Week That Was*. Confident in the power of laughter, Greene 'had the idea that it was a good time in history to have a programme that would do something to prick the pomposity of public figures'. But Macmillan himself was hardly pricked by the satire. 'I hope you will not, repeat not, take any action about *That Was The Week That Was*', he wrote to the Postmaster-General. 'It is a good thing to be laughed at. It is better than to be ignored.'

In fact, the humour of the team of young comics made the politicians seem more accessible. The programme's presenter, David Frost, was to grow from an assiduous quizzer into an articulate interviewer of the great and the celebrated, and even to be knighted. But at the time, we were blundering into playing our early roles, which were too readily received. We were mainly unaware of the changes in our culture that the new novels and plays were signalling. But the fiction of The Movement, *Jill* by Larkin and *Lucky Jim* by Amis and *Hurry on Down* by Wain; the plays of John Osborne and the *Roots* trilogy by Arnold Wesker; and the notorious *The Outsider* by Colin Wilson – all these were informing us of several truths that were already being admitted by the Arts Council of Great Britain. An attack was developing on the metropolis by the regions, probably the most effective since the Great Wen was menaced by the values of the Commonwealth after the Civil War. The élitism and the bohemianism of the London arts Establishment were under inquisition by the puritan scrutiny of the shires. And the long supremacy of Oxford and Cambridge was in the line of fire from the older provincial universities and the newer redbrick ones, which were to arise from the ashes of higher educational opportunity. The Arts Council was beginning to trim its long bias towards centralism and favour a small devolution, a certain independence in Scotland and Wales, a large support for local festivals, and the salvation of the touring theatre.

This outbreak against the chains of Westminster was also a reaction from the hangover of the Second World War, chiefly military conscription. To the children of that global conflict, it seemed a monstrous intrusion upon the peace. My own first novel, *The Breaking of Bumbo*, may have been a pioneer effort, but it was misconstrued as was most of Cambridge satire, as covert nostalgia for the values it seemed to be attacking. I was Trooping the wrong Colour and making an aristocratic comedy out of class oppression and imperial remnants. Other novels redressed the balance, chiefly Leslie Thomas's *The Virgin Soldiers*, Alan Sillitoe's *Key to the Door,* David Caute's *At Fever Pitch,* and David Lodge's *Ginger, You're Barmy*, in which national service was said to be 'like a very long, very tedious journey on the Inner Circle'. The best of the novels of post-war army life was James Kennaway's *Tunes of Glory*, with its clash between rank and command in Scotland. Two plays, Arnold Wesker's *Chips with Everything* – Bumbo from the other end of a class telescope – and John McGrath's visceral *Events while Guarding the Bofors Gun*, profited from the forced experience. Yet when the regretted and talented novelist B. S. Johnson edited his *All Bull*, a collection of reminiscences from national servicemen, he found that most of them had gone into khaki like sheep into a dip. Karl Miller, the Leavisite doyen of literary editors, 'joined like a lamb', while Sillitoe declared that he did not think of it as national service. 'It was conscription, a fact of life . . . Going to war was expected of everybody, if you were a teenager, that is.' And even that self-proclaimed anarchist poet and performer of the 'sixties revolt, Jeff Nuttall, joined up quietly and learned from his service to his country that, most of all and best of all, 'life is a desperate, terrible, magnificent joke'.

The reaction to conscription came after the event. We were inducted before the age of protest. And also we were used to the call of duty from our childhood in the war. We had to *learn* rebellion. In my case the lesson came at university from philosophy and from my own reaction to the Suez crisis. As B. S. Johnson noticed, those Reservists who received their recall papers and sent them back with BOLLOCKS scrawled across them 'were the avant-garde in a movement which was soon to grow to establishment proportions'. So it affected me in my irrational and ill-

thought way. I wrote an article on 'Student Revolt' in an ephemeral Cambridge magazine named *Gemini* in the spring of 1957,
seriously trying to proclaim that the events of the Hungarian
uprising had proved the power of the students:

> Students must learn the methods of their contemporaries
> – strike, boycott, union, picket. These are ugly words,
> but these are ugly times. An ostrich with his head in the
> sand is a fiction; fact is the student who blinds his eyes
> with the past. As in China, so in Cambridge – the dead
> are more important than the living. But China is
> changing – Cambridge hardly . . . Revolt, rebel – there
> are few who ever will, and the dead rot of the hollow
> men, the men of straw, the half-men, and the men without
> arms will suck them down. Before marriage or
> promotion, before interest or age sags our bellies and our
> beliefs, we must smash our fists against the walls the past
> has plastered round us.

Very much a rebel without a real cause, taking as my fiery muse
L'Homme Révolté of Camus, I did not practise what I preached.
Few of my radical contemporaries did. We were bourgeois and
we were being educated well, however much we might condemn
the system which benefited us. In *The Breaking of Bumbo*, I had
tried to say that the worst temptation was inclusion in Society.
From my Cambridge novel, *My Friend Judas*, one sentence was
often quoted by the disaffected. 'Always bite the hand that feeds
you, lest it may pat you on the head.' Gratitude was not on
the agenda. Patriotism seemed the last refuge of imperialism.
Censorship in Britain appeared to be a lipstick on fascism, even
the mild correctives of the Lord Chamberlain to the language of
modern drama in the theatre. In 1959, the Obscene Publications
Act effectively protected literature from interference by distin-
guishing it from pornography – the failure of the prosecution
on the publication of D. H. Lawrence's *Lady Chatterley's Lover* a
year later would prove that a greater freedom of speech was
becoming legally and generally acceptable. The powers of the

Lord Chamberlain were being tested through the device of 'club' theatres such as the Comedy and the New Watergate, where members could view the unexpurgated versions of such plays as Arthur Miller's *A View from the Bridge* and Tennessee Williams's *Cat on a Hot Tin Roof*, directed by the motor of the Cambridge theatre in his undergraduate days, Peter Hall, on his rise to run the Royal Shakespeare Company. Yet *any* restrictions by state bodies were irksome in that time of fledgling ferment.

America was the yeast. In drama and in art, in cinema and in music, that subcontinent suggested the vigour of imminent change. Along with the plays of Arthur Miller and Tennessee Williams came the blast of the transatlantic musicals. I remember travelling down from Cambridge to be shell-shocked by the raw impact of *West Side Story* with its mockery of my fresh-minted radical values. If slum kids were singing, 'We're deprived because we're depraved,' how could they be helped by a welfare state? Out of American photography and style, British pop art was spawning with Richard Hamilton's painted collages and shocking definition of painting as advertising and manipulation of the media:

Popular (designed for a mass audience)
Transient (short-term solution)
Expendable (easily forgotten)
Low-cost
Mass-produced
Young (aimed at Youth)
Witty
Sexy
Gimmicky
Glamorous
Big Business

American excess in building from hamburger joints to cinematic extravaganzas stabbed its high heels into the New Brutalism of our boring, masochistic architecture. A violent cinema for an

adolescent market was setting fashions on the screen, with James
Dean and Marlon Brando as *Jeun'hommes Révoltés* in leather and
jeans and with *The Blackboard Jungle* pulsing with the beat of rock.
Although the jazz revival of the early 'fifties had heralded the
coming of Buddy Holly and Elvis Presley, and although I had
gyrated my army youth away in the cellars off Oxford Street to
the trumpet of Humphrey Lyttleton, the reflex jerk and erotic
charge of the new dance music was a freedom from inhibition
that seemed an emancipation from a straitjacket. America had
always declared it stood for liberty, but this was exported as
ecstasy.

Two of my tutors and my contemporary American fellows at
Cambridge were also my emancipators from the corset of British
restraint. Jack Gallagher put up with my dramatics and paranoia
by entering my delusions and treating them seriously. Often
sleepless and hating imprisonment at night, I used to climb
over the walls of Trinity onto the Backs, there to wander in the
moonlight across the parks between the colleges. I would return
over the spikes and ledges to see Wittgenstein's friend, Piero
Sraffa, toiling under his black skull-cap on his monumental
edition of the economist Ricardo's work. And Gallagher would
always respond to my knock and ask me to help him finish a
bottle of Scotch by dawn. He was a selfless man, who nurtured
two or three undergraduates a year through their self-pity. One
late night when I was at my worst, he helped me draw out the
defences of Trinity in Bren-gun and mortar positions against
the time when *They* came to get *Us*. He told me of visiting André
Malraux twice after the war and seeing the map of a capital city
on the wall, also ringed with defence weapons. The first time,
Malraux was a supporter of the Communists and the city was
Moscow; the second time, Malraux was a minister for de Gaulle
and the city was Paris. Gallagher was the best historian of Africa
of his generation, tough of mind and incisive of pen. He taught
me mental survival and some physical strategies: never to have
one's photograph taken, else it might be used to identify one;
never to give one's correct identity for the same reason; and only

to travel light, preferably with a paper bag containing a tooth-brush and a great many small dollar bills. His example was an inspiration to me when I later became a moral tutor myself: 'You are old enough to deal with your own finances, the police and paternity suits. But if you get into trouble with this College, I will defend you to the death.' He already had over the Suez and Hungary business, and he taught a form of self-analysis as well as a structure of historical inquiry. 'Never say somebody has terrible friends,' he told me. 'You are always somebody's terrible friend.' I certainly was his.

The remarkable Professor Denis Brogan was my tutor in my fourth year, when I decided to read for a doctorate in American History. Both he and Gallagher had come from the same poor Celtic urban roots that I had, and we shared a certain irreverence and lusty cast of mind. Brogan was a memory man; he could forget nothing; he photographed mentally the pages he read. The British expert on the United States and France and their histories, he had run Intelligence into Vichy during the Second World War. He told me of an RAF bombing mission sent to devastate the railway stations of Genoa. As any old port in a night raid will do to dump your load upon, the Lancasters took out the sidings and engines and goods waggons of Marseilles instead. Brogan received a call from Winston Churchill himself, telling him to save the reputation of our Air Force for its pin-point targeting and also our agreement with Vichy over respecting a sort of neutrality. The agents on the ground – Brogan had recruited personally all the women agents on the first week of his appointment – came back with an amazing story. How had London known, when France was unaware, that a huge smuggled shipment of wolfram, the essential ingredient for toughening the armour of German tanks, had been loaded onto trains to depart for the Führerland that night? The Marseilles raid became a textbook story of precision bombing and exact navigation.

Brogan and I would meet for supervisions on the train to London, both of us heavily engaged in metropolitan activities. He taught me to appreciate the old alliance of the United States

and France at the time of the American Revolution, and the
longer *vieille alliance* between France and our country Scotland.
He appreciated the wit of history, its appropriation of successful
errors. Both of us were always interested in women, and Brogan
even persuaded me that Britain was the country of tortured love,
France of the rational affair. He had once proved this to a fellow
French Intelligence officer, when half a dozen operatives from
either country had appeared at a post-war drinks party with the
current women in their lives. On analysis, each Frenchman
proved to be accompanied by his appointed bedfellow, either
wife or *maîtresse* or *maîtresse en titre*, while each Briton was
accompanied by a lady of melancholy or perversity. But my
favourite tale of wartime romance was the occasion on which
Brogan said that he was courting the great-great-grand-niece of
the philosopher Jeremy Bentham. They had taken shelter under
a theatre awning off Shaftesbury Avenue, as incendiaries rained
and blazed from the sky during the Blitz. Tonight was the night
to go to bed together, Brogan had declared. It might be their
last night. But she had replied, 'I would love to, Denis, but you
are not the sort of man I could afford to be caught dead in bed
with.'

Because we undergraduates had been in the army and had
already had our first escapades and affairs, we were treated by
the maverick dons such as Brogan and Gallagher with humour
and tolerance. To me, they were the deregulators of my country.
The study of history had already taught me to compare the
institutions and practices and morality of England with those of
America and of France, where I had spent my long vacations on
the way to Italy. But these two tutors showed me that it was
possible to be a scholar gypsy, owing allegiance only to the inquiry
after the truth, yet existing within the framework of a notable
university. And the other freedom fighters were the young American fellows at the Cambridge colleges, particularly Jan Deutsch
and Roger Donald and André Schiffrin, who soon mocked me
into seeing that most of my assumptions were daft. Their sophisti-

cation and transatlantic point of view left me feeling a fool. They were over clever, overdue and over here.

The contrast between them and the brightest and the best of my generation at Cambridge, such as Karl Miller and Gary Runciman, was not so much the Boston Brahmins against the Apostles, but the Angel Gabriel against the Pharisees. The Americans came with glad tidings of a new world of thought which contrasted to the intellectual hierarchy of Cambridge, clustered round the Apostles under the benevolent discrimination of Noel Annan, the supreme academic arranger of his age – he later called it *Our Age*, claiming that it was controlled by urbane liberal dons of his permissive stamp and mould. The greatest of the philosophers of that time, Ludwig Wittgenstein, may have questioned the very meaning of meaning, but he had accepted, a refugee from Austria to Cambridge, the values of E. M. Forster and the other leading Apostles as a way of life and of introductions. I myself was unknowingly introduced to the secret society in King's College as a prospective member by Denis Mack-Smith, an incisive historian who would become the authority on modern Italian history at Oxford University. I was found wanting in manners and intellect and sent packing without an inkling that I had been interviewed other than for a drink of tea on the Fellows' Lawn. Since then, I have naturally believed that secret societies are the boltholes of timid minds.

Alongside one of the American fellows I relived the American myth of Ernest Hemingway. With Roger Donald, a Polish Countess and Jonathan Spence, a prodigy from Clare College who would become a Professor of Chinese History at Yale, we set off, squashed in a Morris Minor, to begin replaying *The Sun Also Rises* in the Café Select in Montparnasse. Our roles were unclear and queasy. We sat in the café in an edged misunderstanding, Spence and myself opposed to the worldliness of Donald and the Countess. The drive to the Festival of San Firmin at Pamplona and the bull-running was tedious and constipated. We found two rooms over the noisiest bar in town: a single bed in a cupboard for the

Countess; three iron mattresses in a larger space for the young men. Then we were caught in a winnowing process of myth and mayhem and sleeplessness. I recorded the reason for our insomnia:

It was the year of the plastic horn.

One hundred thousand of these tiny trumpets, made from set and tinted grease, had been brought into town to tempt the Basques. They had been tempted. Perhaps a thousand Basques had huge drums and brass horns of their own and could join the hundred bands blowing through the streets of the town. But the other ninety-nine thousand brought their own personal plastic horns. They made the sound of a gale blowing through wrapping paper on steel mesh. It was the sound of a mob of fingernails scratching a wallpaper. It was a rude sound.

At College in Oberlin, Hemingway had stood up higher than the trees. He had walked as a giant, wearing clean prose. He had made writing appear in the fist of any sure young man in Ohio. With sweat and grit, treading in the tracks of the master, anyone could write lean. For Hemingway had shown that the sun also rises in the Fens.

There were two cafés in town in the plaza, decorated by placards stating DAMN FINE FIESTA – *Hemingway.* The Café Kutz was one, and there was another one. They were the two sides of the Spanish Civil War. The Republicans went to the Kutz, the boys for Franco to its neighbour. We went to the Kutz. Hemingway would have gone with us. And there we met Jake, a writer from Oxford called Jim Farrell, who was a friend of Roger Donald. He was a lunger and could hardly swim across the waterhole we found outside town, as the good book told us to do. And there in the Kutz was Bud Trillin, a winsome ugly journalist who spoke immediately to children as St. Francis did to birds. And a Tom figure from *The Great Gatsby,* Jay van Alen, who treated the local distilled *grappa* called Chinchon as an overflowing nipple. 'My pee's turned a shade of *vino clarete,*' Farrell said to Trillin. 'But isn't it interesting how cheap European travel is. You just have to lie in the dark in a cheap room and eat nothing.'

We drank all night. The best joke was persuading the Basques that an automatic cigarette lighter dispensed free white wine. It led to a few firefights and broken noses. In the morning we ran in front of the bulls through the streets to the ring. The first time, I capered drunk among their horns. Then they tossed somebody up in the air and trod on him and I ran like shit away.

I met Lady Brett at the other café. She arrived in the plaza in a white Rolls-Royce with a chauffeur. She looked like a beautiful pug on long legs, and she knew me vaguely from my Bumbo days. She had been asked to Pamplona by the father of a friend. Then she found that only one bedroom was booked at the best hotel, and she dumped him in Biarritz and went on alone with his car and reservations to Pamplona. I was the profiteer, to the envy of my friends. We had the best seats to the bull-fights, *sombra* and not *sol*, and we watched the sickening Hemingway routine day after day, the stabbing down of the proud neck of the beast by the picadors and the missed lunges to the bowed heart by the matadors and the cutting off of the ears for an unmeritable victory. At night, we drank and jived until dawn and ran before the bulls of the next day. About the third night, I was seen to fall off the roof of a car in the plaza onto my head. While I was unconscious, Lady Brett was driven off in the white Rolls back to Biarritz.

So the myth became the fact. Farrell was the incapacitated writer and would die after his masterpiece was done, *The Siege of Krishnapur*, by slipping off the rocks of Ireland into the sea. Lady Brett had come and gone, an elusive transience from a life that none of us could live. And we would now fall apart after our Hemingway adventure. We fled the Basque festival on to Madrid, where Roger Donald had a row with the Polish Countess, who departed angrily. And then as an affront to the Yank, Spence and myself insisted on a visit to the Merchant Navy Club on the Rock of Gibraltar. We enthused over the dark cardboard steak, mashed lumpy potatoes and dried peas, and especially the creased shorts of the blue bobbies playing policemen outside. We split in Torremolinos after spending the night on a hillside: it was hardly the Shangri-la of the aspiring artistic classes. Spence went by train to an *inamorata* in Italy, while Donald drove me back as far as Paris, relentless and unstoppable, determined to be rid of me as soon as possible. In the course of an interminable monologue to keep himself awake, he told me how jejune I was. While at Harvard, he had driven logging trucks in the south and had been on massacres in the *bayous* of Louisiana, where great steel nets trawled in alligators and moccasin snakes as well as tuna fish and crabs, and where massed ducks were blasted from the heavens by pump-action shotguns. This was the real Hemingway, while I was only acting it.

I had secured a Harkness Fellowship to spend nearly two years in the United States at Harvard and Columbia in order to write a thesis on *Prohibition*. I thought I already knew a little on how to escape the restraints of the law into a convenient speakeasy. An autumn voyage on the Queen Mary across the Atlantic into the fall in New England would transport me into a world which would corrode my fantasies. On the boat, I was to meet Philip Roth, but the total misunderstanding between our natures and cultures as young novelists merely would prove to me how much I had to learn from the United States, as a hillbilly from Cambridge. The buzz of the time was the word 'image', and I and my contemporaries were star-struck by the images of America, the richness and wonder and brash confidence of a whole continent, that far glittering toy-shop window in our flight from the rationing and the rigor mortis of our youth.

I was leaving at the crest of a wave that few surfers would have ignored. Later I would translate an epigram by Homer that became a maxim of mine:

> When the tide goes with you,
> 　Ride the tide.
> When it goes against you,
> 　You must still ride.

I had presented a television series called *Lost Without Trace* on how King John's jewels were forgotten in the Wash and T. E. Lawrence's manuscript of *The Seven Pillars of Wisdom* in a bookie's bag at Reading Station. I had dramatized my Cambridge novel, *My Friend Judas*, and it was being put on at Brighton and the Arts Theatre Club in London. And the Royal Court Theatre was staging a musical version of *The Breaking of Bumbo*. I had done the book, Julian More the lyrics, John Addison the music, Kenneth Macmillan the choreography, and Tony Richardson himself would direct. First, Peter O'Toole and then Albert Finney were to play the lead role of Bumbo. O'Toole came and stayed with me in Cambridge and ended singing Irish revolutionary songs and drinking red plonk from a passing policeman's bonnet. The oyster of acceptance lay open at home, and I chose to leave and fail. I did know the elementary rule that whatever silence is, absence is not golden.

Another maxim from Machiavelli also informed my life. He reckoned that opportunity and choice in a man's life were based equally on luck and *vertù*, a word which meant something between skill and quality. But when necessity came, it was the executioner. My career had been farcically easy, too much so for my own good and awareness. I had never even thought I did not know how to write a novel or a play. I had done it and the works were succeeding or successful. My nonchalance and arrogance and the attention of the press had made me a voice of my generation, and I believed that I was, in my lack of introspection.

I had not considered whether anyone could describe his or her own time merely by the luck of personal experience and the skill given by God and genetics and education. Like the jesting Pilate, I had preferred to run away from truth into mockery, and I was travelling to America for an answer to staying in Britain. I was, however, not only one of the last children of the Empire, as Orwell had been, but also of the legacy of antiquity. I could read and write classical Greek and Latin, so that I could balance my sentences, if not my sense or my budget. And I admired Thucyd-

ides above all as a historian. He had intruded himself into his
own text in the Peloponnesian War between Athens and Sparta.
Yet in his whole long work, he only gave himself one sentence
without any justification, that the Athenians selected him as one
of two generals to fight a campaign in the north, that he failed
and took no more part in the war. Such a distance from self
implied the possibility of integrity. If impartiality was possible in
the writing of history, he was our mentor.

So I sailed away from the generation which I was meant to
mirror. I did not. I was armoured in my own solipsism, and yet I
had taken up the trade of my intention, that of the writer. The
luck and success of publication had enabled my pen to proceed.
My friends were all Proustians and believed in saving their
masterpieces in cork-lined rooms until the age of wisdom
allowed their appearance in print. I believed in plunging
ahead with flashes-in-the-pen that expressed at least the
exuberance of the time without the blotter of hindsight. Looking
back on the copious notebooks I kept of the authors I particularly
admired, I see that I selected three other statements which
expressed what I was trying to do, and gave me the persistence
for going on:

> It would be more profitable for the farmer to raise rats
> in the granary than for the bourgeois to nourish the
> artist, who must always be occupied with undermining
> institutions.
>
> ANTON CHEKHOV

> For the first time in his life he is forced to examine
> the values by which he lives. The examination shows
> him that he is the victim of the joke and not its
> perpetrator.
>
> NATHANAEL WEST

You must choose, between the things not worth
mentioning and those even less so. For if you set out to
mention everything you would never be done, and that's
what counts, to be done and to have done.

SAMUEL BECKETT

3

AN AMERICAN AWARENESS

Finding is the first Act
The second, loss,
Third, Expedition for
The 'Golden Fleece'

Fourth, no Discovery –
Fifth, no Crew –
Finally, no Golden Fleece –
Jason – sham – too.

EMILY DICKINSON

New York was already anticipated, but still awesome. It was even taller than its myriad stories, its screens were still wider than the images that it broadcast. But Cambridge, Massachusetts, was a hangdog follower of the older university, and Harvard Square was the redbrick step-sister of King's Parade. I had been attracted to America *in excelsis ego,* flaunting its excesses, not to a carbon-copy campus that could never quite achieve a Tudor or Stuart quad. But as I walked through the alleys of the Widener Library called the Stacks, tenanted by millions of books more densely than by the denizens of Dickensian London and all laid open to my eyes and hands, I knew I was walking through the labyrinths of higher opportunity and learning. Harvard would rescue me from the intensities of my ignorance.

Oscar Handlin, that wisest of eggs from Middle Europe, taught me how to reconcile the new world with the old, and how to research with balance and self-criticism. Otherwise, my encounters were the happenstance of my existence. I roomed with the brother of Sylvia Plath; I had published one of her husband Ted Hughes's first poems in an ephemeral Cambridge magazine. Hughes had always looked and behaved like Heathcliff in the intensity of his love, but Sylvia presented herself as the submissive New England housewife, particularly in the presence of her mother, who lived somewhere in the far suburbs of Boston towards the encircling highway. I was never to understand her later reputation compared with his, the supreme poet of nature of our age: it all appeared as dough compared with beak.

At this other Cambridge, France arrived in America for me. I had given a lecture on young English novelists, reading from my own works in my pride of being out of place. One of my audience was certainly the most beautiful student of her time, Marianne Alexandre. Her auburn hair reached her waist, her grey eyes spilled over into soft lips; she was willow-thin and delightfully alien in every thought and deed. Her mother taught French at Brandeis, a neighbouring and dangerous university, where I was soon going to live with Marianne in a female dormitory, which her mother was meant to supervise. Rather like my moral tutors at Cambridge with their blind Nelson's eye, she turned her myopia on everything she did not wish to see, including my nights spent with her daughter after arriving cautiously with my toothbrush packed in my empty typewriter-case.

Herbert Marcuse was the ruling spirit of Brandeis, and his talk of revolutionary violence was a toxic substance to the heads of the young. The black communist and feminist Angela Davis and the future radical leader Abbie Hoffman were influenced as students by him, and I was pricked by his message in my passing. He seemed a Marx reborn into modernity: the radical fervour of the German Jew translated into the deconstruction of our civilization. He had been active in the revolutionary movement of Rosa Luxemburg, he had helped to found the Frankfurt School of Marxist sociology with Adorno, and he had fled to America in front of the Nazis to preach as scientific history his *Liberation* and also *One Dimensional Man*. His equation of liberalism with fascism in its fight against socialism, the 'comfortable, smooth, reasonable, democratic unfreedom' which prevailed in advanced capitalism as a token of technical progress, appeared to be as convincing as his equation of individual freedom to Marxism was perverse. It was the ancient call to subversion and uprising that was thrilling, to bring down the soft state of things by one swift thrust rather than slow acupuncture.

Set against this regenerative violence was the Parisian decadence of Marianne herself and the elegant French professors at Brandeis and Yale, who were still half in love with easeful death and the romantic nihilism of Baudelaire and Verlaine, Rimbaud and Lautréamont. They posed the question to inchoate and hopeful artists such as I was – How should we fix the vertigos? How reason through the unreason of the senses? Between the red barricades of 1848 and the déjà vu of the boulevards and the sane liberation of the Crimson at Harvard, I was being extricated from my past education and wish ever to return to my own country.

I did, however, go back at Christmas to a monkey called a loris, which Tony Richardson gave to me half-alive after it had eaten his Indian nightingale. I knew then that the musical of *The Breaking of Bumbo* would never happen after the derisive failure of the play of *My Friend Judas*. At its London première, so I was told, the sound of my Cambridge friends hooting and jeering and stamping on my literary grave should have resounded across the Atlantic.

Frankly, America seemed far more exciting and sophisticated and central in world affairs. I remember three of the greater living writers addressing small groups in my various institutions of learning. The first was Somerset Maugham at Eton, who looked like a lizard beyond redemption, and told us that if we wished to become writers, we should copy out the works of Addison and Swift until we were in our forties and then try to imitate them. We thought that he did not want any early competition. The next was the urbane Anthony Powell, who addressed a minimal gathering at a Cambridge college to declare that one in five of the major novelists of the twentieth century had come from Eton College. He had not mentioned himself, but obviously he was, because of *A Dance to the Music of Time* – and he gave hope to others from there. But the third showed true Brahmin finesse, Robert Lowell – addressing a few of the faithful on a wintry night at the other Cambridge and being asked by an intense maiden from Wellesley, 'Mr. Lowell, where do you see yourself in the mainstream of American poetry?' Rocking gently on his heels, blinking intensely through his spectacles, Lowell said, 'Right here.' It was the best of responses; it was the worst of responses, answering nothing. Later that night, we all got drunk together, and I tried to persuade him to sleep it off in my Harvard room. I lost the argument and he drove into a lamp-post and three months in hospital, and I felt intolerably guilty. My words were useless. They carried no conviction.

After the Widener Library, the food of my life came from Elsie's, an early fast food joint where everything was 'to go'. The chubby bustling proprietor was obviously trying to get us to move on from her cramped space as quickly as possible. It was my first lesson in American social mobility.

—Beerwurst, split, to go
—Coffee and apple turnover, to go
—Cream cheese and caviar on rye with pickle, to go
—Root beer, blueberry pie, to go
—Bratwurst on crispy roll and sauerkraut, to go
—Burn the British both sides, English toasted muffin and
  coffee, to go.

So I went further and further from my previous education. The distance was increased by an exaggerated drive across the new continent in an enormous white Buick that was the free gift of my fellowship. We were all under the spell of Jack Kerouac's *On the Road*, with its promise of liberation on wheels; we also could be rolling stones shedding moss and going nowhere except into intense sensation. Marianne and I were married by a mumbling Massachusetts judge after an obligatory blood test; two strollers on the street were our witnesses, and we set off for San Francisco with Jonathan Spence, now at Yale, as our fellow traveller, sharing the expenses and dangers of the honeymoon. High in Wyoming, Marianne had a haemorrhage, which became a miscarriage. We were turned away in Spokane in Washington State by a Puritan doctor who wanted nothing to do with poor travellers in such trouble – she might have bled to death – but we found Samaritans in a Jewish hospital in San Francisco. They gave her eight pints of blood even though I could not pay the bill except by instalments. With that extraordinary combination of greed and generosity, caught between the supermarket and the heart, that characterized the nation, they told us that the blood cost thirty-three dollars a pint, but if we could find eight free donors, it would only cost eight dollars a pint. In the end, strangers bared their veins – Park Rangers and cowboys – on our drive back, the

casual and spontaneous giving that told me that I was in a new
world of easy acceptance and warm feeling. So we were spared
two hundred dollars of blood money.

In San Francisco, the Beats were setting up shop at the City
Lights bookstore. Running it was the editor of their protest, the
gangling poet Lawrence Ferlinghetti, who wrote a pamphlet
called *Tentative Description of a Dinner Given to Promote the Impeachment of President Eisenhower.* We all lived then in fear of a strange
rain from a mushroom cloud which would kill friends like Timothy Birdsall; but I had not yet read such an indictment of the
great strategist of the last Just War of our childhood:

> And after it became obvious that the strange rain would
> never stop and that Old Soldiers never drown and that
> roses in the rain had forgotten the word for bloom
> and that perverted pollen blown on sunless seas was
> eaten by irradiated fish who spawned up cloudleaf
> streams and fell onto our dinnerplates . . .

> And after it became obvious that the Great Soldier had
> become the Great Conciliator who had become the
> Great Compromiser who had become the Great Fence
> Sitter who actually had heard of the Supreme Court's
> decision to desegregate the land of the free and had
> not only heard of it but had actually read it . . .

> And finally after everyone who
> was anyone and after everyone who was no one had
> arrived and after every soul was seated and waiting for
> the symbolic mushroom soup to be served and for the
> keynote speeches to begin
> The President himself came in
> Took one look around and said
> We Resign

Actually, President Eisenhower did not resign because of Ferlinghetti's pamphlet of May 1958, but he was finishing his two
terms in office, and the election looked exciting. The rabbity
and rabid vice president, Richard Nixon, was being challenged

by the charismatic war hero from Harvard, John F. Kennedy, who delivered his words in a staccato flat beat that sent us more than the phrases of his speech-writers. He was the body and movement of youth and action. I was lucky enough to secure a press pass for the Democratic Convention in Los Angeles from the *Observer*. I took the bus down to stay at a flea-pit hotel on Pershing Square off the local Skid or Snow Row at the cost of three dollars a night. I was then sympathetic to a poem that I read on the Greyhound Bus down in the ephemeral *San Francisco Supplement*, by a poet called Bob Kaufman, who was temporarily in the Beat scene and wrote on its other hipster drug centre, the Co-Existence Bagel Shop, where 'time is told with a beat'. His poem on HOLLYWOOD 59 seemed about right:

> Impatient Cadillacs, trading in their owners for more
>   successful models,
> Lanky Calypso singers, caught with their fads down,
>   trapped in beat coffee cups,
> With small-chested actresses, bosomed out by the big
>   breast scene,
> Unsympathetic dope pedlars, who refuse to honor credit
>   cards,
> Carping critics, refusing to see what's good, just because
>   it isn't present,
> Lonely old DE MILLE divorced God, seeking a new
>   producer,
> With a couple of rebuilt commandments,
> HOLLYWOOD, I SALUTE YOU, ARTISTIC CANCER OF THE
>   UNIVERSE!

I again felt a minnow in the mainstream of history. What Larkin and The Movement stay-at-homes were doing seemed to me to be parochial and off-stage. Thom Gunn and Ted Hughes, the best of the Cambridge poets of my time, had also come to America, where it was essentially happening, and Gunn would stay in California, following Christopher Isherwood and preceding the artist David Hockney.

Presently I was thrown into the Democratic Convention,

watching the two-time loser Adlai Stevenson sling away his late surge among the delegates with a quip. He posed in the California sun with a snowball symbolizing his gathering backing among the delegates, but then he had to say, 'I can see my support melting down my sleeve.' One of the best presidents that America never had, Stevenson would rather have wit than the White House. At a meeting of the Texas delegation with cheerleaders dressed in pompoms and the Stars and Stripes, Lyndon Johnson ranted red-faced as a turkey's wattle in an effort to spike the Kennedy bandwaggon. And I met the next president himself at the Massachusetts delegation, where he gave me an inscribed copy of his book *The Strategy of Peace* in return for five dollars for his campaign cause. His eyes were lidded with exhaustion, his skin was brown with cortisone for the pain in his back, he walked like a zombie, yet there was already a command and a presence in him. My instinct was to feel safe in his hands.

We returned to New York to find the attack on our emancipators in San Francisco already under way. It had predictably come from an apostle of Leavis, Norman Podhoretz, who had escaped the ghetto into the success of a scholarship to the Cambridge of the Fens, and had returned to lambast the new liberation theologians of his homeland. To him, they were the know-nothing bohemians. As the Angry Young Men had seemed too old for me, so the Beats were too far gone for Podhoretz. 'The fact that Kerouac is thirty-five or thereabouts was generously not held against him.' Bohemianism was no longer fashionable, certainly not to the Leavisites, but Podhoretz did admit that the lifestyle of the highway gypsies was attractive. Yet their philosophy was dangerous. 'It is hostile to civilisation; it worships primitivism, instinct, energy, "blood". To the extent that it has intellectual interests at all, they run to mystical doctrines, irrationalist philosophies, and left-wing Reichianism. The only art the new Bohemians have any use for is jazz, mainly of the cool variety.' These were exactly the arguments that were later used against the ethos of D. H. Lawrence, the John the Baptist of the Leavisites – except for jazz, of which he was unaware. But Podhoretz thundered on.

'Sex has always played a very important role in Bohemianism,' he declared, rather forgetting that sex also had something to do with the creation of the human race, which might be losing, but not without sex. Anyway, the Beat generation suffered not only from a hostility to intelligence, but also from a pathetic poverty of feeling. In a ringing finale, Podhoretz put his case:

> How can anyone in his right mind pretend that this has
> anything to do with private property or the middle class?
> No. Being for or against what the Beat Generation stands
> for has to do with denying that incoherence is superior
> to precision; that ignorance is superior to knowledge; that
> the exercise of the mind and discrimination is a form
> of death. It has to do with fighting the notion that sordid
> acts of violence are justifiable so long as they are
> committed in the name of 'instinct'. It even has to do
> with fighting the poisonous glorification of the
> adolescent in American popular culture. It has to do, in
> other words, with being for or against intelligence itself.

This was quite a counterblast against the youth revolution, which had already begun in the United States before it would spread to Europe in the 'sixties. We found an apartment in a brownstone house in Greenwich Village, which we shared with another Harkness Fellow, Anthony Howard, a journalist of insatiable political curiosity. I took the subway occasionally up to Columbia University to see my supervisor, the leading social historian of his time, Richard Hofstadter, whose sceptical inquiries into American reform movements were my chief influence other than the geographical investigations of the French historian Braudel. Hofstadter was wise and ironical about the truth of the trade, which I was learning. 'I have written five or six books, which are called seminal,' he told me. 'The trouble is that I could have written each of them in a dozen different ways coming to a dozen different conclusions. And if I had done that, each version would still have been called seminal.' All that winter through to the following summer of 1961, I was writing my social history on *Prohibition,* a work that could have been written a hundred different ways and which came to be called seminal.

I was asked to be a Founding Fellow and Director of Historical Studies at the brand-new Churchill College, still building at Cambridge in England, and I accepted. For I had no job when my American Fellowship was over, and with a young wife, we were existing on my grant as poor as Bowery cockroaches. Two may live as cheaply as one, but certainly they cannot wear the same clothes – or could not then. Although the young students and the action painters wore a winter uniform of jeans and lumberjackets under the sprinklers of the dusty lofts they were beginning to colonize on the Lower East Side, it was not our style. Richard Smith was there, another British Harkness Fellow who was a bridge between the abstract expressionists and pop art with his enlarged images of a watch and a cigarette packet, also Jasper Johns and Robert Rauschenberg, in a building on Pearl Street off Fulton and the fish market. The Village had been and still was the haunt of the emigré artists to Manhattan, although rising rents were already driving them downtown. Two blocks away was the house where e.e. cummings had lived and the saloon where Dylan Thomas had drunk himself to death. It was ten minutes' walk to the Cedar Tavern, where Jackson Pollock and his mates had met for beers between their fusillades and salvoes at the canvas. By now, Pollock had killed himself in a car crash, but his wake went on in the bar. Larry Rivers even did its menu in a painting in 1960 – Bean Soup .35, Beef Goulash 1.25, Lamb Shank 1.00, Hawaiian Ham Steak 1.35, Lima Beans, Boil. Pots, Salad, Home Frys. The first flight of the nascent gay liberationists against police harassment exploded outside another neighbouring pub. But this was election time, and the threat to the Village was chiefly political.

Carmine de Sapio, a ward heeler with Italian connections, was the supreme power in the Village. He had put money into the construction of two high-rise piles of condominiums on the far side of Washington Square, the only park and meeting-place of the Villagers, where anyone could converse in peace or play guitars or hustle at chess. De Sapio had promised to drive Fifth Avenue straight through the middle of Washington Square so that his two spires would have the fancy address of One Fifth Avenue, which would double their value. And when he called a meeting in the Village at an old armoury building, where Harry Truman was coming to speak for John F. Kennedy as the Democratic president to succeed him, I went there and saw true democracy at work. I arrived early and the ex-president was late, so we were entertained because of the nostalgia vote with Irish tenors and fiddlers rendering 'The Wearing of the Green' and 'Sweet Adeline', while Italian tenors delivered us 'Santa Lucia' and 'O Sole Mio' to the last tear-drop.

There was a sudden commotion at the back of the hall, where the seats were already packed with the party faithful of longshoremen and vendors. Past the bouncers and strong-arm men at the door the new constituency of the Village surged in, the students and the artists and the young bourgeois executives, all waiting for Harry. And when he came, short and feisty in a light blue suit, 'Give 'em Hell' Harry Truman gave them hell. 'I told the American farmers what to do, and they didn't listen to me and they put in the Republicans, and now they're listening. And I'm telling them again, put in the Democratic candidate, John F. Kennedy – he's as Irish as some of you are.' And the chant rose from the back of the hall. 'Put out de Sapio – Save Washington Square – Give him hell, Harry.' And Harry heard, and passed on the message to Robert Kennedy, then intending to run as a carpet-bagger for senator in New York, and he told his brother, and the Village voted the Democratic ticket, and Carmine de Sapio soon disappeared into the obscurity he had come from, and Fifth Avenue has never run through Washington Square.

This was my lesson in the power of democracy. Its heroes and presidents, Truman and Kennedy, could still hear the cries of the people and knew the political machines well enough to make reform work. It was direct and effective, and when it grew corrupt, it could be mended. The vote was what mattered, and demographic and economic changes meant that no party boss could manage his ward for ever. Politics was also exciting. There was the possibility of immediate change for the better, a long remove from the hidden manipulations of Britain, where the mandarins of Whitehall and the Establishment appeared to answer to nobody except to their ministers in that secrecy which was called national security. In America, the citizens could tell even the president. In England, the children were told what to do.

On New Year's Eve, we were asked by a southern woman writer to a party in a block of apartments with a plate-glass shatter-proof door near Columbia University. While I was chatting to a cadaverous actress who was playing the whorehouse madam in Genet's *The Balcony* and was introduced as a whorehouse madam and looked like a whorehouse madam – nature imitating artifice – Norman Mailer made an entrance with a Brooklyn minder and one of the serial wives he had stabbed a week before, missing her heart by inches. He had been committed to the Bellevue mental wards, she had not preferred charges, and now she was egging him on to his challenge to fisticuffs or arm-wrestling with cries of, 'Why don't you give 'em a lecture on murder, Normie?' The minder propositioned every unavailable woman with four-letter invitations, Mailer failed to get into a fight, and when the trio left, we all heard the splintering of the shatter-proof door, and the siren song of Mailer's wife, 'Normie didn't do it, I swear, Normie didn't do it.' Normie said he didn't and the minder swore blind that nobody had done nothing, so they walked off into the night leaving our southern hostess to pick up the pieces. It quite cured me of my previous admiration for Mailer's invitations to assault the American dream.

I found in Manhattan the most brilliant and critical minds that I had met, even at Cambridge. American higher education seemed to sharpen the wits. The professors and their assistants at Columbia University, the New York publishers and museum curators, the artists and the actors, appeared to be able to temper an intense Americanism with a certain worldliness and regret from central Europe, as though their tongues were full of old

honey scraped from the bottom of a new jar with a switchblade.
But they were all under the extreme pressure of life in this insane
metropolis. Although Hemingway had defined genius as grace
under pressure, this forced display of intelligence under the stress
of earning enough to live well threatened to burst the cooker
and blow the lid. My three better American friends were to kill
themselves over the next few years, so that I would feel that
Broadway was Suicide Alley. But at that time, I merely revelled
in their deadpan charm and ability to get by with exquisite performances worthy of a Chaplin on the skating rink of the Rocke-
feller Plaza.

Marianne and I were overwhelmed on our travels by the energy
and the scale and the opportunity of America. I would write my
own tiny Kerouac picaresque novel about free-wheeling across
the continent, east to west and north to south. Only one chapter
of *The Hallelujah Bum* is now readable in its limey Beat lingo. It
praises the wonder and the splendour of bridges and cranes and
highways, the very works of man that transformed the crossing
of the United States, already defined into squares by Thomas
Jefferson, that magnificent architect of the grid-iron stamped on
the ground that turned North America into a gigantic waffle,
when seen from high as a pie in the sky. I tried to imitate Walt
Whitman and Hart Crane in extolling the iron deeds of the
pioneers, and to follow the Beats in their distrust of the soft
consumer times to come:

> Bridges, cranes, highways, take me with you. Walt would
> have loved you, only he died too soon. But he had
> people to love, to hosannah in an exult of frontier. Now
> the people are rotten and patched and only what they
> built is fine, and the last hope is in the things and in
> people seeing the last hope in the things they have
> made.
>
>   I sing the body plastic
>   I believe that you are to stand or fall with the soul of
>   the New World

Toupee, dark glasses, deaf aid, red-running nose,
Face lift, mask, cream, profile surgically Roman,
False lashes, teeth, teats, smiles, bowels in the purging,
Flesh sweetly firm in Maidenform,
Hips, hip-sockets, hip-strength, supple in sinuous
    corsets,
Womb, man-root, love-perturbation rising at dirty
    pictures,
Woman and all that is a woman's vanity-case
I demand that you let my gushing rivers interpenetrate
    your Kleenexes
While I bestow upon your fierce and athletic
    bubblegum, artistic musical popcorn, rude-muscled
    candybars,
From Spearmint, from Saltwater Taffy,
All the seedpips in the jamjars, all the nipples in the
    bra bars,
All the mixes, all the cookies, all the fabrics, all
    synthetic
        Pioneers! O pioneers!

It had been the great privilege and luck of our time in San Francisco and then in New York to see the pioneers of the youth decade of the 'sixties already at work, unconscious of what they would unleash. We hardly ever know the effect of what we do. If we did, we might be circumspect. In Manhattan was the beginning of the confusion between advertising and art, merchandising and media and the message. When Jasper Johns produced his two bronze-cast and hand-painted cans of Ballantine Ale for Leo Castelli's gallery, it was because Willem de Kooning had said of the art dealer that you could give that son of a bitch two beer cans and he could sell them. Robert Rauschenberg was also producing for Castelli his *Coca-Cola Plan* with three coke bottles caught within a wooden structure with wings. Although both artists would distance themselves from later practitioners like Andy Warhol, who did little more than confuse advertising with art, the two of them had translated the images of the small screen and the supermarket into the art gallery by the beginning of the 'sixties. In doing so, they had speeded the process through which 'the arts' were being engulfed by the sounds and images produced by a consumer and mechanical society. A work made by hand for a patron was fast becoming a product to be reproduced by an assembly line for a mass market, as Warhol would practise in his multiple screen prints of screen icons such as Marilyn Monroe. The fine arts were being lost in the new technology and commerce. While the Middle Ages had included war and love in the *artes*, 'the arts' in modern times would now incorporate comic strips and the design of soft drink bottles. Folk art and popular art would vie with the fine arts for the attention of the people and win for a while.

Motion and performance were also becoming a part of painting. Where Duchamp had depicted movement and hailed the end of naturalism, the kinetic and performance artists began to ingest or act it out. The witty machines of Tinguely, which might auto-destruct, or the body-painting and the incoherent chants of the new urban tribal ritualists were removing all permanence and standards from creative works. As one commentator was to write on the exhibition called 'The Machine' which I saw at the Museum of Modern Art: 'The future of art seems no longer to lie with the creation of enduring masterpieces, but with defining alternative cultural strategies. But in destroying the formal divisions between art forms, and in their casual moves from one expressive medium to another, individual artists do continue to demonstrate new attitudes towards art and life. As art and non art become interchangeable . . . the artist defines art less through any intrinsic value of the art object than by furnishing new concepts of life-style.'

This was the crux of the matter – what my friend the jazz-singer and art critic George Melly would call the pop arts in Britain: a 'revolt into style'. It was not only a style of life that was seen as a work of art, but a style of dress and behaviour, of speech and of clothes. Each person was, in a sense, his or her own work of art. Narcissus was the god of the new generation. All standards of art should be dethroned; an alternative or counter-culture should be found. Any cultural heritage must be rejected in favour of instant creation.

In the United States, the first emancipators into present sensation, Jack Kerouac and the Beat poets of San Francisco, the heirs of the anarchists and the decadent French poets, would distinguish themselves from the pop artists and the hippies of the 'sixties. But they had opened a Pandora's Box and loosed the consumer children of the machine age. The bridge was to be Allen Ginsberg, who translated anarchism into political action. His chanted poem 'Howl' had already mesmerized the young of San Francisco and Berkeley and would make him the mouthpiece of protest against authoritarian Washington and the future American involvement in the war in Vietnam. A dependence on drugs and a sexual free-for-all would pit the alternative culture against the old moralities and traditions. 'Howl' did not even suggest fixing the vertigos or the reasoned disorder of the senses, but self-destruction on the pretence of recreating the revolutionary libertarianism sought by William Blake:

> I saw the best minds of my generation destroyed by
>   madness, starving hysterical naked,
> dragging themselves through the negro streets at dawn
>   looking for an angry fix,
> angelheaded hipsters burning for the ancient heavenly
>   connection to the starry dynamo in the machinery of
>   night . . .

The assault by American youth on traditional values was backed by its spending power. As consumers, the young were the mass patrons of the objects of the alternative culture – records and posters, designs on T-shirts and Coca-cola cans. A dealing collector's market grew up in these products of instant consumption. Their images were ubiquitous and too powerful to avoid, except through some belief that political activity still mattered. We still had the capacity for change. And the election of John F. Kennedy to the White House did not open another Pandora's Box, where only the unlikely emergence of hope kept humankind from committing mass suicide. The president's speeches about a New Frontier offered the possibility of making things different. Yet many of us, even the foreigners, did believe that it was not what America could do for us, but what we could do for America. And that spirit sent Marianne and myself driving south into the states where the freedom riders were going on their trail buses, and then on to Haiti by air, unknowingly at the time of the Berlin crisis. History was again rocking our luck.

The freedom riders from C.O.R.E., the Congress of Racial Equality, were testing segregation along the highways. The *New York Post* called their voyages across Alabama, enduring beating after beating, 'as daring an exploit as any ride in a space ship'. Some of the Greyhound buses were bombed and burned; the blacks and whites seated together were clubbed with lead pipes and baseball bats. We merely found the south caught in a time trap, where Jim Crow generally still ruled. At Rock City, a garden gnome fairyland among some boulders, there were three drinking-taps, the taller labelled WHITES, the middle one COLORED, the lower DOGS. To advertise a fried catfish restaurant in Mississippi, the effigy of a burned and lynched negro was hanging from a tree branch. It took very brave people to drive unsegregated and hand in hand across that retrograde land. And yet, there was a saving grace in southern wit and black humour that seemed able to defuse the crisis. The River Styx divides Florida from Alabama; below the new road bridge and by the rotting ferryboat was a sign, CHARON RETIRED. And the one cabaret club revue that we attended in the Original Absinthe Bar in New Orleans was dedicated to the freedom riders and called *Nobody Likes a Smart Ass*. Its humour was a revelation: you couldn't say that sort of thing yet in England.

'Get to the back of the bus, you nigger bastard.'
'I'm Jewish.'
'Then get off the bus.'

'Say, boy, where do the coloured folks hang out around
here?'
'On that tree.'

'I hit two niggers driving in Mississippi. It was an accident
– but I got both of them. One came through the
windscreen into the car, and the other was hurled a
hundred yards ahead. The Highway Patrol came along,
and they charged the first Negro with Breaking and
Entering and the second with Fleeing from the Scene
of the Crime.'

A Negress looked at her reflection:
'Mirror, mirror, on the wall,
Who's the fairest of us all?'
Voice off:
'Snow White – and don't you forget it, you black bitch.'

Such cathartic humour reflected the situation and was far closer
to the gut and the bone than anything we could imagine in
Europe. Satire, as always, was telling the truth and mocking the
bigotry of the backwoods and the *bayous*. We flew on to Haiti,
where we had been told that the Olofson Hotel in Port au Prince
was a Gingerbread Palace, and that this black republic, independent for more than one hundred and fifty years, would show
us how relaxed such Caribbean self-governing islands could be.
Instead, it made Mississippi seem enlightened. Graham Greene
had not yet reached there to make a vicious farce of it in *The
Comedians*. We arrived a year or two in advance to be met by his
lethal *farceur*. When this pintpot piece of black velvet danced too
close to my wife at the Gingerbread Palace, she said sweetly to
him that I would kill him. He ran away under her shoulder and
did not call in the *Tontons Macoutes*, the local midnight killers of
the Duvalier government. It is wonderful how we chance our
arm when we are too young to reckon the consequences.

And so it went on, our politics of well-meaning ignorance. I
had my head sculpted by the ascetic Monsieur Dimanche, who
said, 'My hatchet is my paintbrush.' He found in the lump of

oak which he was attacking, twin devils' horns on the forehead of my long face. He wished to have liberated from the wood an Archangel Gabriel; he had chopped out a silly Satan. He was gracious about it and explained the faults in the grain, saying, 'When I was poor again, God sent me this dream about a monk. So I knew you were coming. I even chose a piece of wood to make you in. Of course, you do not come from the east. But I am making your head stylized thin and long and white. For that is what I see in you. You are the spirit of the monk. As long as I have my Christ, in my studio and in my purse, neither shall be empty.'

Of course, I was not what he saw in me or sculpted: I was merely giving him the dollars he had to have to live at all. Yet it was a truly testing time. We met an opposition family of the old Creole aristocracy, which had ruled Haiti before Duvalier and his slogan *LE NOIR DUVALIER AU POUVOIR*. I had boasted that I knew people in the new Kennedy administration in the United States. I was given some two hundred detailed pages of the tortures and killings of the dissidents in the island recently, and I was told that the old Eisenhower administration still maintained a detachment of Marines at Port au Prince to bolster the régime. I put this evidence among the leaves of my papers, prepared to saunter with it through Haitian Customs, in the blitheness of my folly.

Then the Berlin crisis came upon us. The rains dripped down, long and silver, on the thatch restaurant of the Gingerbread Palace. There were southern planters there as well as *Tonton Macoute* spies. I was gloomily considering how far the two hundred dollars in my pocket would take us towards South America before the nuclear rain began the following day. Could we beat this fall-out to another tropic? But like the Suez crisis, it ended in a farce. Khrushchev blustered; Kennedy saw him out; the Berlin Wall went up; the air-lift to the besieged city soared in. Another necessity became a joke of decision. We flew back to Miami, and the thorough Haitian Customs officials searching my baggage did not look through the pages of my manuscript. After all, they spoke French, and why the hell should they leaf through this nonsense in a lesser language?

I would later write on my meeting with Monsieur Dimanche and on this Haitian experience in an American magazine. One paragraph will suffice:

> A sudden spatter of rain fired a volley on the roof of the Gingerbread Palace. The repeating rifles of the drops spluttered their requiems. Haiti has only two seasons, the season of dust and the season of mud. This was the muddy season, and it rained each evening for one hour. Somewhere beyond the horizon, real rifles would cough out men's lives, and corpses lie along the beaches of Cuba. Revolution and counter-revolution, rich and poor, each for all and all against all – must that be the way of the Caribbean? Only the Dimanches of the world were excused from these considerations. For them, God was the good. They could carve Him so. Through the ethical glasses on their eyes, they could see only the good in others, and, with this strange insight, could shame men into goodness, from the very weariness of doing evil. To Dimanche, I was a monk and Haiti was a heaven. His inexplicable expectation in us prevented us from doing what we wanted to do, to act like the Devil in hell.

We returned to the United States without a fuss, and I went to see Arthur Schlesinger, one of my professors at Harvard who had a niche within the Kennedy circle. We met at a safe house in Massachusetts, and I showed him my evidence from Haiti. I asked him to withdraw the American Marines until there was some social justice there. And incredibly, it happened. My foolish and presumptuous voice changed American policy by a jot and a tittle. And I believed that we still lived in a time where the Lone Ranger could affect global policy, at least in America. Democracy actually worked.

We sailed home on a French liner, the old *Liberté*. To us it seemed a freedom of the revolutionary spirit. We could do things that might change things. Many years later, I said to the poet

Christopher Logue that the American Revolution was the first of
all European revolutions. No, he insisted, it happened after the
French Revolution. All the history books in the world, I said,
would prove that it happened ten years before the French experiment. 'I'm interested in the truth,' he said, deflating me, 'not
the facts.' At that time, the truth seemed to be that Kennedy had
rekindled the radical hope in the world, and that France, with
its extraordinary historians and philosophers of youth and exis-
tentialism, was not far behind. The melancholy was the train
journey home from Southampton through all the low suburbs
into London. What a flat grey sky, what creeping houses, what a
little land.

4

THE TERRIBLE OBLIGATION OF HOPE

> The interrogation and even the modification of the
> past . . . is now no less plastic and docile than
> the future.
>
> JORGE LUIS BORGES

We returned to England to meet John Osborne's reaction to the Berlin crisis that had not killed us with nuclear rain in Haiti. He had written 'Letter to My Fellow Countrymen', attacking the Conservative prime minister and the Labour leader of the opposition, who had supported the action against Russia:

> There is murder in my brain, and I carry a knife in my heart for every one of you. Macmillan, and you, Gaitskell, you particularly. I wish we could hang you all out, with your dirty washing, on your damned Oder–Neisse Line, and those seven out of ten Americans too. I would willingly watch you all die for the West, if only I could keep my own minuscule portion of it, you could all go ahead and die for Berlin, for Democracy, to keep out the red hordes or whatever you like.
>
> You have instructed me in my hatred for thirty years. You have perfected it, and made it the blunt, obsolete instrument it is now. I only hope it will keep me going. I think it will. I think it may sustain me in the last few months.
>
> Till then, damn you, England. You're rotting now, and quite soon you'll disappear. My hate will outrun you yet, if only for a few seconds. I wish it could be eternal.

Although Osborne later in his memoirs declared that he had libelled his own passionate confusion 'by omitting any grace notes of rigor or irony', at the time this ultimate anger was a stimulant to us in our fear of death. But there was a difference between us. As Buenos Aires imposed on Jorge Luis Borges 'the terrible obligation of hope', so President John F. Kennedy had imposed hope upon us. And that hope, as Borges also stated, was 'the memory of the future'. We believed, or thought we believed, that the American Eagle had warned off the Russian Bear and would continue to do so. We believed that Kennedy would create a New Society in America, which might again become the beacon of the world in example as well as in image. Our belief may have been naive and would be disappointed, but that is how international politics seemed then – the passion of our anger and our revolt might be turned into a change of human society, probably in America, hardly in Britain.

We bought a short lease on a small flat below the Georgian roof of a house in Soho Square. We wanted to live as metropolitan bohemians, not as provincial academics in damp and draughty Cambridge digs. For Churchill College was a construction site. My teaching quarters were in a prefabricated hut. I shared a thin wall with George Steiner, whose melodious rant wonderfully instructed me on the literature of the four cultures he knew – German, French, English and American. He and I were the sole representatives of literature and history in a new college of twenty-five Fellows, nearly all of whom were scientists. Some had won the Nobel Prize and most had worked and were working on the three revolutionary inventions by which Cambridge altered the twentieth century – nuclear fission, computer technology and genetic engineering. I had come there to be in the forefront of radical change in the shape of the world. Although I knew nothing about science, at least I would be there.

As most of the young felt, so did I, hating and fearing the atomic and hydrogen bombs and the politics which they spawned. And I was teaching in the heartland of the atomic Establishment. The paradox was that I knew that the forces of destruction and creation were both present. The old could be annihilated just as the new could be remade by machine and gene. After the bombing of Hiroshima and Nagasaki, the leading Australian physicist Mark Oliphant had said, 'This has killed a beautiful subject.' He had been a pupil of the great Lord Rutherford and he had supported the open exchange of scientific knowledge. Theoretical physics were now constrained by secrecy, contorted by military application, and convulsed by moral doubts among the scientists.

Indeed, the British atomic bomb tests in Australia had proved the graveyard of the ideals of the Cavendish physicists. Although some sites for nuclear fission tests were offered in the United States under American supervision, the British government decided to conduct its own independent experiments in a Commonwealth country.

Supervised by Sir William Penney, the first director of the Atomic Weapons Research Establishment, a series of atomic bombs had been exploded. The first device was loaded into an old frigate and blown up offshore. The British navy feared that the Russians might smuggle a bombship into an English port and detonate it as an atomic Trojan horse. The effects of such an attempt were the object of the test. Unfortunately, a large radioactive cloud was carried by the wind over the Australian mainland, contaminating huge areas. It was the first of some hundred explosions of atomic weapons, three more of which led to fall-out on British aircrews and naval personnel, on Australian towns and on Aboriginal settlements, leading to loss of life. In spite of the known results of fall-out on the Japanese survivors of Hiroshima and Nagasaki, the British government allowed the testing of thermonuclear weapons above ground in conditions that led to a deterioration in health and to early deaths of servicemen and civilians.

Scientists working for the government on defence could no longer pretend innocence about the effects of their actions. The weapons they designed would probably be used, even if they were only tested. They did not warn the military well enough about the dire consequences of detonating nuclear weapons. And although they became more important as advisers to governments and general staffs, they still claimed that they had hardly any influence on the employment of their inventions. The more responsible physicists did do something to put pressure on their administrations to cease trying out nuclear weapons in the atmosphere, which could carry clouds of pollution world-wide. Yet no major cabinet minister or general or admiral came from a scientific background. And the specialist advisers and scientific peers created by the needs of the Second World War did not have the power to change the decisions of their governments. Their terrible inventions were not under their control. Although they had made these Golems, they could and would take no responsibility for the use of what they had wrought.

The master of Churchill College, Sir John Cockcroft, was himself in that position, as was another Fellow, the leading apologist for the responsibility of the scientists, C. P. Snow, later created a life peer as well. Both were heavy men, who made a virtue of their bluffness and their affable bumbling, their disguise for their long understanding of the labyrinths of power. Cockcroft had himself been a pioneer in splitting the atom and had risen through the laboratories to run the British nuclear research establishment at Harwell, while the chemist Snow had also advised many governments on scientific affairs while labouring alongside Anthony Powell in writing a contemporary British Proustian series of a dozen novels, *Strangers and Brothers* as against *A Dance to the Music of Time.* These were the honest furrows of a plough-horse compared to the pirouettes of a pen-master. In one essay reflecting on the ethics of his own past, Snow wrote about the trouble of getting onto any kind of moral escalator. No one knew whether one would ever be able to get off. When scientists became soldiers, as Snow told me, they gave up something imperceptible of the full scientific life. It was not a matter of intellect, but of morals. This was a moral price which sometimes had to be paid. 'Soldiers have to obey,' Snow finally decided. 'That is the foundation of their morality.' It was not the foundation of scientific morality. 'Scientists have to question and if necessary to rebel.'

Snow was not stating that loyalty was without virtue or that all rebellion was good. He was pointing out that loyalty could become conformity, and that obedience carried to the limit could become destructive. More crimes, as Nazi officialdom proved, could be carried out in the name of obedience than ever were in the name of rebellion. Snow himself had become a government official rather than a wartime scientist, and he had fallen into the moral trap of conformity. He was liable to hide behind an institution and refuse moral choice, and he was painfully aware of it.

Snow had already delivered at Cambridge a memorial lecture on the opposed 'Two Cultures' of science and the arts, which had made him a global name and would shortly fall foul of the invective of F. R. Leavis. In a criticism of that lecture, the distinguished scientist Michael Yudkin later declared that government ministers probably never had understood properly the hazards of nuclear tests. They could not evaluate scientific evidence because they were not trained scientists. Thus they had to rely on the opinions of their advisers, who usually stated their views with more dogmatism than the evidence warranted. The specialist advisers themselves might distort or fail to mention evidence that might prejudice a chosen policy. The ethics of the Cavendish were often mute in the corridors of Whitehall.

Yet if the splitting of the atom at the Cavendish had finally led to a secret of causing mass death, it also led to a secret of all life. Sir Lawrence Bragg, a founder of crystallography, had become a director of the Cambridge laboratory. He was particularly interested in solving the structures of proteins, then thought to contain the genes which transmitted hereditary traits. But recent research in New York had suggested that deoxyribonucleic acid or D.N.A. molecules might be the carriers of genetic material. In 1951, a young American biologist, James D. Watson, had come to the Cavendish to work on the structure of proteins in a unit led by the Austrian emigré chemist Max Perutz. He soon developed a partnership with the brilliant and temperamental physicist Francis Crick, whom Watson said was rarely in a modest mood, even if he might one day be considered a Rutherford. Using the patient work of the London physicist Maurice Wilkins on the D.N.A. molecule, Watson and Crick began to speculate on the genetic origins of life. The great American chemist Linus Pauling was also experimenting in California. Three groups were competing to discover the primary secret of human biology, a discovery which would be as momentous as splitting the atom.

The front runner, Wilkins, would be a loser. As Watson observed, Wilkins had escaped into biology only to find it as unpleasant 'as physics, with its atomic consequences'.

There were important differences in understanding between biologists and geneticists, chemists and crystallographers and physicists. The Cavendish unit managed to bridge these gaps. Using the shape of a double helix, the form that Leonardo da Vinci himself had created in his staircase at the Château de Chambord, Watson and Crick solved the problem of the structure of the D.N.A. molecule. In a letter written from the Cavendish on 12 March 1953, Watson outlined the discovery in crude diagrams. It was the beginning of all genetic engineering and the biochemical changing of human society, twenty-one years after nuclear fission was performed at Cambridge, a dozen years after the seminal work of Turing on computers that cracked the code, eight years after the dropping of the atomic bomb on Hiroshima, simultaneous with the making of hydrogen bombs and the poisoning of the atmosphere with radioactive fall-out.

As Percy Bysshe Shelley wrote of the west wind, so the Cavendish Laboratory was destroyer and preserver. Even the finding of the structure of the genes could have terrible consequences. Since fundamental changes in the shape of living things could now be developed, Mary Shelley's fantasy of Frankenstein approached reality. We could not only alter the plants and animals on the earth, but also ourselves. James D. Watson himself was horrified by the probability of cloning and the reproduction of identical human beings. Great controversies and legal measures would arise about scientific meddling with ordinary human reproduction. Sperm could be frozen and banked, babies conceived in test-tubes. We could, indeed, begin to remake ourselves, for better or for worse. Meeting him later on the road to Washington rather than Damascus, I asked him about these awesome possibilities. He said that cloning must never happen.

Francis Crick was also a Founding Fellow at Churchill College, which turned out to be more conservative than Winston had been. When China briefly invaded northern India and withdrew, the talk at the high table was not of the merits of Mao and Nehru, but of how much money the college would have made in investing in tea-plantations in Assam; their share-price had plummeted, only to bob up again. John Maynard Keynes, who had made the fortune of King's College with similar plunges on the stock market, was rubbing his dry finger-bones in his grave with glee. At the dons' dinners, we never solved the problems of the world or even our own. We talked of building the college and money – I suppose, the important things right there and right then. But for a young radical with a foot on the accelerator, it was a red light on Global Street.

I was more and more aware that my Cambridge year or years of satirists were not revolutionary. They were incapable of replacing the Establishment except with its heirs or with themselves, blunted, like Bumbo, by the process of easy inclusion into the right ranks. Those who were actually changing human society – the Fellows of Churchill College – were far older and wholly impervious to our assault. They ignored the cause of nuclear disarmament, which served as another chance for the arts graduates to attack the technocrats who had invented the monstrous atomic weaponry. The new *Frankenstein* was Stanley Kubrick's *Doctor Strangelove*, subtitled *How I Learned to Stop Worrying and Love the Bomb.*

The original atomic fission had been performed in the Cavendish Laboratory, and the literary puritans of Downing College did not allow the physicists to forget it. Their attack was on the Cavendish's chief interpreter and only major novelist, C. P. Snow. By charging him and denying his premise of the 'two cultures', F. R. Leavis only proved that the 'two cultures' were more antagonistic than ever.

In his previous memorial lecture of 1959, C. P. Snow had made some simple, but important statements that reflected on his experience and widely influenced his time. By training he was a chemist; by vocation, a writer. He had a ringside view of one of the most creative periods in all physics. He had intimate friends among both scientists and writers, but the two groups

kept apart. It was their different little societies which he had
pinpointed, in his lecture, as two cultures. To him, 'culture'
meant, anthropologically, a group living in the same environment, linked by common habits and assumptions and way of life,
and a development of the mind. He thought that the literary
cultures of Chelsea and Greenwich Village shared a common
language, but to them, the scientists at the Massachusetts Institute
of Technology might have been talking Tibetan. The intellectual
and practical life of the whole of western society was being split.
As far as the new scientific revolution was concerned, literary
intellectuals were 'natural Luddites'.

Exaggerating his case, Snow dismissed most leading writers of
the nineteenth and twentieth centuries as pessimists without the
social hope of the scientists, who had the future in their bones.
Snow here equated literary culture with 'traditional culture',
which did not wish the future to exist. The gap between these
two cultures, scientific and literary-traditional, was growing wider
in England where there was early educational specialization and
where social forms were crystallized. In Victorian times, Lord
Salisbury had his own laboratory at Hatfield, the prime minister,
Arthur Balfour, was interested in natural science, and the leading
civil servant, Sir John Anderson, had done research in inorganic
chemistry at Leipzig. 'None of that degree of interchange at the
top of the Establishment is likely, or indeed, thinkable, now.'

The separation between the scientists and the non-scientists
was greater than ever. Academics at Cambridge had ignored
the Industrial Revolution, which had enriched them and had
separated Disraeli's 'Two Nations' of the rich and the poor into
Snow's 'Two Cultures'. Yet even more significant was the new
scientific revolution which Snow dated from the 'thirties and
the use of atomic particles in industry, largely the creation of the
Cavendish Laboratory. The innovative industrial society of electronics, atomic energy and automation would make society cardi-
nally different and enable the western nations not only to benefit
their own populations, but also to bridge the abyss between the
rich and the poor nations by exporting their technology. The

danger lay in the split of the two cultures both at the universities and in the government, by which the scientists who managed the new revolution could not communicate their social hope to the administrators. According to Snow, time was running out for western societies to close the gap between their cultures. History was merciless to failure, nor would we in the West write it. But Snow failed to foresee the coming to power of a prime minister with scientific training, Margaret Thatcher, and the collapse of socialism in Marxist eastern Europe in the face of superior western technology.

Yet at that time, Snow's plain language and simple dialectic appealed world-wide. It provoked a vicious assault at Cambridge from the self-elected guardian of the university's essential values, F. R. Leavis. As provincial and rigorous and condemnatory as any regicide in the Civil War, Leavis hated Snow for his international success, his loose definitions, and even his literary reputation. To Leavis, Snow was portentously ignorant – but a portent of an ignorant time in which Leavis was considered a sage and a master-mind and a guardian of the values of the heart of England.

At another memorial lecture in 1962, attended by a crowd of hundreds of undergraduates and dons, Leavis claimed that he was not enjoying the murderous field-day. In fact, his words breathed envy; his tongue was malice incarnate. He demeaned the university traditions that he claimed to be defending. He talked of Snow as an intellectual nullity, as undistinguished as it was possible to be, incapable of posing or answering problems. As a novelist, let alone as a scientist or thinker, Snow did not exist. In Snow's major novel, *The Affair*, science was a mere word, the vocation merely postulated. Snow's lecture on the 'Two Cultures' was a document in the study of the cliché. Snow was as ignorant of history as of literature. Leavis used the minor tools of a Wittgenstein to brand Snow's statement about scientists having the future in their bones as not a meaningful proposition; he forgot that most of his vilifications of Snow were meaningless too. He rightly pointed out that Snow had not defined 'culture' exactly and had slid from 'literary' to 'traditional culture', as well as dismissing the worth of the major literary figures of the previous hundred and fifty years. Leavis concluded in vainglory. He was not a Luddite. Human intelligence was needed to respond to the challenges of the new technology. The proper study of Cambridge was language. The centre of the university should be a vital English school. Twenty years of running the critical magazine *Scrutiny* had taught him that the academic was the enemy and the academic could be beaten. He and his disciples were, as they knew they were, 'the essential Cambridge in spite of Cambridge.'

This rancorous attack, which was so venomous that I left the hall, signalled not only the division of the 'two cultures', but also the split in the values of the old and the new Cambridge. As much as he was condemning the significance of the scientific pre-eminence claimed by Snow, Leavis was attacking the old Apostolic pursuit of self-gratification and style, which still informed much of the Cambridge English department and the London literary reviews. Ironically enough, many of the younger Apostles who were becoming the new literary editors were profoundly influenced by Leavis and by his teachings. On the whole, they were the very puritanical and provincial professionals that he liked his students to be. But in this worst display of his vindictive and righteous self-justification, Leavis proved that he could scrutinize the faults of every leading figure, but not his own.

The most astute of the comments on the controversy that so acutely exposed the many little rival 'cultures' and traditions at Cambridge was written by a research biochemist, Michael Yudkin, for the *Cambridge Review*. Although praised by Leavis for denigrating the use of the phrase 'two cultures' when there were many 'cultures', Yudkin agreed with two of Snow's theses. There was a failure of contact between scientists and non-scientists. This failure was unfortunate and probably dangerous. But Yudkin did not think any significant improvement was possible. With his claim that society's hope now lay with the scientists, Snow was pursuing the falsely optimistic idea of a new Renaissance. There would be no bridge across the gap between science and the arts. There would only be the atrophy of Snow's traditional culture, which would be gradually annexed by the scientific one until only a single culture remained. In his last words on this commentary, Snow seemed to accept some of Yudkin's criticism and pessimism, saying that Renaissance man was no longer possible; England had lost even the pretence of a common culture.

The scientists were no Dr. Strangeloves. The best of them, particularly at Cambridge, did try to stop the pernicious fall-out from the testing of nuclear weapons in the atmosphere. As Sir Peter Medawar wrote, scientists feared the effect of radiation on genetic materials; but 'a principal social function of science is to act as scapegoat for the blunders and malfunctions of its political masters.' The old Cambridge Apostle Bertrand Russell had first suggested international conferences on science and world affairs in a manifesto drafted in December 1954. The declaration was signed by Einstein shortly before his death and by other leading scientists. Cockcroft supported the idea and began representations, which were to lead to the first of many Pugwash conferences; at them, experts from both East and West sat down to exchange information and differences. It was at these early Pugwash meetings that the conditions for the Partial Nuclear Test Ban Treaty of 1963 between Russia, America and Britain were unofficially established. In Churchill's famous phrase, jaw-jaw was always better than war-war, and the physicists responsible for nuclear fission demonstrated that they still had some influence on their governments.

It was high time to reach a limited agreement. After the débâcle of Suez, the British government had followed the American example in moving from an expensive conventional defence policy towards a cheaper one of massive deterrence. Fewer armies and navies, more nuclear weapons and the means to deliver them. It may have been true, as one officer at Suez remarked, that an H-bomb could not keep the canal open, but a strategy of deterrence based on the new hydrogen bombs allowed the British government to cut down its army by a third, to end military conscription, and to reduce its defence spending from eleven to seven per cent of its gross national product. Sir Anthony Eden had been wrong about the consequences of the Suez adventure. He was also to prove wrong about placing too heavy a reliance on nuclear weapons at the expense of conventional forces. 'If continents, and not merely small islands were doomed to destruction,' he wrote, 'all are equal on the grim reckoning.' They were not equal in the smaller wars short of nuclear war, as the Suez crisis had proved. But the possession of the hydrogen bomb gave Britain the status of a great power, even if she had not the resources to support her pretensions.

For good or ill, Britain persisted in the pursuit of independence through nuclear deterrence. But nuclear power could not change British society by itself, nor finally preserve it. The well-being of the country depended on an economic revolution based on scientific invention, the computers and biotechnology also developed at Cambridge. It did not depend on a military solution. If C. P. Snow exaggerated the gap between the 'two cultures', he was correct that electronics, the peaceful use of atomic energy, and automation would make society radically different.

Further inventions in electronics would spawn the computer revolution which would make Cambridge itself the Silicon Fen of England, with Sir Clive Sinclair and his competitors setting up shop around the abilities of the scientists of the ancient university. Atomic energy would still be the force that kept the perilous peace between the great powers, but more beneficially, it supplied the electric grids of nations short of less dangerous fuels. The arms race of deterrent weapons still continued in successive escalations. In 1957, the Russians had put into operation the first intercontinental ballistic missile and had sent up the first sputnik into the heavens, creating a 'technological Pearl Harbor' for the Americans, who had quickly riposted with their own missiles and spacecraft. To protect themselves militarily and economically, all governments with the necessary technological expertise pushed forward with new defence systems and industrial innovations at whatever cost to existing societies.

The third industrial metamorphosis had begun, and it had begun largely at Cambridge. That revolution which the Cavendish had helped to start was so awesome in its application that no literary Apostle, no arts professor, no master of the media, and certainly no politician could gauge its consequences or adequately describe its future. It could only be attacked and misunderstood in its significance, as F. R. Leavis did in his deadly personal assault on C. P. Snow. For lethal it nearly was. Shortly after the visceral lecture, Snow had a minor operation. As he was suffering from great stress and distress, his heart stopped under the effect of the anaesthetic. He was clinically dead for five minutes, until his heart was massaged back to life. He and his wife, the novelist Pamela Hansford Johnson, ascribed this setback to the Leavis vituperation. When he told me of it, his anguish and his wife's loving concern touched me. George Steiner and myself were two of the few dons at Cambridge to speak out and write on behalf of Snow's integrity and honesty, and against this slow death by a thousand envies. The result was that George Steiner was never given even a mere lectureship in English at the university, although he was to become Professor of Comparative Literature at Geneva and he was incomparably the most brilliant speaker at Cambridge with the greatest knowledge of western literature. My own works were to incur the distaste of the Leavisite literary editors during the decades to come. It was a Lilliputian war about greater matters than which end of an egg to break, a microscopic squabble about a macrocosm. But then, as solitary human beings, we can only understand well what personally happens to us. One thing was proven: how unforgiving Cambridge was.

At the end of the 'fifties and at the beginning of the new decade, C. P. Snow had postulated that there had been a rupture between two cultures, science and the arts. In point of fact, three cultures were already dividing like an amoeba. Not only was there a split between a scientific and an artistic culture, but both of these cultures were considered élitist in an age of spreading mass democracy which had its own standards – particularly in popular music and in art – and where advertising techniques on television

were changing the perception of images. The leading patrons of
culture, the government departments and committees in charge
of distributing funds for education or research, the British and
the Arts Councils and the local authorities, pursued what Keynes
had advocated after the war – standards of excellence which
might educate a larger audience. But there was a searching of
souls among the governors that this policy of excellence, which
Lord Reith had also advocated at the British Broadcasting Corporation and which his successors were steadily eroding, might
be wrong for the times. Perhaps there was a lower common
denominator in the cultures of Britain – and this should be
patronized. This was precisely the fear of T. S. Eliot in his *Notes
towards a Definition of Culture*: that mass education would adulter-
ate and degrade culture, preparing the ground for the barbarian
nomads of the future – an accurate prediction of the diluted
Dadaism, the pop art and music of the youth 'culture' of the
next decade.

For the riches bred by the new technology were granting a
vast spending power to the young, who had been taught to be
consumers, not to be patrons. The incessant barrage of advertisements on American television had educated the new generation
in spending on various appealing products, particularly on
gramophone records and tapes. This vast and immediate power
of consumption was creating fresh arbiters of taste, semi-literate
pop stars and artists, who used the devices of advertising and
mass production to produce works of 'art' that had the quality
of instant recognition. Thorstein Veblen had accused the Gilded
Age of the American moguls of conspicuous consumption; this
modern age was guilty of spontaneous consumption. And the existing standards of culture and art were to be the victims of that.

The destruction of the fine arts had been a strand in contemporary Europe from the Decadents through the Dadaists to the
Lettrists and the Situationists, who considered culture merely
something to be overthrown and replaced with events. To them,
capitalism masked its repression through spectacles rather as the
Roman emperors had used circuses to placate the people. Their

strategy was to oppose the mass media by other spectacles, instant and subversive and humorous. Works of art should obliterate themselves, such as Metzger's nylon canvas eaten away by hydrochloric acid, or Tinguely's self-destructive machines in the garden of the Museum of Modern Art in New York, which indeed, as I saw, were gone almost before they were perceived. Masterpieces should become consumables. Then they could not be stored or considered. They were only part of a process of change. They existed in their own destruction rather as the accumulated treasures of a Viking chieftain had been consumed by fire after his death on his burning ship. Creation as destruction – this was the death of sponsored art which could not conserve the finished work.

Abstract expressionism was the first schism between American and European culture. The drips of Jackson Pollock had no meaning and no content. The viewer interpreted the splodges and brushstrokes as he wished. Lack of beauty was in the eye of the beholder. The pop art which followed attracted the new consumer culture of the young with its superimposition of advertising images on those of art, with its insistence that brand names were also titles of aesthetics. When its extreme practitioner, Andy Warhol, said that he wanted to be a machine, he seemed to resolve the conflict between the sciences and the arts, between the technology that made the young so rich and the pictures they wished to consume with their money. It asserted the triumph of mechanical art and the destruction of the values of the fine arts.

Such a resolution appeared to be a final solution to the conflict between the three cultures with their differing patrons and consumers. Yet the permanent remained the enemy of the instant, the abiding was the foe of the non-existent. Charles Snow still lived, and I never forgot what he told me about the afterlife. When his heart had stopped and he was clinically dead, he said that he had left his body and looked down upon it. His spirit or soul, in which he hardly believed, left his warm corpse before returning to its place. Possibly there was some resolution in things through the reconciliation of the spirits of mankind.

5

JUST TO BE ON THE SAFE SIDE

At a meeting between Harold Macmillan and President John F. Kennedy, the British Prime Minister asked his nuclear expert, Sir William Penney, how many hydrogen bombs would be needed to finish off Britain. 'Five, I should think, Prime Minister,' Penney said, then added: 'Just to be on the safe side, let's say eight.'

The Civil War in Spain had been the opposite case: then Russian tanks had defended the Republic against fascism. There was no Just War possible now, not with western imperialism joined by eastern imperialism, confronting each other with nuclear weapons that might destroy all humanity. The fiasco of the Suez adventure had proved that there were only two great powers in the world. Without the support of one of them, nothing much could be done. Emotionally, the Russian assault on a European country was more devastating to radical thought than the British attack on a canal in the eastern Mediterranean. 'I cared more about Hungary,' the novelist Margaret Drabble told me at Cambridge. 'The Empire had better go, anyway.'

The consequence of Suez was, indeed, that the Empire went, under the astute direction of the British prime minister, Harold Macmillan. The winds of change that he released to blow across the last of the British colonies confirmed the doldrums of the Suez invasion and, at the personal level, the futility of my father's life as a Colonial Police commissioner, who was soon forced into early retirement. America and Russia were the only great powers now: yet the new Conservative defence policy of increased reliance on nuclear weapons stimulated the just cause of the Campaign for Nuclear Disarmament, which concluded at Trafalgar Square an annual march of forty miles from the Atomic Weapons Research Centre at Aldermaston. Although the government hardly altered because of the Suez débâcle or the protest marches, a process of change was begun. The children of the last Just War were breaking down the gates of the Establishment.

I joined an Aldermaston march more from personal grief than political conviction. Timothy Birdsall had died of leukaemia, and we held it to be the result of overground nuclear testing. He was the most amiable and funny of men. His cartoons for the *Spectator* and *That Was The Week That Was* showed a deft and immediate originality that was as spontaneous as his humour. Looking through his memorial volume *Timothy*, edited by Michael Frayn and Bamber Gascoigne, I am still struck by the piercing sympathy of his satire. A graduate squats in the street, his upturned mortar board as a begging-bowl: behind him, a placard – AFFLUENT SOCIETY TO SUPPORT. A wife looks at her City husband over his breakfast newspaper and says, 'Darling, where *is* the Free World exactly?' Two schoolboys in shorts and blazers pass an evening newspaper poster scrawled with K.'s BIG BOMB, and one says to the other, 'What are you going to be if you grow up?' Timothy had two small children who did grow up and a marvellous actress wife, who played in *Look Back in Anger* at the Royal Court Theatre. His loss turned our satire into sympathy, our mockery of politics and society into a terrible urge to change them.

He was already dying when the Cuban missile crisis had wonderfully clarified our minds. Writing about it later, the best critic of modern British culture, Bryan Appleyard, declared that the yeast of the 'sixties was not pop music or sexual liberation, but the conviction of the young after the Cuban affair that they were living on borrowed time. As much as sex and drugs and rock music, mass death defined the decade. There were many ways to go – heat and blast and the slow poisoning of radiation. 'So we threw the last party, survival was not an option.' Historians argued about whether Cuba was the most dangerous crisis of the Cold War, or Berlin. But nothing matched Cuba for symbolic and imaginative power, as a crisis of horrific and slow-motion purity. 'It happened at the pace of a game of postal chess' between the young god Kennedy and the shoe-banging peasant Khrushchev. The worst was that Cuba was only about atomic war. It began with intermediate-range nuclear weapons in clearings in Cuba. Conventional weapons had nothing to do with it. If it had gone wrong, there was an apocalypse. 'We would go from peace to terror to our skin coming off like gloves in minutes.'

This prescience of instant annihilation was summed up in the acronym M.A.D. – Mutually Assured Destruction. The strategists of the major powers had made the use of nuclear weapons appear inevitable at one time or another. It had been the subject of my third novel, *The Project*, in which a nihilist physicist set off the terminal rocket as a war game. It made Marianne and myself say that we refused to have a child in the circumstances, but would only adopt an orphan from the Third World. Both as an attitude and a belief, we did live in fear of death. And the dying of a friend from the polluted and irradiated atmosphere confirmed our darkest suspicions and sent us marching from Aldermaston towards Trafalgar Square. But the leaders of the Campaign for Nuclear Disarmament were increasingly moving from one just cause, which could attract anyone who did not want to die, into the many panaceas of the Left. They 'edged the whole organization towards protest not only against the bomb, but against hunger, old age pensions and the whole gamut of socialist grievances'. So they destroyed its universal appeal, and that pure protest seemed to us to reside only with the Anarchists. Just as George Orwell had supported the democratic Left in Spain against the totalitarian Socialists, we felt that our commitment was to freedom of speech against the bomb above all.

As it was, we were attacked by the police in front of Westminster Abbey and the Houses of Parliament, our flags were ripped down, our guitars were broken, and in a confrontation of extreme absurdity, I found myself pulling up a red and black banner from under a police boot like a rebellious American colonist feeling his liberties had been trampled on. I was then struck a blow in the chest by the police officer, who announced, 'I'll put you inside.' I hit him back in the chest with the brilliant riposte, 'I'll put *you* inside.' We glared at each other, the free-for-all drove us apart, and I found myself running across Parliament Square and up the Mall, waving a tattered banner of freedom for all the world, like Pudovkin's Mother with the wrong flag.

My recklessness was part of my political incoherence. I worked by passionate instinct, not by party politics. As a Fellow of Church-ill College, I was in the heart of the atomic Establishment. Yet here was I running with the Anarchists, whom I suspected were the last of the free. I knew their history, that they were far greater in numbers than the Bolsheviks and should have taken over in the Russian Revolution. But, of course, true to their principles, they could never organize. But I also knew that they were not a party so much as a contradiction of all parties. President Kennedy and the United States had kindled my hope or memory of the future, and if something was to be done to change Britain, only the Labour Party appeared able to do it. So I wrote to its leader, Hugh Gaitskell, out of the blue from Soho Square, even though he had routed the unilateral nuclear disarmers within the party. I told him that the style of his speeches was terrible. I said that I would act as his speech-writer without pay and try to give him the style of a Kennedy, who had inspired us with the products of his script-writers. I was a historian of America; I thought I could do that for the Labour leader.

Incredibly, Gaitskell replied and accepted. It was the gall of my Cambridge contemporaries that we did offer ourselves, and if we were any good, things happened. Gaitskell was only receiving two thousand pounds a year to aid his expenses as leader of the opposition, and he could hardly afford a secretary. He had expensive tastes and depended on hostesses such as Ann Fleming to run his social life for him. He may have responded to my mixture of social awareness and youthful radicalism, but what he wanted was the Kennedy jokes and apt quotations from the classic writers. These I did provide, particularly in an article designed to save the Euston Arch from destruction. But then he threw away my speech on joining the Common Market at the Labour Party Conference and turned against it, evoking a thousand years of history as an excuse for staying out. In my hoity-toity way, I told him that I would not write his speeches any more if he ignored my efforts. But when his ratings slipped again in the polls, he recalled me, and I realized in my ignorance that I was working for a great man, a true lost statesman.

On that occasion, the shadow cabinet had been meeting in the leader's office, while I waited outside. As they filed out, their salute to the alien youngster was characteristic – George Brown's

jocular 'Hello, comrade'; James Callaghan's polite 'Good morning'; and Harold Wilson's suspicious glare. But when I was called
inside, Gaitskell disarmed and shamed me. He said that he knew
from his daughters, who had recommended me to him, that my
generation spent their holidays in Europe and supported entry
into the Common Market, but that the members of his generation felt a guilt about the Empire, and that they could never
put our obligations towards the Commonwealth after an entry
into Europe. As he spoke, I thought of my father and his imperial
service that I had repudiated. And yet, Gaitskell continued, he
could be convinced that he was wrong. He might well be so, and,
if the circumstances were different, he would have the courage
to change his mind. His argument and his decency and his
frankness made me feel ashamed of the arrogant innocent that
I was. I went on writing his speeches. His stock soared, he was
going to Moscow, he would certainly win the next election,
ending the long Tory hegemony. And then he went to hospital
with pneumonia. And there he died, too young, on the threshold.

Hope died with him – the hope of changing things within the
Labour Party and the country. He was the first revisionist Labour
shadow prime minister, and the little man who would follow him,
Harold Wilson, would weasel and widdle away the election victory
which he inherited. Gaitskell looked to the Democrats and to
Kennedy in America for his inspiration in turning his party into
the natural majority party of Great Britain. We were all then
under the influence of things American except for the Marxist
left wing, and Gaitskell was trying to eliminate their influence in
the party.

This second dying and killing of hope affected us even more.
Satire seemed a blunt instrument, a cosh for caring. It was significant that even on that vehicle of deflation, *That Was The Week
That Was*, my friend Bernard Levin delivered a eulogy on the
dead Labour leader: 'That he *did* save the party he loved was not
the least of his achievements. The tragedy is that it was to be the
last. And the tragedy is not his alone, but the tragedy of all those
involved in, or even affected by, the struggle for freedom and

social justice, those twin causes in which he so devoutly believed, and in the selfless service of which he lived and died. "The ideals of democratic socialism," he said, as he conceded defeat on election night in 1959, "have never shone so brightly". If they shine less brightly today than yesterday, it is because of his passing.'

Soho had also been a killing ground before we came to live in the Square. The very name of the central London village was originally a call to the hunting dogs pursuing a hare to its death. Many of the old Fitzrovian painters and composers and poets had been hounded to their graves after the war, the victims of booze and fags – Nina Hamnett and John Minton, the two Roberts Colquhoun and MacBryde, Constant Lambert and Dylan Thomas, who had already foreseen his end in his last poem, calling himself 'an old ramrod dying of strangers' – and pints and chasers. There were still Francis Bacon and Lucian Freud to be seen at their lunches in Wheeler's in Old Compton Street; but we could rarely afford to get beyond the bar, where they would serve half a dozen oysters and a glass of Chablis and free olives and brown bread and mayonnaise for twenty-one shillings, a guinea a head. And there was the French Pub, that last hangout of the Soho bohemians, the poets and the plastered artists, pissing their lives away.

Already the conditions for writing poetry in Fitzrovia were in decline. George Barker saw that young poets could no longer create and eat at the same time. 'It is already impossible for them to drink and write as they wish: the beer is no longer singing beer.' For economic and social reasons, artists had begun to move from Soho by the early 'fifties, because of the rise of crime and rents, which could be afforded only by strip-tease shows and pornographic bookshops. The Fitzrovians who stayed in the area had to be able to pay for it – or so George Melly found when Lucian Freud took him on the occasional binge to the Stork Club where the hostesses served whisky in teapots outside licensing hours. The sting of war and bohemia was already blunted.

The future of writing and the arts would be less concentrated, yet more restricted and overly cautious after the middle 'fifties, the suburban celebrations of John Betjeman, the provincial pastorals of Philip Larkin. State patronage would increasingly make for safe production for subsidy. Some noble and unfashionable romantics would continue to laud the lost past and intermittently try to live as they had then; but even they were aware that their peers had departed and that modern times were replacing the beery universities of their fledgling days.

As literature fled from the garrets and pubs of Soho, music entered by the cellars and the clubs. It was the first youth culture that Britain had ever seen, and it grew from the protest songs of the exploited. I had heard Joan Baez sing in a voice more piercing than a bleeding nightingale in a coffee house off Harvard Square in 1960, and Pete Seeger a year later in Greenwich Village. And now Ewan MacColl, who was separated from Joan Littlewood and her Theatre Workshop in the East End, was bringing the folk songs of the Depression 'thirties to the jazz and skiffle players of the 'fifties. In a benefit for the Marxist newspaper, the *Daily Worker*, MacColl had sung a black American chain-gang prison song alongside Ken Colyer's Jazzmen. The banjoist with Chris Barber's Jazz Band, Lonnie Donegan, was becoming the great 'skiffle' star with his version of 'Rock Island Line' and 'John Henry', borrowing a black American style and giving it a British twang. (It was a skiffle group in Liverpool called The Quarrymen that gave John Lennon his musical start.) Tennessee Ernie's 'Shotgun Boogie' and 'Sixteen Tons', the blues of Muddy Waters and Bo Diddley and Chuck Berry, the rock of Buddy Holly and Elvis Presley, and the cool sound of Charlie Mingus and Thelonius Monk – these galvanized the traditional jazz bands of Humphrey Lyttleton and Chris Barber from a homage to Louis Armstrong and Charlie Parker into another beat. We would go to their clubs off Oxford Street and Cy Laurie's in the basement of Mac's Rehearsal Rooms in Windmill Street; then we would progress to Ronnie Scott's in Gerrard Street and later in Frith Street, where his club still endures in spite of the maestro's sense of humour. At other times, we went to the Marquee, first in the basement of the Academy Cinema and afterwards in Wardour Street, where the new Rhythm and Blues groups were playing, and where the Rolling Stones made their West End opening. In the same street was the Flamingo under the Whiskey A Go Go, where the mods went on their scooters to applaud Georgie Fame and the Blue Flames. For us, it was the time and the place to be, so we could listen to the experiments in new sounds that were exploding in the firecrackers of our new age.

The Beatles from Liverpool were the phenomenon of their time. John Lennon once said that their effect was greater than Jesus Christ's, and even George Steiner said that they spread the *lingua franca* of English across the world more effectively than the Bible. They were taken very seriously indeed: a work by Lennon was selected by Kenneth Tynan to appear on the stage of the National Theatre. Effectively, they and the Rolling Stones and a few other British pop groups replaced American images and sound, and British literature and religion as the major influences on the young. Sport endured, particularly football, and the pervasive film culture of Hollywood. But otherwise the Beatles and the Rolling Stones became the voices of the 'sixties.

There was a conflict between the two groups, although Lennon and Paul McCartney had given Mick Jagger his first successful number, 'I Wanna Be Your Man'. 'And that's how it came about that the Beatles came to the rescue of the Stones,' Andrew Oldham remembered, 'and provided them with the song that was going to establish them as a popular recording group.' Paradoxically, as the manager of the Stones, Oldham was turning his middle-class boys into the apparent toughs of their age, the bards of violence, while his opposite Brian Epstein was changing the Beatles from Scouse louts into young Etonians with floppy hair and charming manners and classless accents. The Stones were roughened, the Beatles were polished smooth. And in those years of protest and anger, the universal love-songs written by Lennon and McCartney seemed anodyne to me beside the snarl and loathing of the strutting Stones. As yet their message better suited my feelings.

Along with English literature, The Movement had already lost its eminence and its way. It was symptomized in the jazz criticism of its guru, Philip Larkin, who showed his insularity and resistance to change as well as the paucity of his ear and his perceptions. When he equated Charlie Parker with Pablo Picasso and Ezra Pound, it was because he disliked all three of them. Their works of art were 'irresponsible exploitations of technique in contradiction of modern life as we know it'. Larkin failed to see that his view of modern life as he knew it was circumscribed and retrograde. To him, modernism in painting and cool jazz did not help 'us to enjoy or endure'. It compelled us to wade deeper and deeper into violence and obscenity in one long screech or a blank canvas. The fact that Larkin's own private letters revelled in abuse and smut was not the subject of his public criticism.

Equally irrelevant now seemed the postures of the Angry Young Men, most of whom were ageing fast into a right-wing reaction from their previous protests. Although John Osborne still backed the staging of my musical, *The Breaking of Bumbo*, it had been killed off by Tony Richardson's flirtation with Hollywood, where he was directing an appalling version of William Faulkner's *Sanctuary* after the success of his early Woodfall films in England. And at Cambridge, I only met Kingsley Amis once, although he was also a Fellow of a college there. I was asked round for tea at his house with his first wife. His son Martin was playing in the garden, a shrimp who would grow into his father's superior. Kingsley recalled this sole and pleasant encounter in his memoirs, in which I was condemned to the role of the mean Scotsman in a pub, who cannot stand a round of drinks because he has left his wallet behind. Poor Kingsley probably could not remember the name of another Scottish writer to afflict with that hoary old Sassenach story.

The pessimism of that borrowed time, the feeling that we were living under the dark nuclear umbrella, put Marianne and me under the influence of the blackest wit of his post-war Oxford generation: known as Deacon to the other undergraduates such as Kenneth Tynan because of his solemn style and utterance, he dominated his friends as Larkin had, but through his magnificent pessimism and bleak vision. 'I was not laughing,' he once said to me when I took him to a comedy in the theatre. 'The sound you heard was a glottal spasm or premonitory rictal death rattle.' He never elided a syllable nor used an apostrophe, but he spoke the perfect prose of Hobbes or Swift, every phrase considered to each dead stop. His conversation was usually about himself and his survival in his Mayfair maisonette which was decorated as his own *memento mori*. 'I died many years ago,' he used to say to us. 'My subsequent activity has been to maintain this status quo.' A sufferer from tuberculosis, he had been operated upon. 'They removed a lung and whatever other organ they could reach. I recovered sufficiently to participate in my diurnal death throes. I must go back to isolation. It has its horrors, but the horrors of knowing one is not alone in this world are incomparably worse.'

We had met him at a drinks party – he swore it was the only one that he had ever attended. My book on *Prohibition* and his only novel on his Swiss sanatorium years – hailed by Graham Greene as one of the greater books of the century – had been printed by the same American publisher. At the gathering in William Sansom's garden in St. John's Wood, Deacon was smitten by the beauty of Marianne, although he praised my own novel, *The Breaking of Bumbo*. When he gave us his address and telephone number, James Michie almost had a seizure: how had we penetrated into the hermitage of the most solitary recluse in London? We became two of the few people that Deacon ever saw. We were entranced by the long dark pain of his body, the brown melancholy of his eyes and his sonorous prophecies of woe. 'The world is a vast concentration camp,' he told us, 'each generation of prisoners handing on its torch of suffering to the next.'

His home was his hibernation and proved his biological determinism. He compared the futility of human life to the photograph on his wall of five fishes, all eating each other while they were being clutched by a squid, itself being swallowed by a larger apparition. Mankind also ate itself, but wearing kid gloves. On the wall of his bedroom, Deacon maintained the cross-section of a live ant colony, so that he would be reminded of a superior organization for living. On his chimney-piece, a small skull grinned out of a wooden box marked *Égalité*. A huge beetle, as large as a child's hand, *goliathus giganticus*, was trapped for ever in perspex, its six legs spread beneath its black and yellow back. There was a painting of a face as the sacred one in the Holy Shroud, rotting away into an obscurity of canvas; a silver medal with a skeleton shaking hands with a skeleton and the inscription SEMPER; a music box which turned around and about a white mouse supporting spectacles on its nose, reading a book named TIME; while a nanny goat clutching a hundred dollars lay on a psychoanalytical couch, circulating gently to the tune of 'Round the World in Eighty Days'. Otherwise, leather-bound books in English and French on oak shelves, Balzac and Dostoevsky, Proust and Sade, Schopenhauer and Kierkegaard, lined the walls of this collector of strange things. The wallpaper and the drawn curtains were grey in the museum or mausoleum of a life in limbo.

We agreed on admiring the talent for self-destruction of a Balzac, a man who could describe his failings to perfection and continue to do them for the impish glee of ruining himself. Deacon's stories were told with such deprecating humour that we could only weep or laugh. Yet to weep would mean offending him as a gentleman. Therefore we had to laugh with a cheerful brutality and so confirm him happily in his incurable pessimism about the human race. Our dialogue was a running gag at death.

I would say, 'You seem to want your living to be as much of a problem as possible.'

He would reply dismissively, 'Why not! Our servants can die for us.'

'You'll be the only man who has himself buried on a bed of nails.'

'Pointing inwards.'

'So you won't be able to rise on Judgement Day.'

'Or outwards, so the pallbearers will bleed for me.'

'How in fact do you see your funeral?'

'As set out in my will. I request no flowers, no music, no public announcement, no service and no mourners. My charred remains to be tipped into the nearest municipal ashcan. The last time I redrafted my will, my solicitor said he hoped I would modify the stringency of these instructions. I replied, "Gladly. I was flattering myself by suggesting there could be any mourners. Strike out no mourners! Utterly otiose! A waste of time, ink and paper." '

Then he would roar with laughter, but remain deadly serious. He was a great raconteur of death gone wrong. He told me a story of leaving his Swiss sanatorium to buy a revolver and kill himself. It was hard to buy the weapon. He had to pledge the gunsmith not to kill anyone but himself. He went back to his hotel suite and decided that it was too grand to stain with his gore. He progressed to a night-club with a friend, became drunk, went to sleep in the bath, nearly drowned, but was saved by switching on the shower in his last convulsions. Then he put the revolver in his mouth, was too weak to press the trigger, hated the taste of the gun barrel and ordered coffee and croissants instead. With his breakfast came the hotel manager, who insisted that he left the suite immediately because a dignitary wanted it. To him, suicide was a form of slapstick. Deacon often took his temperature with the gun instead of a thermometer – he could not tell the difference. He had probably breathed so much down the barrel that it was clogged with rust.

Deacon's attraction to Marianne was through French and Edwardian Decadent literature, particularly Rimbaud and Verlaine, Lautréamont and Oscar Wilde. One of the few people capable of writing flawlessly in two languages, she published two elegant novels in English, *Paradox Lost* and *Watcher in the Park*. The first was an account of a lesbian affair in Paris with a café singer: the heroine was only seventeen. The second was about a twelve-year-old girl enticing and then condemning to prison a retarded male exhibitionist, so that she was more sinning than sinned against. These perverse texts alienated the wives of the last of my conventional friends from Eton and Cambridge. The words were far too far from Leavisite puritanism. They marked the distance I had travelled from our old common ground and the new byways I was exploring. My own next novel, *The Raker*, was a dance of love and death. Shown on the cover, which was one of Deacon's collection of Edwardian fantasy postcards, was Pierrot talking to Pierrette, their heads the sockets of a skull, their champagne glasses its teeth. The epigraph was Emily Dickinson's poem 'The Lost Gentleman':

> Because I would not stop for death
>   He kindly stopped for me
> The carriage held but just ourselves
>   And immortality
> We slowly drove, he knew no haste
>   And I had put away
> My labour, and my leisure too
>   For his civility

The novel ended with the Raker's suicide. His last note was meant to be that of Socrates, after he had drunk the hemlock. 'We owe a cock to Asclepius,' Socrates had said, referring to the God of Healing. The Raker died at the point of writing, 'We owe a cock to ass.' His hand then failed. The night before, somebody had visited him and bored him until dawn with talk of taking his own life, only to receive a postcard in the afternoon, 'Why didn't you?' This was a true story told to me by Deacon.

Such pessimism and perversity appeared to us to suit the temper of the times under the mushroom cloud. Soho itself seemed to be cocking a snook at death and trying to recreate the Berlin days of the 'twenties, while life still lasted and homosexuality was still criminal. At the Huntsman, the gays danced together to rock records in the cellar, convivial on cappuccino. At the Fitzroy Tavern and the Golden Lion, the boys flounced to meet the older men over a pint or two of bitter. At the French Pub and Muriel Belcher's Colony Room, we could find Francis Bacon and Lucian Freud. But the only artists we could afford to collect were Elisabeth Frink, one of her bronze birds, and Brigid Reilly with her eye-boggling squares, and Souza, an Indian painter of landscapes that looked like jewelled Rouaults. Soho was not wholly the home of the new music and the youth culture. It still clung to the older artists and always to the cinema and the cutting-rooms off Wardour Street.

More than perceptions from America, the cinema supplied the images of our world. We haunted the British Film Institute in London, the Museum of Modern Art's cinema in New York, the Cinemathèque in Paris. We were known to refuse an occasional important dinner party in order to see a new colour print of Eisenstein's *Ivan the Terrible*. The magical novelist Angela Carter, whom we met, also confirmed the importance of the screen in her déjà vu of the 'sixties. We thought at the time that we had become 'classless' and that we were involved in the creation of an expanding European intelligentsia. There was a new kind of intellectual mobility. Angela Carter saw *Breathless* in 1959, and her experience of the new decade could be logged by Jean-Luc Godard's movies rather as T. S. Eliot's people had counted out their lives by coffee-spoons. She responded to this cinematic way of seeing the world far more than to the Leavisite version she was given at university. 'The last words of *Weekend* – *fin du cinéma, fin du monde* – heavens! how they struck home. Because towards the end of the 'sixties, it started to feel like living on a demolition site – one felt one was living on the edge of the unimaginable. There was a constant sense of fear and excitement and, of course, it was to do with war.'

The war was within us as much as it was without us. In Paris, where we had bought a ground-floor apartment in the rue Campagne Première, the images of the past and the present were exploding. At Chez Rosalie in the same street, the old lady in charge had accepted paintings in return for dinners since the 'thirties. In her *cave* were stored numberless and unknown Utrillos and Picassos and Van Dongens, the old painters of Montparnasse. Her death while we were there caused a treasure hunt underground in her ancient trunks: all were mildewed, many were holed; rising damp and rats had destroyed everything – enough canvases and drawings to furnish a new Modern Art Museum. My French literary agent's husband recalled Modigliani coming round the tables at the neighbouring Coupole to sell his nudes, drawn on paper. He was a *chic type* and so he was given dinner, which he paid for with a sketch – immediately scrunched and discarded when he left the table. It had seemed merely another scrawl from another café artist.

On a side-street by the Coupole and the Dôme, a new film bar opened, the Rosebud. Named after Citizen Kane's boyhood sledge and dying word, the place played cool jazz and attracted the generation formed by the American cinema, now translated into the French *nouvelle vague*. Our gods at the time were Godard and Alain Resnais, whose *Hiroshima Mon Amour* and *L'Année Derni-èreà Marienbad* seemed to have done what T. S. Eliot had achieved in poetry, to have created a contiguous past and present and future, a confusion of the years by screen cutting that mocked the steady running of the hours. And Godard made us see each moment afresh. The master of the unexpected, he altered our vision of what we thought we already knew. In time – and I must flash forward – I was to become the publisher of seven of his screenplays, and I met him twice in Soho, when he was filming there. Our encounter encapsulated what his films meant to me. A small man in large glasses and a crumpled brown raincoat appeared in my office, announced himself, and asked for all the money I had in the bank in used five pound notes next Wednesday. What did I want in return and how much did I have?

'Eleven hundred pounds, Monsieur Godard, and I want *Weekend* and *Wind from the East*,' his current revolutionary film.

At my bank, I was treated as if I were robbing it, not collecting my balance. All in used five pound notes, what was the purpose of this transaction? I stated that this was my affair and put the loot into a large brown-paper bag. When Jean-Luc Godard appeared again on Wednesday as clandestinely as he had first come, I gave him the bag and a sheet of paper to sign about publishing his screenplays. He signed the page without reading it and did not count the money. I could not resist saying what I was thinking.

'Monsieur Godard, I feel as if I were in one of your films. And you are playing Belmondo robbing a bank, except it is yourself.'

He gave me one of his rare thin smiles.

'Something like that,' he said and left.

I never saw him again.

We entered into Godard's scenes as onto an unfamiliar, but predictable terrain. His films insidiously took over our lives and changed our behaviour and our perceptions. The paintings of Francis Bacon would have that same quality, the structure enabling the viewer to step into the space and room of a private horror. Also at the Rosebud were some of the Situationists, whose subversive playfulness and mockery was to incite a real revolution at the end of the decade – something the Cambridge satirists never could do. Guy Debord and his friends, particularly the Scots anarchist Alexander Trocchi, a founder of *Merlin* magazine with its obsession for publishing Samuel Beckett, would cross our paths in their demonstrations that the oppressive machinery of state capitalism was constantly masked by the sensual pleasures of the entertainment and culture industry. They did not even approve of Jean-Luc Godard. A cartoon in the *Situationist International* headed the picture with the slogan BUT TOTAL REPRESSION CREATES A LANGUAGE OF TOTAL DISSENT. And in a Paris bar, a girl approached a man, a bubble in her mouth:

'What about a movie?'

'No, there's only a Godard and he is just another bloody Beatle. C'mon, let's go to my place.'

'PHEW! That was a close shave.'

In trying to define the Situationists, George Steiner put down their view of the rest of us. 'Like Osborne's "Entertainer" we strut about in a bankrupt side-show playing parts we loathe to audiences whose values are meaningless or contemptible. Culture itself has become frippery and grease-paint. Our very revolutions are melodrama, performed under stale rules or make-believe; they alter nothing but the cast. Hence the Situationist-Surrealist battle-cries; "Revolution must derive all its poetry from the future . . . Work must be suppressed and replaced by a new form of free activity . . ." '

These heady cries from the Rosebud were echoed at Shakespeare & Co., a bookshop named in honour of Sylvia Beach, who had published Joyce's *Ulysses*. The place was now run by two Americans, Mary and George Whitman, from premises in the rue de la Bûcherie on the Left Bank facing Notre-Dame across the Seine. Here most of the visiting British and American writers flopped or congregated, including Ferlinghetti, who had found in its relaxed welcome an inspiration for his own City Lights bookstore in San Francisco. Otherwise, the American travellers went to the cheap and tolerant Beat Hotel in rue Gît-le-Coeur off the Place Saint-Michel, where the aged Madame Rachou would clear up nearly everything that Ginsberg and Corso and Burroughs and their associates left in a mess behind them. Ferlinghetti again expressed so much of what certain people of my generation were trying to relive in his 'Adieu à Charlot (Second Populist Manifesto)':

> You Whitmans of another breath
> there is no one else to tell
> how the alienated generations
> have lived out their expatriate visions
> here and everywhere
> The old generations have lived them out
> Lived out the bohemian myth in Greenwich Villages
> Lived out the Hemingway myth
> in *The Sun Also Rises*
> at the Dôme in Paris
> or with the bulls at Pamplona . . .

The Coupole was our usual restaurant, however, and most of Paris passed through its doors, looking for one another. The 'thirties paintings on its pillars, the paper tablecloths and the first-come, first-served principle of seating made it a democratic magnet for the artists. The tide was flowing away from Saint-

Germain, where the tourists far outnumbered the old habitués
and the Deux Magots was already printing on its napkins and
bills – RENDEZ-VOUS DES INTELLECTUELS. Jean-Paul Sartre himself
had already fled to the Dôme beside our café, and we would pass
him, blinking with grey myopia through his glasses at Simone
de Beauvoir or a visiting girl of the sort that de Beauvoir had
characterized in *L'Invitée*. There were fewer literary and artistic
groupies left in Montparnasse than in Saint-Germain, which had
surpassed its neighbour on the Left Bank in the 'fifties, but now
was surrendering the tricolour of the arts again. A rare
excitement, a whiff of revolution, a sureness of culture, pervaded
the crossroads of the four great cafés on the Boulevard Montparnasse, the Sélect and the Rotonde, the Coupole and the Dôme.
It was the scent of caramel-coated roasted nuts and crêpes with
calvados at this best encounter-ground of all the world.

We knew that we were in the left circles of the right cities at
the right time. A certain self-consciousness of our role as part
of the expanding European intelligentsia still hung over us. The
former literary editor of *Tribune* and collaborator with George
Orwell, T. R. Fyvel, published a series of interviews called *Intellectuals Today: Problems in a Changing Society*, in which he treated
us with the seriousness of a French interviewer who believed
intellectuals actually existed and could influence their societies.
When he asked me about how my life in London and Paris had
given me ideas on our cultural structure, I had the gall to reply:

> I should like to put in a word for élite culture within a
> mass culture. Although it is now unfashionable to say this,
> I think education for élite culture cannot only have
> practical merits, but can be seen to have them. Eton,
> for instance, has its annual intake of seventy precocious
> scholars. By their interaction, the members of this élite
> within a closed society are undoubtedly competitively
> forced ahead. The social links forged in this society can
> be valuable, as George Orwell found later. Culturally,
> these early interchanges can be valuable, too. There's a
> literary anthology, I think, where one writer in seven is

an Etonian. In my time we were conscious of the literary
generation of Cyril Connolly and George Orwell as the
one at Eton before us.

When I am in Paris, I am very aware of French
advantages in both their general and élite education.
True, the rigidity of their university system stultifies
efforts, especially among historians. Those dry, safe,
empty subjects they choose for their doctorates! But their
advantage in élite culture starts in adolescence, at the
Lycée. The *bac* is a great examination. A visitor in Paris
like myself hardly meets a Frenchman who hasn't passed
through it, and the all-roundedness, the essay writing, the
power of expression required – these link French
businessmen and technicians to intellectuals in a unique
way.

On top of that, the Grandes Écoles give an education
which is fantastic in its length and scope. English friends
are flabbergasted when I describe it – I can quite believe
that the educated top French administrators are the best
going – and the system is something we should try to
adopt, *ceteris paribus*. French élite education seems far
more appropriate to contemporary society than our more
social equivalent, whether it's Eton and Kings or
Bradford Grammar School and Balliol – more
appropriate because more clearly thought out.

Asked why I had written mainly about the United States of
America when I was occupied with France, I replied that it was
so with many of my contemporaries:

It's not only my own case. It is perhaps as curious that
today the Channel should be a ditch wider than the
Atlantic as it was that the Mediterranean should have
been a British lake in the nineteenth century. Or
perhaps it is inevitable. America is today, of course, what
the Grand Tour was to the nineteenth-century sons of
gentlemen; only America also pays for study there.

I suppose one's first new civilization to comprehend is
always a challenge. I wanted to understand America as
soon as I thought about it. In a sense, we Westerners are
all *Americans* now, if we accept the power factor of our

age, just as all nineteenth-century educated people
tended towards England – in love or hate.

I was then asked whether I agreed with the American analysts
who were saying that our society had become so complex that
we had reached the end of political ideology – an increasingly
fashionable question.

No, I don't think we have reached any such era. 'Ideology'
is still too useful a way of putting across various political
thoughts in a simple and emotional form. What we have
perhaps reached is the end of certain over-extended
European political ideologies.

But in America, an ideological concept such as 'liberty'
is still enormously important. In the vast spaces there,
one can still feel an attachment to liberty as an almost
sensual concept. Ideology as a political instrument is
effective if couched in terms understood by ordinary
people. As soon as I heard the American Vice-President
Lyndon Johnson speak of 'the Great Society', I realized
that here was an ideological concept for piecemeal
pragmatic reforms which can even survive a good many
failures. The Great Society, the New Frontier, the New
Deal, the Square Deal, all these phrases mean something
and have their political function in the United States in
a way often not understood by Europeans.

In Europe, of course, we have recently witnessed the
failure of several embattled ideologies. Especially in
Britain. One result of lack of ideology is that the young
tend enormously towards becoming competent. It's
almost as if one were to occupy key positions in order
that when ideological aims return – and these things do
seem to move in cycles – one should be ready. If at the
moment one can do nothing about the course of affairs
in a world of technocrats except to take one's own
technocratic place in the scheme, then let this be done
properly.

With the one individual exception of de Gaulle, the
current lack of ideology in European thinking may also
be due partly to a lack of leaders, a temporary lack of
charismatic personalities.

A further point is that if today one has talent within the great communications industry, one can grow rich very young, if one wants to (at least in England, not so readily in France). This embrace of wealth is the thing which has always tended to corrupt the talented, but today the process has been so speeded up that talented young writers can almost at once wallow in the cornucopia – get there practically the first time they set pen to protesting paper. And the English governing classes have always invited rebels to join them – they're adept at that.

Yet there is another side to it. For instance, John Osborne, by his financial success, has practically reached the position of an eighteenth-century gentleman of independent means where he can say what he chooses – can afford his 'Damn you, England', and all kinds of total rebellion in words.

I also said that my own rebellion was taking me from socialism towards anarchism and populism. And when I was told that my fiction struck a note of fairly profound anxiety, I knew the answer:

I could say: 'I'm pessimistic about nuclear disarmament.' So are many. But I've also been pessimistic about avoiding nuclear war. Historically viewed, people have never piled up arms without using them. These are just generalizations, but in the 'sixties I have supposed that my life expectancy was about four to five years. Agreed – when I lived in Paris I found few French intellectuals who shared my anxieties. But the French are the most walled-in nation; they're going through a period of extraordinary, introverted nationalism.

On the other hand, one can't, of course, live day-to-day life except on the possibility that the nuclear stalemate will continue. Still, if I have worked hard, tried to hurry, to produce – a partial reason is this background feeling that time may be short.

My thoughts about our three societies and cultures at the time reflected a growing pragmatism and a reluctance to make a drama out of a minor moral crisis. This was reflected in the affair of the Churchill College chapel. There are probably more Anglican chapels to the square mile in Cambridge than in any other town in England: the bigoted history of the university towards Roman Catholics and those of other faiths was notorious until recent times. We had opted for an inter-denominational chapel in our new college, where those of various faiths could wheel in the Cross or the sacramental symbol of their choice. A certain wealthy Anglican clergyman gave twenty-five thousand pounds towards the construction of a Church of England chapel, and the gift was accepted by the master. At a special meeting of the twenty-five Fellows, the two doyens of the scientific Establishment, the agnostic Charles Snow and the embattled John Cockcroft, challenged each other. The speeches were those of another age and might have been spoken in the controversy over Charles Darwin's *The Origin of Species*. Eventually, the vote went by thirteen to twelve against the Anglican chapel. But within twenty-four hours, Lord Cockcroft had broken the opposition, approaching each of the rebellious thirteen with the statement that he might resign as master and destroy the nascent College unless we changed our vote. Eleven did so, but Francis Crick and myself would not. It was a matter of principle. Either the Fellows ran our policy by our votes or the master did as an autocracy. And both of us soon resigned our Fellowships, although Cockcroft assured me that I could come back when I changed my mind.

At the same time, an intense friend of mine and another novelist and historian, John Caute, decided to resign from his sinecure at All Souls at Oxford in protest against its refusal to reform itself into a teaching institution. We discussed our strategy: to dramatize our decision and attack our institutions; or to stay mum. He published an article in *Encounter,* 'Crisis in All Souls'. I did not speak a word, any more than Iago had after the death of Othello. Seven years before, I would have rushed into print as I had over the Suez crisis, sure of my rebellion and my righteousness. But I had been offered another travelling fellowship to America which would take me back to Harvard and San Francisco, there to write about women's rights. And I had been asked to adapt Dylan Thomas's unfinished novel, *Adventures in the Skin Trade*, for the theatre as well as being engaged on a plethora of other projects. I was finding it impossible to do what my fellow novelists and teachers of Americana Malcolm Bradbury and David Lodge managed to do, to accommodate an artist's life with an academic one. In all, the opportunity outweighed the morality. and decency and discretion overcame publicity.

So Marianne and I sailed back to New York on the old *Île de France*, in anxiety and in hope. After the Berlin crisis and the Cuban missile crisis, we thought that John F. Kennedy and Nikita Khrushchev might well preserve the nuclear stalemate for a few more years, so that we might be able to work on some of our plans. It was a limited hope, but there was hope, to be shattered by three bullets fired in Dallas in conspiracy or madness.

6

THE ILLUSION OF COMPETITION

Why haven't we seen a photograph of the whole Earth yet?

STEWART BRAND

For my mother's generation, the question was, 'Where were you when you heard France had fallen?' That was the moment that the game seemed to be up, the Second World War lost. For my generation, the question was to be, 'Where were you when you heard that Kennedy was shot?' It did seem then that the final whistle had been blown on hope, the Cold War lost. I was researching for my book on women's rights in the Smith College archives and I had broken for lunch off Harvard Square on that late November day. I was asked to write a piece about that afternoon, which was later reprinted in *A Tribute to John F. Kennedy*, which collected some of the words about the grief, which had brought the whole nation to tears.

> Today, Harvard weeps for her favourite son. John F.
> Kennedy was a Harvard man. No one could forget him.
> Harvard was in his mind, his dress, his tongue. He knew
> he was meant to rule, with courage and integrity.
> Although he was rich, he was taught that his duty was to
> serve the poor.
>
> Harvard and Massachusetts used to be a power in the
> American Government. For more than a century, they
> had lost that power. John F. Kennedy put Harvard back
> in the White House. Not since Woodrow Wilson had
> such an educated man been President.
>
> But if Kennedy did much for Harvard, Harvard had
> done much for him. Once it had been a centre of the
> Abolitionists, who had helped to free the Negro slaves.
> Now it was a Harvard man who was trying to push
> through the greatest freedom for the Negro in a hundred
> years.
>
> Kennedy had been destined for academics. Until the
> death of his elder brother, he had chosen the library
> rather than the hustings. Even in politics, he remained a
> Harvard man. When in the Senate, he was elected as

a member of the Harvard governing body by the largest
vote of graduates up to that time.

As President, he did not forget Harvard. His advisers
were often drawn from Harvard and the Massachusetts
Institute of Technology. And he could be faithful enough,
while occupying the most powerful place on earth, to drop
in on a Harvard football game only a month ago. Land
by the Charles River has already been set aside to build
a library to house the Kennedy papers.

If John F. Kennedy did not forget Harvard, Harvard
did not forget him. When he was shot, work stopped. No
one spoke. All listened to the wireless.

No one spoke in the Yard or in Harvard Square.
Occasionally to a stranger or a driver, a voice said, 'Have
you heard?' Or simply, 'He's dead.' In Widener Library,
a girl wept with hysteria.

Outside, on the grass, the grey squirrels were the only
things that stirred. The students stood still, alone, in
groups. The air was dazed. There was a silence. No one
could move or speak. The flags fell to half-mast.

The bells in Memorial Church began to toll. One
student hit a tree with his fist. Again and again, he hit
the tree. An unknown man lay on the grass on his
stomach. He was crying.

Harvard's President, Nathan M. Pusey, said that John
F. Kennedy, 'was one who made wise and effective use
of the world of learning and we mourn him as a friend.
His only ambition was to serve his country and he gave
his life for it.'

A line of students stood by the newspaper stand in the
Square. No one could believe the news. 'Did you hear?'
'Yes.' 'Is it true?' 'Yes.' And they waited for the newspapers
to say in print what they feared to believe in themselves.

Harvard has lost more than an honorary Doctor of
Laws, who was given his degree with the inscription, 'brave
officer, able Senator, Son of Harvard; loyal to party, he
remained steadfast to principle.'

Lost is an intellectual in the White House, a good
historian, a man who believed in learning and in
compromise for peace and in the values of the mind.

Government must go on. Harvard must go on. She has
made Presidents before and will make them again. If

there are tears and silence now, they are to mourn a great
man, who would have laughed at the child in Harvard
Yard who asked *if* America would get another President.

That piece showed something of the contingency of history. Since
his death, no American president has been more vilified, his
Camelot by the Potomac displayed as a mythical carapace of
broken promises and dreams. But it was not so at the time, when
he was the best hope of the western world. The other tributes to
him from such diverse creatures as Willy Brandt and Dr. Albert
Schweitzer, from Saint-John Perse and Norman Mailer, paid
homage to his courage and to the security he seemed to give us
all. As with the death of Hugh Gaitskell, *That Was The Week That
Was* put aside its satire to salute his passing:

> When Kennedy was elected three years ago, it was as if
> we'd all been given some gigantic, miraculous present.
> Suddenly over there in Washington was this amazing man
> who seemed so utterly right for the job in every way that
> we took him completely for granted. Whenever we
> thought about the world, we had that warm image at
> the back of our minds of a man who would keep
> everything on the rails. Now suddenly that present has
> been taken away from us when we thought we had still
> five more years before we need start worrying again . . .
> Behind the trappings of the image was the first western
> politician to make politics a respectable profession for
> thirty years, to make it once again the highest of the
> professions and not just a fabric of fraud and sham . . .
> Kennedy was simply and superlatively a man of his age;
> who understood his age; who put all his own energy and
> the best brains of his country into solving its problems
> and who ended up in more cases than not by doing the
> right thing at the right time because he had gone about
> it in the right way.

So the Oxbridge mockers came to mourn an American who gave
us expectation, a kind of guardian to us, a sort of guide. The
Raker of my novel had been described by Daniel Defoe in his

Journal of the Plague Year as the cleanser of rotting corpses from the streets and houses of the metropolis, and I was now studying the Muckrakers of American journalism, who delved into the dark areas of the lives of even the reformers, 'guys who poled through the sewers in glass-bottomed boats'. These ditchers and diggers would destroy the faith we had that we had found an amazing president who was superlatively a man of our age; but they could never remove the inspiration and the élan he had given us, the true grit and the quick wit. When Marianne and I drove south to research in Washington before crossing the continent to California, we visited twice his austere grave in the Arlington war cemetery under snow. 'A pile of pine-branches over the grave,' my diary recorded. 'On the green needles, five soaking military caps – one for each of the armed services, and a blue shoulder-strap. A simple black lamp kept a flame burning in the sleet. Kennedy's death, as much as his life, was done with quiet style.'

We had bought a green-and-white Pontiac, and were wandering free and slightly afraid. 'The pleasure and horror of living in the trunk of a car', my diary also stated, 'is to find out that we can shrug off things, dear things, all possessions. We can live in no-time and no-place without *dead*-lines – in the past of research or in the infinite present – and we discover that all we miss are five or six people we have left in Europe. We would blow over the earth, dirt in the wind, if love of friends did not make us mud.' The rolling wheels and unravelling highways did reel the spools of our minds, until we came to the deep delta below New Orleans, where we stopped by a roadside graveyard. 'The dead here were poor. They buried themselves as best they could. The families with a few hundred dollars had built traditional dolls' marble houses for coffins above the swamp. The rest did what they could – a small oval of stone, a wooden cross, a mere lump in the ground. It was so wet that, for the first time, we smelled human carrion. Yet above, the Spanish moss was light on the winter trees.

We trod on a path of white oyster shells. Only the marsh beneath made even the crosses crooked.'

We shook off the hood of death at Mardi Gras in New Orleans. As the fifteen flamboyant floats of the Krewes came by, the capering shapes on them were dressed as Greek gods, with masked faces. We, the people, howled at them, 'Throw me something, mister,' stretching our imploring arms. And the gods of the Krewes threw down beads and necklaces and plastic alligators and purple rabbits with winking eyes – baubles for their screeching beseechers. Behind them, the drum majorettes swaggered their Lolita bums and the brass bands played and the motor-cycles sang their sirens to the crowd, and the last of the lost of the old jazz bands played, little old men blowing their horns and banging their drums in black suits, like the Scots tribesmen I came from, with only two tunes – a celebration or a lament, a stomp or a blues.

Driving across America was to stitch together a continent by road-signs. How many more miles to El Paso or Albuquerque, to Reno or San Francisco? The numbers dwindled, the Rockies loomed. When once more, it was proved that the east coast did connect to the west, I thought dear old Bishop Berkeley was proved right. Maps were no good. We had to affirm the flip seaside of the United States personally, otherwise it might only exist in the mind of God. It was our good luck that in that other Berkeley to the east of the Bay Bridge, there were new beginnings, in the revolt of free speech, and the search for the liberty of the spirit through psychedelic drugs. Again, fortune timed our arrival in a fond place.

Just before we reached San Francisco, there had been a mass sit-in at Berkeley, followed by many arrests and the surrender of the faculty, which declared that free speech on any topic including revolution was tolerable on campus. With these constitutional rights won, the students there were beginning to demand power, just as the constricted Beat movement was starting to expand into the global cult of the hippies. Our guide was the thin and wise, wide-eyed and yellow-brushmopped Stewart Brand, whom

we had first met as a G.I. photographer in Soho Square through
a mutual friend. He had told us of sky-diving, 'like the first cold
separation at birth, a free fall into being alone with another free
fall near, an even colder separation into death.' We had set up
shop in an empty apartment on Vallejo Street off North Beach
and under Telegraph Hill. We had furnished it for a hundred
dollars with a bed and a table and chairs from the Salvation
Army, all painted white. The second-hand cost nothing in the
United States, which only wanted the new; food and wine were
half the price they were in Europe; this land was a cut-price
paradise. Among the metal jams of the tailfins of the automobiles
in the adjoining car park, an old Chinaman denied his age with
precise calisthenics.

Across the street was a commune, and there was living again
our friend Stewart Brand, who was to become one of Ken Kesey's
Merry Pranksters and the founder and the undertaker of *The
Whole Earth Catalog*. But now he was experimenting in the future
with a young Ottowa Indian woman called Lois, who wore a silver
disc in the middle of her forehead, and Tom, who had played in
the Atomic Band before he dropped out, and a Pre-Raphaelite
Jesus Christ who could fix the third gear of your truck quicker
than your head. The use of hallucinogenic drugs to achieve a
further reality had already spread from Timothy Leary's pioneer-
ing psychological experiments at Harvard, and L.S.D. and marijuana had reached the Beats through Allen Ginsberg and others
of the City Lights congregation. The Californian poets had
experimented before Leary: Michael McClure, in *Scratching the
Beat Surface*, recalled Francis Crick from Churchill College buying
one of the hundred and fifty copies of his *Peyote Poem* in 1958
and including two lines from it in his book about discovering
biogenetics, *Of Molecules and Men*:

THIS IS THE POWERFUL KNOWLEDGE
    we smile with it

To McClure, the use of this verse showed the important reaching out from science to poetry and from poetry to science that was part of the Beat movement and would be part of the hippie surge. As a Christmas card, Stewart Brand was to send me a drawing of the starry night sky with a round hole in the middle and the query, 'Why haven't we seen a photograph of the whole Earth yet?' We would, but our first introduction to his new culture was a commemoration of the death of Aldous Huxley, when we were assured by our local commune and its Berkeley friends that dozens of them had accompanied the British prophet of science and magic mushrooms on his last trip beyond the moon by the use of hallucinogens that he had recommended. Later, beside an extraordinary night bonfire on Stinson Beach, the spirits of the Shamans were called up by Carlos Casteneda and our Indian friends with green shapelessnesses appearing from the flames as banshees, reminding me of the old Scottish inscription:

> All is botgastis and eldritch fantasies:
> Of brownies and bogillis full this buke.

I had no time to take psychedelic drugs and lose my mind. I had two books to write – a biography of America's least and worst president, Warren Gamaliel Harding, as well as the book on women's rights. The study of Harding was called *The Available Man* and showed how the insignificant and the incompetent could rise to the greatest office on earth by being the chosen compromise and the glad-hander without enemies. It added to my growing disillusion about the power of anyone to put into effect political reform. And the book on women's rights, *The Better Half,* also seemed to show that the long Victorian battle for the vote had lost its ideals when emancipation was achieved. Its success was the failure of its hope. But I did prophesy that just as the first struggle for feminism was begun by women supporting the rights of black men in the south, so the new women upholding the freedom riders and Martin Luther King's campaign for black equality would end by demanding their own fulfilment. Certainly, the politics of protest were livelier at Berkeley than they were on the Aldermaston marches. It was the capacity of mediocre politicians to change anything that was in doubt. With our young leaders dead in their prime, what would we hope to achieve?

Even our fear of nuclear death seemed to induce a creeping detachment. In the commune over the way, Tom told me the strange story of how he had become a drop-out, the prototype of the hippies, many of whom adopted their new style of life as he had in a protest against the wealthy conformity of their middle-class homes. Drafted into the army, he had found himself in a special military band in Nevada, because of his ability to play the horn. Their detail was to march out onto the white desert flats and line up facing a row of empty gilt seats, as in the opening of the Ionesco play *The Chairs*. Generals and Pentagon officials would appear from Jeeps and nowhere to provide an audience, while the band played 'The Star-Spangled Banner'. Then an almighty blast would detonate from behind their backs, and the bandsmen would drop their instruments one by one, in spite of orders to play on and never turn to view what blew to the rear. Yet they would look backward to see a vast mushroom of smoke spreading across the blue heaven, and then Tom would look forward again, and see:

> On the faces of the important persons, there was one
> fixed expression in common – horror. Tom might have
> felt hope because of this, that men for once might not
> use the power in their hands against other men. Yet
> these were the men responsible for making the atomic
> cloud. If they were responsible for the explosion and
> were horrified and still went on and on making
> explosions, seven times, and seven times seven, what
> then?
>
> Then Tom looked beyond the chairs to the spill of
> rocks and scrub and sand that made up Nevada. And
> he knew for certain that the land did not care what men
> did or whether they were there. None of their acts would
> make the least difference. Men could be gross or flip,
> earnest or despairing, believing or indifferent, men of

war or of peace. The vast indifference of Nevada would outlast them all.

So I recorded my growing hopelessness about the possibility of political change in a short story, *The Atomic Band.* And I read an essay by a pioneer of jazz and poetry, whom I admired in California, Kenneth Rexroth. In his piece on 'The New American Poets', he declared much the same despair about the decline of the Beat writers and the rise of the hippies, which I was witnessing. The beatniks were like the teddy boys, mods and rockers of Britain or the *stilyagi* of Russia. Just as the tyranny of the Tsars had produced the original nihilists and a new breed of anarchists, so the threat of imminent nuclear extinction had made the literature and example of violent alienation very popular among the young. 'Today, it's an up-to-date version of the banner of my youth – FREE LOVE, FREE LIQUOR, FREE MONEY. In other words, it is no longer alienation, but revolt. However revolting its conduct, revolt it still is.' What disillusioned Rexroth still more was his perception of the rising of flaming youth as a rite of passage, not as an education for an artist. The beatniks of yesteryear were the bankers of tomorrow, who would parade their eroded standards. Their conspicuous expenditure of spirit would result in conspicuous consumption and social status. And yet, 'vestigial remnants of their adolescent ideologies [would] survive to become the accepted mores of their middle age.'

An alternative to political responsibility was being offered in California as the Situationists had suggested in Paris and Huizinga had written in *Homo Ludens.* It was the power of play to alter society. South of San Francisco, in Perry Lane, in Palo Alto and then in a log cabin in a redwood forest gorge near La Honda, Ken Kesey was gathering his Pranksters together before setting out on his rainbow-painted Hieronymus Bosch of an International Harvester school bus. Theirs was a continental trip of the mind and the body, fuelled more by psychedelic drugs than gasoline, travelling across the frontiers of the senses and the states. They played games with the cops and the laws; they mocked authority and pissed on probity; and they were to find their dandy scribe in Tom Wolfe's *The Electric Kool-Aid Acid Test*, which was like Heisenberg's Uncertainty Principle in trying to describe a phenomenon after it had already moved on.

In San Francisco, we were watching a passage from protest to play power, from the shibboleths of radicalism to sacerdotal drugs. Timothy Leary was to preach that his League for Spiritual Discovery was a religion. 'The sacraments marijuana and L.S.D. should only be used by initiates and priests of our religion and only used in shrines.' These were the bread and wine, the holy body and blood of his new cult. 'L.S.D. is ecumenical. God is not Christian. He doesn't speak Greek or Latin. When you contact God as we have you realise that His energy and His blueprint were going on long before man worked out these verbal formulas.' The psychedelic revolution was a spiritual revival, which would change American culture. Jazz and rock music were becoming psychedelic, as were the new styles of design and poetry and even architecture. 'I tell young people today to drop out of Power Politics because it's an old man's game of competition. New political solutions will grow out of small groups of people living together away from large cities.' Leary's revelation was not original. The genetic code, which he considered to be the main instrument of God, had been telling us the same message for thousands of years. Each of us must search inside the self. That was his primary conclusion. 'Nothing you do outside is important unless you're centred within.'

Seeking such an inner journey and a serene detachment as we left San Francisco, we accepted a gift of an L.S.D. solution in a tiny glass bottle with a cork stopper in return for all our Salvation Army furniture. We intended to take the drug in the Arizona desert, in Navajo or Hopi country, to see whether we might enter their ancient dreams. I had already set myself what I called the hardest question in my diary. Should I gratify my urge to live and develop myself or should I try to help others in general? 'The crippling egotism of wishing to write or the sense of continued failure of trying to do some good. To be proud or to lose – is there another choice?' A refuge in detachment was being offered. As a new Candide, I was being told to cultivate my *karma* rather than my garden. But when we reached the unearthly and solitary dream landscape of a dry creek near Monument Valley, we found that the cork had blown and the volatile genie had fled the bottle.

We lay down anyway and apart. And without a drug, both of us had our first trip through time. With our heads pillowed on bleached rocks, we *were* – or seemed to be – the split and curved and weathered shapes about us. We were sky, dust, stone. Hours were minutes or no time at all. And afterwards, since we were sleeping most nights in the Pontiac, looking through the car windows at mesas and stars to wake in the silence and sun, we were reaching a new understanding at last, which we found at the Bandelier National Monument. We looked through tall trees and over a stream at the large ruins of an ancient pueblo of cliff-dwellers. This time, as we lounged on the grass in the sun, we were both conscious of our flesh. I peered forward and saw the tip of my nose. I framed the cliff dwellings with a crooked arm to block the brightness. I was seeing pictures logically. I felt myself a pipe of food and shit with the mind separate. Only the inward closed eye saw no flesh. Here the Indian symbols were the essence of things: cloud, deer, rain, thunder, life.

And beyond the cliffs we knew was Los Alamos, where the atomic revolution had plotted its primary explosions. We had visited the White Sands by Almogordo. These were under snow, white on whiteness. The gypsum dunes were a lost and solitary world, but on each side of them was a Missile Range – 'the largest testing ground in the free world', in the words of the local advertisements. By Almogordo, the first atom bomb had been detonated to begin our age, pale cloud over mineral waste. 'The sands advance,' I had written, 'the era recedes, by inches.' While we stood alone on a dune, a rocket had been launched beyond the crested mountains. A long roar, a reverberate clapping, no noise, a bleach of space, an end of the world.

Remembering this, we went on to the San Ildefonso Pueblo.

Among these log and adobe cabins, we found the studio of Maria
Martinez and her son, a noble and sure man. We talked of art,
of how the toy canoe with the water painted on its side *was* a
canoe in water, of how the celebrated blue Egyptian hippopotamus with lilies painted on his flanks *was* a hippopotamus in a lily
pool by the Nile. We bought a silver box with the essence or
symbol of a turquoise deer in a forest on the outside. I still did
not understand. We visited the museums of Santa Fe, and then
we drove out to the Great Sand Dunes. It was cold and night.
We were alone in the campground in early May. We lit a fire.
The dry wood flared. I looked into the flames. I saw red deer
skulls with branched antlers of yellow. The fire was not *like* red
deer skulls with antlers of yellow; the fire *was* red deer skulls with
antlers of yellow. The thing seen with the inward eye through
the outward eye *was* the thing. A great bird with forked wing and
tail was black in the blue night sky.

At the end of these experiences, I began to paint again, and I
even wrote a manifesto. I had withdrawn into privacy. No more
public declarations at any price. So my audience was Marianne,
my discovery an interior journey. My movement was only an
instinct and an intuition with one follower, who was my wife. My
Irrealist Manifesto had much to do with the famous Surrealist
one of André Breton. It read:

> There is no metaphor. The thing perceived is the thing.
> The mind is the eye, for it can see the essence of the
> thing.
> The symbol, either traditional or perceived by the artist,
> is to the mind the whole species of the thing.
> The irreal is the inwardness of the thing seen.
> The irreal is the free mind and eye seeing a thing
> through the knowledge of the love and the habits and
> the past of the thing.
> When the eye observes, it concentrates on the thing
> observed. The background merges in the thing, when
> observed with care. Irrealism concentrates on the *shape*
> of the thing, and includes its setting within that shape.

Irrealism puts a form seen by the mind on the facts of nature.

History and botany and ethnology are important to the irrealist, for the mind cannot perceive a thing and the background in a thing, without the knowledge of why the thing is.

Anything seen by the mind is the content of irrealism. Its form is governed by what is pleasing to the mind and by the shapes and patterns and symbols made by nature and humanity.

Irrealism is the country of the inward eye, reflected in the chosen objects seen by the outward eye.

As in meditation, the irrealist concentrates on *one thing alone.* Within that one thing, within its necessary shape, the irrealist places all things that make the one thing in harmony with its setting.

The irrealist must explain in words to the careful looker what the eye can comprehend as a whole. The catalogue of a museum should be a series of footnotes to the inward eye, to allow the mind to appreciate both the harmony and the meaning of a thing.

There is no harmony without meaning for the irrealist.

The way to the abstract for the irrealist is through the symbol.

Freedom is the use of colour and symbol within form.

The journey continued – my diary tells me now – to Bryce Canyon in Utah, where –

Irrealism came to be. We arrived at evening and reached the bowl which the Piute Indians called 'red rocks standing like men in a bowl-shaped canyon'. We set off down the mountainside through hammers, spires, pinnacles, thrones of rock, in lilacs, scarlets, oranges, whites, and reds. Beyond the great temples of stone standing round a throned god on an altar were white cities with red battlements. Night fell. The moon was so bright that our shadows were crescents of pitch on glitter dust. We walked through gorges, teeth, molars of black rock. The dust and stones were files on our feet, and the star specks above were powder in our eyes. We toiled up

an infinite S of trail from a throat of cliff. As we looked
up, we were Jonahs in a whale-mouth of black teeth and
silver tongue. The moon-shadows brought out the terrible
fangs of eroded rock. On top of the canyon again, we
saw the massed gape of rocks, the helmets of hundred-
foot men in ranks. We were alienated. We were not men.
For men are but the shadows of nature. The men first
found a cave in rock, then built a cave in imitation.
Cities are indifferent copies of this fantastic junkyard of
shapes of stone and earth. Marianne saw the shapes as
God's *atelier.* Here He found all the shapes of creation,
chose a few at random, suffused life into them, and
loosed them. To me, they were the essences of all shapes,
flesh eroded away to the inner core of all things. Later,
the next day, we saw them as armies, dragons' teeth,
fantastic Aztec-Assyrian torture-areas where prisoners
were catapulted and impaled and hunted through gorges
by eagles and skewered by arrows, faster than the blue
swifts that sheered about the canyon. The cruel and the
macabre is also irreal, for there is no morality in
the forms of nature.

Later, the next morning, Marianne lay in the pose of a
sleeping coati mundi, a leg and an arm and hair on
each side of a root, while I looked at the valley of red
and white shapes pricked by green arrows of firs. I was
a tree. My eye was the eye of a tree inside bark. My two
legs were roots. Flies did not settle on me, for I was not
flesh. Noise was far away, filtered by holes into my sap.
An irrealist poem appeared in print within me:

> In the white hill
> With white thighs
> The river canyon lies.

I wept with joy. I have not done so for years. I was, in
wonder, a living thing, *part* of the view.

Irrealism begins with the shape, the form, 'The white
hill.' Then the background of the shape is included
within it, for the chosen thing *includes* the setting. The
poems of Blake or *haiku* are often irrealist in this way,

for they describe the thing, and the *moment* of time and place in which a thing always is.

After Bryce Canyon, both Marianne and I knew we must only write, paint, make, be. There is nothing else. To be in nature is all of joy, to imitate it well is all satisfaction.

If I emphasize these experiences, it is because they did change my awareness and my diary still tells me that I felt it there and then. T. S. Eliot's understanding had come true. Time past and present and future were all the same. In that flow, competition was as meaningless as destiny. There was still opportunity, but that was a question of chance, not of will. This applied even to the possibility of political change. Necessity had struck down our leaders of hope. God only knew if and when any others might take their place.

And so we drove back from the American west to take a French liner back to England. I had been offered another job before my insight into irrealism, teaching American history and political philosophy at University College in London. It would support us and give us much free time in one of the metropolises that were the foci of our lives. What I could not foresee was that the revolution of the young in music would turn towards protest against the powers that were and come close to unseating them all. And I could not imagine that such hard flame would temper the fine spirit of Marianne into a blunt steel.

7

SHEDDING ONE'S SICKNESS

One sheds one's sickness in books – repeats and presents one's emotions to be master of them.

D. H. LAWRENCE, *Essays*

'The modern artist seems more often to *create* his sickness in his work,' the British critic A. Alvarez wrote in the summer of 1965. The creator gave himself over to his sickness for the sake of the range and intensity of his art. 'He cultivates not his own garden but his psychosis, or at the very least his psychopathic tendencies.' The result was that all phenomena were seen within. Romantics had made nature the object of their radical aesthetic politics, while the moderns appeared utterly unaware of the world outside. The reasons were two clichés. Contemporary artists were forced to inwardness by the sheer size and engulfing blankness of industrial society, while their inheritance of the concentration camps and the threat of a nuclear holocaust compelled a personal extremism and an endless series of underground tests upon their own selves. 'But the fact that it is the Americans rather than the Europeans or Russians who have responded to this situation with such artistic alacrity is due', Alvarez thought, 'to their particular genius for loneliness, which creates these conditions even despite the environment.'

Later Alvarez was to write extensively on suicide, including the death of his dear friend Sylvia Plath. What he did not mention in his present article was the stress of the city which drove the lonely man, who felt himself an outsider, towards suicide. Before we had sailed away from New York to return to London, our best friend there had killed himself, because of the corruption of his success, with sleeping-pills in front of his ten-year-old daughter who became my ward. As her guardian I advised her mother to pull the child out of her school in Central Park, where drug pushers already besieged the gates, and to return to England, if she wanted her daughter to survive the appalling trauma which her father had inflicted on her. Of my two principles in life, the

first is the most important: *Never harm the innocent.* The second
follows from it: *κινεῖ ὡς ἐρωμενον*, Aristotle's words: *Move towards
what you love,* and so encourage society to give all its citizens the
opportunity to move towards what they love. The young were
doing that, anyway, without the helping hand of the authorities
in the 'sixties. But our leaders and our friends were still being
struck down, as if we lived in plague years. Both of my editors
and friends in New York, Roger Klein and Peter Ritner, were
soon to commit suicide from metropolitan pressure and the
judgement of an age, in which a publisher could hardly come
out of the closet. Death still seemed to be our cloud.

Returning to our flat in Soho Square in London, I began to
teach my students at University College. And I found that I was
already old to them. Seeking to please me, a bright lad said that
he admired my novels. When I asked which one, he answered,
'Your *historical* novel.' With a sinking stomach, I realized that he
was referring to *The Breaking of Bumbo* about the Suez crisis,
already old bowler hat and desert sand to him. So instant were
communications now in this psychedelic decade, that the 'fifties
seemed to date from the Flood. *Avec nous, le déluge.* I appeared a
part of the Establishment, which the young wished even more to
destroy, particularly now that the increasing American involvement in the war in Vietnam had made our subject as touchy as
unstable napalm. I found it difficult to explain a faith in the
martyred John F. Kennedy, when he had already been sending
the Marines to Saigon before Lyndon Johnson escalated the
whole affair into an American disaster in foreign policy in
the Pacific even greater than its conquest of the Philippines
some sixty-five years before. I could only say that all revolutions
eventually became reactionary, and that the American one was
now merely interested in conserving its own security.

The Free Speech Movement at Berkeley and the poetry of
protest of San Francisco had already crossed the Atlantic to the
Albert Hall. There in June in 1965, four hours of modern poetry
were read to the seven thousand of us who filled the great dome.
It was the first of what would be called Happenings. Under the

strange dominance of Alexander Trocchi, the bards of the new sensibility and politics chanted and paraded their verses. In his black sunburst of beard, Allen Ginsberg spoke as if from the Prophetic Books of William Blake on 'Who Be Kind To', and Lawrence Ferlinghetti produced a refrain on how to solve the Cold War through physical love:

> For there is a time to kill
> and there is a time to kiss
> but the trick of hate is loose in the labyrinth
> *dies irae dies illa illa illa*
> and ticks carry diseases but kisses carry love
> which is also infectious
> And there is a time for war
> and there is time for a piece of love
> So get ready General
> Ready Get Set Fuck
> *kyrie kyrie hallelujah* . . .

Yet Adrian Mitchell, with his deadly northern seriousness, brought home to us that far Asian war, and it would never leave us until the Americans were forced to leave Vietnam, and until the petty revolutions of the young in many of the capitals of the world were put out. But on that particular day of annunciation, Mitchell played with the blues and the old Second World War dance called 'the hokey-cokey', building his chorus by a line more after each verse of 'To Whom It May Concern':

> I was run over by the truth one day
> Ever since the accident I've walked this way . . .
>
> Heard the alarm clock screaming with pain,
> Couldn't find myself so I went back to sleep again . . .
>
> Every time I shut my eyes all I see is flames.
> Made a marble phone book, carved all the names.
>
> I smell something burning, hope it's just my brains.
> They're only dropping peppermints and daisy-chains . . .

Where were you at the time of the crime?
Down by the Cenotaph drinking slime . . .

You put your bombers in, you put your conscience out,
You take the human being and you twist it all about
    So scrub my skin with women
    Chain my tongue with whisky
    Stuff my nose with garlic
    Coat my eyes with butter
    Fill my ears with silver
    Stick my legs in plaster
    Tell me lies about Vietnam.

The fallen Recording Angel of this First Happening was Peter
Lorrimer Whitehead, who would be my liaison to the images of
those curious days. He filmed the event and also published it in
his own press as an illustrated book, *Wholly Communion*, naturally
distributed by City Lights in the United States. He would later
print the screenplay of Godard's futurist thriller *Alphaville* and
entice me into taking over the publication of many of the classical
screenplays of the world. But for the moment, he was filming
Wholly Communion and following it with another view of London
in the later 'sixties, caught on the wing in a trapped and fugitive
emanation, possibly the most piercing of all the documentaries
of that classic time, *Tonite let's all make love in London* – a phrase
from Allen Ginsberg.

Probably not since the radical eras of John Pym and Francis
Place had the small publications available in little bookshops
been the fuses of future rebellion. In his analysis of his combust-
ible years, the novel *Snipe's Spinster*, Jeff Nuttall declared the
importance of those reading places. The rendezvous of the
underground were not the pubs or clubs or discothèques, but
the bookshops, such as Better Books in London, Peace Eye in
New York, Giat Froget's in Paris, City Lights in San Francisco,
and The Paperback in Edinburgh. The peaceniks read continu-
ously: Marx and Engels and Russell and Fromm; Hegel and Sartre
and Heidegger and Shaw and Nietzsche; Kerouac and Ginsberg

and Corso and Ferlinghetti; Osborne and Lessing and Burroughs and Beckett; Rimbaud and Joyce and Aquinas and the *I Ching.* 'And they saw about them a vast drift of people so ignorant and consequently so bored with their empty lives they walked willingly and eagerly towards the big bang and the big numbness, lubricating their slippery progress with the usual rationalisations about the facts of international power and the spirit of Dunkirk.'

Against this rising tide of radical sentiment, the Prime Minister Harold Wilson played King Canute, retreating step by step as the salt waters soaked his feet. His chief liability seemed to be his tendency to sink in the water of American policy in Vietnam. He did, however, have one bait to throw to the shoals of sprats nibbling at his toes – the old temptation of inclusion, which was engulfing my generation of rebels and satirists. Through his favoured minister, Jennie Lee, the widow of the firebrand Aneurin Bevan, he gave money to the burgeoning arts through the Arts Council of Great Britain, then headed by Wilson's lawyer, Arnold, later Lord Goodman. A million pounds a year more for the national arts budget did allow for policies to aid youth and innovation, but these signified little. No new seeds of culture grew from this late dose of fertilizer. As Lord Goodman admitted, 'We never expected a new Art to emerge, and it didn't.' In a speech in the Guildhall soon after his appointment as chairman of the Council, he put out his programme for the arts along with his fears. New audiences had to be cultivated for the arts, but they would not be gained without a struggle. The pop groups were winning. 'At best we are holding our own; if we are to be a civilized and cultivated nation; if the standards which mean something to you and something to me, are to be maintained, we can only win this battle by teaching people what are the worthwhile things in life . . . History will not grant us a moratorium.'

There was, indeed, no moratorium. There were the revolt of youth and the demonstrations of an 'alternative or counter-culture' across the cities of Europe within a year or two. But although the forces of the Establishment were to win the final battle, the

Arts Council did not win in its efforts to include and guide from its new and larger office in Piccadilly. The new Activities Committee which was set up became the butt of ridicule and ingratitude. Although it included some of the activists of the counter-culture, these did not think as did their older colleagues. Lord Goodman noted: 'Many of the young people clearly did not like the Arts Council and did their business with it only because of the allure of its money and its premises. Of this, with great candour, they made no secret. They produced magazines containing caricatures of the Arts Council's hapless chairman, depicting him as an octopus, of which his only comment was that the tentacles were too few and too short.'

This effort to reach the young seemed to them patronizing and inadequate. They could only laugh at Goodman's reasons for trying to reach them at all. The point was not to serve the Arts Council, but to replace it. The hand or tentacle which doled out funds to some new activities must be severed. Even Goodman realized that his Activities Committee might not be viable. 'It has discovered that the major myth is the belief that it is employing a common language. It has, to some extent, underrated the resentment arising from the very fact of its intrusion. It has also underrated the self-contained and palisaded character of the "activities" and the fact that the occupants of the palisades regard themselves as a community developing along their own lines and requiring nothing from the Arts Council, except possibly its premises and its funds.' Up Piccadilly, towards Park Lane, young squatters were planning to take over a mansion. On its white stucco facade, they wrote: WE ARE THE WRITING ON YOUR WALL. They were not on the wall further down the street. Their challenge was to be contained and their demands limited to pittances and then snuffed out during the next decade. In defeat, however, their legacy would be a bitter one. Until their failed *putsch*, the Arts Council had been seen as the friend of the artist. Now they saw it – as they saw most of the artists over twenty-five such as myself – as barriers to self-fulfilment, to moving towards what they loved.

The young Clive James, still a student at Cambridge, foresaw the failure of the new protest movement in a letter to the underground magazine *Oz*. As long as the underground preached revolution it was setting up its own defeat. The revolution it demanded would be the worst thing that could happen to it, as it would be destroyed by whatever force emerged to administer the resulting chaos. 'In its heart of hearts, of course, the underground has no plans for revolution, since this would mean taking over an industrial society which is too complicated for it to understand.' By instinct, if not by brains, the underground was aware that continued industrial progress was the necessary precondition of its own survival. Its significance was not as a political movement, for political movements were not in themselves creative. All they could create was the possibility of creation. And James himself could remain basically for the underground only until the point where it went irrational by conviction.

Yet that was what Richard Neville, the editor of *Oz*, wanted and described in *Play Power*, his account of exploring the international underground – a modern version of *Homo Ludens*. To him, the Provo movement in Amsterdam was the touchstone of subversion through games and happenings, which the Situationists had advocated in France. It was a rebellion without a cause. No Dutch soldiers were dying in Vietnam. No ethnic or social groups were being victimized. Provo was against the very existence of the established order. The reason for Provo's actions was 'to *provoke* – spontaneously, flexibly, relentlessly'. This meant painting K for Kancer on every tobacco advertisement while smoking marijuana, advocating laughing gas in the church organ for a royal wedding, and distributing free white bicycles for everybody to ride round the city. Marianne and I spent a weekend in Amsterdam sleeping in the enormous circular dogbasket of a surrealist painter called Franz, who was painting Marianne like Janus with a face of light and of shadow emerging from a desert rock. It was then a city of gentle experiment, a far remove from the violence to come.

In *Play Power* the rise of the underground in London was charted from the cosmic poetry occasion at the Albert Hall through the Happenings organized or disorganized by the first of the alternative papers, the *International Times* or I.T., through the Electric Garden and Middle Earth to the Arts Laboratory of the American Jim Haynes, one of the founders of I.T. and its nightclub U.F.O., where the Pink Floyd and the Soft Machine were the house bands. Haynes had an uncanny and lanky ability to charm money from the stone-fisted, only failing with the Arts Council, where Lord Goodman thought that he advocated a drug culture. He even charmed a few pennies from me, but then it was obvious that I.T. and the Arts Lab were providing playgrounds for the aspirations of the young. As Haynes testified in his modest autobiography, *Thanks for Coming!*, I.T. was an important paper and a community paper. There were weekly listings in which free publicity was given to any interesting or alternative events. 'The free announcement idea encouraged a lot of individuals and groups to create who wouldn't otherwise have done so. I really felt that there was a direct link between the amount of publicity generated about alternative events and the number of events that materialised.' This was a stimulus for people to do more, and I.T. was appreciated 'because there was always something outrageous in the paper, or mad, or absurd'.

The foundations of the Arts Lab, in an old warehouse in Covent Garden, wrought more than even Haynes imagined. It would not only set a style for the community arts centres of the future, but it would bring back to the run-down Strand the dramatic pleasures of its grand Edwardian days. The idea of using interconnecting spaces for the various performing and electronic arts and of allowing programmes to happen as the artists were available and the audiences arrived, this produced the pattern of controlled anarchy in which Jim Haynes excelled – a Compère Ubu of the Underground. During the two years he ran the place, Haynes made it an extraordinary experience in which nobody knew what would occur, although something always did – such as Jane Arden's musical *Vagina Rex and the Gas Oven*. In the end, he was not able to raise the support he needed, and had to close. But he demonstrated what he thought happened to the 'sixties, and he encouraged the doomed hope of the young that changing the world might still be possible. He thought that up to the 'fifties, the dominant image was of a class-ridden and stratified Britain. He saw 'the working-class kids with their noses against the window-panes looking in on the upper-class kids having a good time'. The 'sixties changed the point of view. Now the upper-class kids had their noses pressed against the panes watching the other kids having a good time, and they wanted to join in the fun. Accent and social background and class no longer mattered. Everyone was welcome who could contribute to the social joy and energy of the time. Anyone could talk to anyone and wear anything. The colourful clothes and long hair of the 'sixties were emblems of tolerance and novelty, experimentation and delight.

Certainly Haynes was right from my point of view. Old Etonian and former Coldstream Guards officer I might be, but I never had any trouble in communicating with Haynes or the Beats in San Francisco. There was no question of being spat on, as I had been in the streets of Cambridge, from seeming to have had a privileged inheritance. Briefly, a great classlessness pervaded all, and everybody seemed to want to learn. Asked by a friend to lecture in a Californian 'university without walls', which still gave visible degrees, I was preceded by a guru of sorts, who did not use words so much as strike gongs, so that all might join in his inner meditation. I fiercely defended the use of words and particularly the learning of Latin and Greek, so that we might understand the roots of what we were trying to say. I received rounds of applause, the guru silence – which did not mean to say he was not appreciated more.

This period was a 'revolt into style' – the term used by George Melly to describe the pop arts in Britain. It was not only a style of life that was seen as a work of art, but a style of dress and behaviour, of speech and of clothes. Each person was, in a sense, his or her own work of art. Narcissus was the god of this new generation. All standards of art should be dethroned. An alternative or counter-culture must be found. Any ancient heritage must be rejected in favour of instant creation. The problem was that anyone who declared themselves an artist was an artist. Nobody needed much talent to create a masterpiece. No meaning would be given to 'the arts' except that which was produced by self-expression. Art was what any artist did.

In the United States, two different movements were spreading out in ripples that would lap the Himalayas. These were called the hippies and the Yippies, while the outrage against the expanding war in Vietnam, where so many of the killings of the G.I.s were of black men, led to the violent response of Black Power, first of the Muslims and then the Panthers. The distinction between the cool or hip movement and the hippies was well-defined by one of Kesey's Merry Pranksters, Tuli Kupferberg. 'The hip person, the "hipster" had to work for it, the hippie is to the manner born . . . the change from hip to hippie was a change from hard to soft.' The centre moved from the east of the city to the west in San Francisco, from North Beach and Telegraph Hill to Haight-Ashbury, where the world's first psychedelic shop was opened on the New Year's Day of 1966, and provoked an immigration of a hundred thousand flower children to the district. Equally, the serious Free Speech Movement at Berkeley spawned the Yippies, or Youth International Party, a protest movement inspired by play power, a gambol with Allen Ginsberg and Abbie Hoffman and their like against the war in Vietnam. Hoffman declared in *Revolution for the Hell of It* that the crowd in their march on the Pentagon war office in the October of 1967 tried to exorcize and levitate the huge building, concluding that 'the peace movement has gone crazy and it's about time' – and even Norman Mailer was arrested. It was, as the *Liberation News Service* reported, 'guerilla play-fare' with the accompanying pop groups that included The Jefferson Airplane and Mother Earth and The Fugs. As Richard Neville bitterly observed, the Yippies were 'politicised acid freaks, or as Paul Krassner once put it: "they're hippies who've been hit on the head by a policeman." Doped, they stumbled into politics backwards.' Instead of acquiring an ideology from a textbook, they found their politics and their liberty through a lifestyle. 'They extracted their world view from an intense, electrifying generational communion, which taunted authority, and like a poultice, brought out the worst of it.'

The Yippies tried to abolish the distinction between theory and action, as the hippies tried to convert play power into a love-in or a drop-out. The outer protest among the masses of the young was being translated into an inner search. Nowhere was this interior metamorphosis more evident than in the career of the archangel of political song, Bob Dylan. To the rising Black Power movement, he had seemed its white voice. At the Green-wood rally in Mississippi in the July of 1963, he had sung 'Only a Pawn in The Game' about a black activist shot dead by the Ku Klux Klan. It had been the opening track on the second side of his album, *The Times They Are A-Changin'*, and he seemed to have picked up from Woody Guthrie and Ewan MacColl and Pete Seeger the gift of writing lyrics of instant radical protest, nasally intoned on a twanging guitar. But soon after Kennedy's assassination, Dylan was invited in New York to accept the Tom Paine Award for his work in the black civil rights campaign; at the time he had given up protest, saying: 'There's no black and white, left and right, to me any more. There's only up and down, and down is very close to the ground. And I'm trying to go up, without thinking of anything trivial such as politics.' In point of truth, he was trying to go within his own self as the hippies were, as the Beatles were teaching the young to do.

The difference between the two dominant British groups of apostles of the young, the Beatles and the Rolling Stones, was one of direction. As with the Angry Young Men, one lot was trying to kick its way in, the other lot was trying to kick its way out. The Beatles were singing faded drug lyrics, 'The Yellow Submarine', and L.S.D. or 'Lucy in the Sky with Diamonds', advocating global love and inner peace through fixes and yoga and Indian medi-tation. The Rolling Stones were progressing towards violent action against authority, which would be epitomized in 'Street Fighting Man', a response to the urban violence of the year of

1968, when most of the cities of Europe would be threatened by radical action, as they had not been since 1848, a hundred and twenty years previously.

The radical lyrics of the Rolling Stones were appealing more and more to student and black activists. George Melly analysed a split in the pop scene after 1967, particularly when Mick Jagger was busted on a drugs charge. A distinction was to appear between soft and hard pop, the same sort of distinction as between the hippies and the hip. Hard pop had come out overtly against the Establishment. 'There was no danger after that summer of pop becoming officially acceptable. It was tolerated but only just, its heroes were harassed at regular intervals and that, from the teenage viewpoint, was enough to endorse its continuity.'

To the Black Muslims and the Black Panthers, the pop songs of aggression were sweet music in their ears. During James Meredith's march to Jackson in Mississippi in 1965, the shouts of 'Black Power' had punctuated the singing of 'We Shall Overcome'. New leaders were emerging on the west coast, Stokely Carmichael and Huey Newton and Eldridge Cleaver, and on the east coast, the charismatic and tragic Malcolm X. There was a beginning of division. The blacks now did not want any help from the whites. They would strike for their own power and take it, if they could. In Cleaver's future diatribe, *Soul on Ice*, he would exalt violence and rape against an oppressive white culture, and he would be suspicious of 'The Negro Celebrity'. Most black celebrities to date had been entertainers and athletes, and whenever a crisis arose with racial overtones, one of them was 'trotted out and allowed to expound a predictable conciliatory interpretation of what's happening'. It was a far distance from the notorious Black Power slogan – HAPPINESS IS A WARM GUN.

Violence had exploded, indeed, onto the London stage in Peter Brook's version of Peter Weiss's *The Persecution and Assassination of Marat as Performed by the Inmates of Charenton under the Direction of the Marquis de Sade*. Very much influenced by the theories of Artaud, the play shocked and terrified the audience. When

I saw it, I seemed to join in the sadism and madness of the French Revolution. At the time, my diary recorded, 'Seeing something as artificial as this is still a knife in the bowels of mercy.' Brook's later piece on Vietnam, named *U.S.*, was a failure, because the recurrent television images of burning human beings and of naked and screaming and running small girls were far more horrible than anything that could be staged, even though it included the repetition of Adrian Mitchell's poem 'To Whom It May Concern'. The intent was to make the audience feel guilty, which we already did. The effect was to annoy the watchers with the moral superiority of the portrayers.

Peter Brook pronounced on the *Marat/Sade* play that 'violence is the natural artistic language of the times . . . it's our reality, there's no way round it.' It provoked a debate in which many of the leading artists of the period were asked to contribute, including John Arden and David Hockney, Roy Fuller and V. S. Naipaul, Alan Sillitoe and the neglected Colin Wilson. But Thom Gunn, with his special knowledge of the male motor-bike gangs in California, and Norman Mailer made the most cogent contributions. To Gunn, those who declared that art was impossible under the shadow of the Holocaust and the atomic bomb were being melodramatic. It was a matter of knowledge without experience. 'Our obsession, however true we may make it of our inner lives, has almost no correspondence to any external reality of a writer's life in England (or a good many other places).' Never before had it been possible to walk through the streets of London in such safety. 'We would have to wait around a long time before we saw even a street fight. Compared to the contemporaries of Tennyson or of Dryden, we have practically no personal experience of violence. There is a peculiar danger, then, to our cult of violence in literature. It takes the form of a nostalgia, it is an attachment to the idea of something we do not have and do not seriously want.'

To Gunn, the two best poets of violence writing in the English language were Robert Lowell and Ted Hughes, both of whom I knew as gentle men of internal conflict. Their sickness, as D. H.

Lawrence had long ago suggested, was shed in their works, where they repeated and presented their emotions of violence in order to be the master of them. Having witnessed the aftermath of Mailer's attempt at stabbing his wife, I found his views on two kinds of violence fascinating. 'One is personal violence – an act of violence by man or woman against other men or women. The second kind is social violence – concentration camps, nuclear warfare.' Social violence created personal violence as its antithesis. Juvenile delinquents were violent because their spontaneous expressions were cut off by institutional deadenings of their natures. 'Threatened with extinction of our possibilities, we react with chronic rage. Violence begins, you see, as the desire to fight one's way out of a trap. Moral questions over the nature of one's violence come only as a secondary matter. The first reaction, the heart of the violence, is the protection of the self. The second question, the moral question, is whether the self deserves to be protected.'

Although I believed in fighting for what one most loved, violence could go a knife too far. It was hardly the most necessary form of self-expression or escape from a trap. At the converted locomotive shed of the Roundhouse in London in the summer of 1967, the psychiatrist of liberation, R. D. Laing, called a fortnight's conference on 'The Dialectics of Liberation – Towards a Demystification of Violence'. Although violence was as much internal as external, as Gunn and Mailer knew well, Laing argued that the responsibility for aggression lay with a warped society. Mental health services and a police state operated a guerrilla war against the sick in the name of law and order and peace. The conference itself, however, turned out to be more of a carnival, where communication ended in a play break and a denial of all authority. And as the *International Times* reported and I saw and heard: 'Ronnie Laing and Stokely Carmichael drew crowds of over a thousand and Stokely's Black Power rally was a surprise; instead of demystifying violence, the crowd cheered frenziedly at every mention of violence. Non-violent actions were booed – racism was once again affirmed.'

What else did the organizers expect, given the temper of the times? Carmichael had been born in Trinidad and was considered the leading revolutionary in the United States. He spoke of the need for 'counter-violence'. He quoted the new icon of his times, the Cuban Che Guevara, on the hatred of the enemy that forged his comrades into cold killing machines. He opposed Allen Ginsberg, chanting a mantra and singing that Burroughs's gay drug writings gave 'the best analyses of the present consciousness existing in the west'. For Carmichael, there was no revolutionary element in the hippies. At best, they were neutrals. They were not friends. And even when the old Herbert Marcuse reached the platform and preached another version of play power, 'an aesthetic reality, society as a work of art', his attack on the repressive balance of liberal society did not convince us that the solution was a trip to inner space rather than to overt aggression.

Something between hope and adventure and faith took Marianne and myself to Limehouse. Because of romantic reasons about the incredible city of London, I had always wanted to live in Soho and the docks and the Parks, by bohemia and the river and the green. We had discovered six derelict houses in Narrow Street on the Thames in Limehouse. Blitzed in the Second World War, they had been built in the eighteenth century. In a later novel of mine, *Magog*, I described the scene from the point of view of an anti-hero of power and authority:

> Magog had himself been seduced by the view from the
> derelict houses, which still had barge-builders operating
> from the cellars. The buildings were set on a wharf on
> an outer bend of the Thames, so that the eye was carried
> by the sweep of river towards Greenwich on the left and
> Tower Bridge on the right. Facing Magog across the
> Thames, two factory chimneys made a rifle's foresight to
> aim the view, while day-and-night sounds of machinery
> and wreaths of smoke flew with the gulls and the swans
> over the water from the working of ENTHOVEN and
> ESSO on Lavender Wharf. Around them, gutted ruins

and a rubbish tip, where trucks emptied wastes down
canvas chutes into barges to be towed away. On either
side of the river, warehouses squatted and bulked below
the arms and torsoes of the iron cranes that were spiders
in the blue fog of the morning or else were skeletal in
the low slant of the evening sun. Below Magog, on the
north foreshore, the long coffins of the Thames barges
had slats over their maws and red-painted decks, the same
size still as the galleons which had been made there in
the first Queen Elizabeth's time, when Raleigh had sailed
off to found Roanoke and the whole of North American
history had been a dream of adventurers seeking
Eldorado from the East End. Scrubby tugs also lay on
the gravel bank, their hatches lime-green, navy-blue-
funnelled, rust-arsed and ready for reconditioning to
leave a cleaner wake. At the end of the buildings, the
back of a pub called The Grapes (Charles Dickens drank
here) and beyond, another great chimney of a power
station smutting the air so that black rain fell on the
twin giant cranes that walked away downriver into the last
light, two red lamps shining at the edge of their
platform. To the west, the river crooked its vein into the
heart of London, with a Wren church spire pushing up
its white bill in the midst of a nest of the iron-boned
cranes. On the rim of the City, Tower Bridge held up its
two manacled wrists, while the street-lamps dressed
themselves in single file to confine the water o'nights.

Such mystery and brutality of place, such stark demand
of beauty, such harsh vision, made Magog decide to keep
a hidden place there for himself. And when the long
narrow studio was finished, with its white-painted pine
walls leading out to a balcony that jutted over the tidal
Limehouse Reach, so Magog could stand on his rope-
caulked deck of beams and steer like Captain Ahab
towards the two chimneys across the river when the
storms hammered at the skylights and the barges banged
against the watergate of the house trembling like *The
Victory* at anchor before Trafalgar, then Magog knew why
he was there, playing the sea-dog at the muddy ditch
from where England had grown to Empire, black
factories, coal-dark bricks, iron ships, the docks of
London where any sailor could drop down in the foc's'le

1 The author in New York

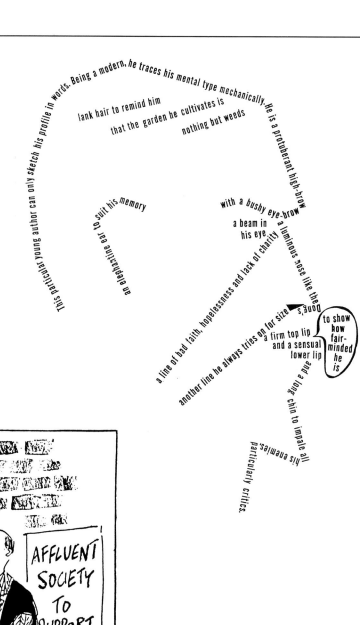

This particular young author can only sketch his profile in words. Being a modern, he traces his mental type mechanically. He is a protuberant high-brow

lank hair to remind him
that the garden he cultivates is
nothing but weeds

with a bushy eye-brow
a beam in
his eye
a luminous nose like the

an elephantine ear to suit his memory

Donne's

a line of bad faith, hopelessness and lack of charity

another line he always tries on for size
a firm top lip
and a sensual
lower lip

and a long chin to impale all
his enemies,
particularly critics.

to show
how
fair-
minded
he
is

AFFLUENT
SOCIETY
TO
SUPPORT

By TIMOTHY

2 Portrait of the Artist
as a Young Manuscript, 1958

3 Cartoon by Timothy Birdsall

the Original Absinthe Bar
400 Bourbon - Corner Conti
CABARET THEATRE pre-sents
the Fudgeripple Follies
or Nobody likes a Smart Ass

MONDAY thru SATURDAY
9:30 and 11:30 pm
For Reservations · Phone TW 1 · 4502 or 523 · 8730

5 Marianne and Andrew in Soho Square, 1963

6

7 David Hemmings in Antonioni's *Blow-Up*

8 Malcolm McDowell in Lindsay Anderson's *If*

9 French street art, 1968

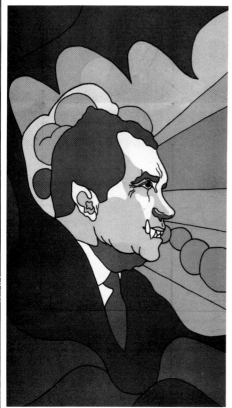

10 Tania la Guerrillera, Cuba, 1968
11 President Fidel Castro, Cuba, 1968
12 President Richard Nixon,
   Cuban Popular Art, 1968
13 Che Guevara, Cuba, 1968

14 Mass rally in Pyongyang, North Korea, 1969

15 Marianne in Pyongyang

16 Marianne and Timon

in a cone of yellow light from the deck lamps and begin
like Conrad's Marlow to say: 'A funny thing happened to
me on my way to Penang last voyage . . .'

So he would go down to Limehouse to watch the great
cargo ships from the four corners of the world as they
were towed into the wharves by the tugs. Sometimes he
saw a couple of floating cranes move slowly past, hanging
the low sun on the gibbets of their frame, the *London
Hercules* and the *London Titan.* Once he saw a red-sailed
Thames lugger making a bloody patch towards
Greenwich, once a four-masted clipper training ship,
once even a painted galleon like the Ancient Mariner's
boat mysteriously making towards the sea without noise
or sails, by opening the air in front and closing it behind,
presumably set on course for the new Eldorado of film
sets in Spain. But most evenings, in the decay of trade
and night and main, there were just some bumping tugs
pulling strings of barges loaded with bales of old paper,
or a few lighters croaking their way across to France, or
some navy cadets toiling at the oars in whalers on water
too dirty even for a shrimp to survive in, or perhaps cold
youths in racing-sculls which made a plaything of this foul
river that had once floated counter-Armadas. For the
little diesel freighters of rebuilt Rotterdam were now
taking most of the trade of the continent away from the
London docks, as Europe slowly began to unite and
Britain stayed in her cold island, waiting for destiny to
visit again and give her another opportunity or carry her
away.

Limehouse was, indeed, the finale of the imperial dreams, its
docks deserted, half its houses fallen into a wasteland of bomb-
sites, a whole generation of dockers neglected by even Labour
governments, which knew what a safe seat it was in the House of
Commons. If violence was the theme of the time, Limehouse
certainly was rich in aggressions, with memories of the Chinese
gang wars and Jack the Ripper's murders and now the bullyboys
of Cable Street and the Kray brothers still terrorizing the turf or
rubble. The local version of shooting grouse on moors was pot-
ting rats with air-rifles on the gravel foreshore or cornering them

with terriers in the iron barges, where the excitement of the bloodbath led to one famous docker biting off the heads of the rodents – until his false teeth slipped. There was none of the proletarian nostalgia of Arnold Wesker's plays in the East End. The dockers all marched for Enoch Powell, when he warned against the rising tide of immigration to Britain. 'What, Andrew,' they said to me in the pub, 'you never shared a toilet with them?' I had not often, but when I pointed out there must be only three or four immigrants among the ten thousand registered London dockers, many of whom had worked on unloading ships for generations, they thought I had missed the point. They wanted to have no competition, to keep things as they were. And I knew that the word comrade did not always extend beyond the white cliffs of Dover.

Narrow Street was the first riverside private development in the East End of London and would prophesy the regeneration of the docklands twenty years later, culminating in the giant cigar case of Canary Wharf. One of my neighbours, a young doctor named David Owen, would become a politician and split the Labour Party which had denied Limehouse for so long. But the beginning of the move from the middle of London to the peripheries and the world of the working classes was being paralleled all over the country. The centre was not holding, nor were the places of ancient tradition. The trend was most evident in the new pullulation of redbrick universities, which I was sent to cover in a series of articles, endeavouring to find out whether Oxford and Cambridge, London and Edinburgh would still continue to rule the minds and the opportunities of the land.

Oxford had been the first university in England, founded eight hundred years before; Cambridge was the second, created by refugees after a riot by the Isis. They had blocked the founding of new universities at Salisbury and Northampton and Stamford during the reign of King Edward the Third, who did not want any more of these unruly institutions 'except in the places where universities are now in some sense held'. This duopoly had continued through the Civil War and the Commonwealth, destroying

John Milton's hope of founding colleges and universities in every city. A hundred and fifty years ago, at the defeat of Napoleon, there had only been two thousand university students in the whole kingdom. But then Durham and London Universities were founded, followed by twelve in the major provincial cities, and also the Universities of Wales. These were called redbrick universities because of the poor quality of their buildings. Bristol University opened in a terraced house, and Liverpool and Leicester in disused lunatic asylums. But after the Second World War, eight new universities were founded in areas starved of higher education, and in visiting these, I found an extraordinary expectation and a tendency to design them in *ziggurats* or stepped pyramids, harking back to the original source of our education and literature, Sumeria and Babylon and *The Epic of Gilgamesh*. Although unachieved, the pyramids of the University of East Anglia would house the most successful of these new experiments. The Sainsburys would build there the most modern art gallery in Britain in a steel hangar, while the novelist Malcolm Bradbury would provide an antidote to F. R. Leavis, teaching a new generation of young writers influenced by American models, rather than a provincial criticism that stifled any creative urge.

Symptomatic of the collapse of the centre was the rise of the Liverpool poets on the back of the Beatles. Where John Lennon was held to be a new Elizabethan lyricist to match Andrew Marvel, Brian Patten and Roger McGough and Adrian Henri appeared to be urban Wordsworths, the bards of the northern streets rather than the lakes. They also declaimed their poems and songs with jazz backing to audiences of thousands. There was a renaissance of popular spoken poetry in the provinces on the model of *Wholly Communion* in the Albert Hall. And the Liverpool poets stuck to their mother city, finding the magnet of the metropolis too repulsive. They would not be sucked down, as the Irish and the Scots usually were. Brian Patten put well the need to avoid radical metropolitan chic in his 'Party-goers':

The charming young publisher, lean dark handsome
    host to the intelligence
in the thick carpeted living room
    has his causes on display and labelled like butterflies.
    The nouveau-poor
suck up the atmosphere.
    This room is all vanity, all temporal power.

The loss of my centre and a slow disintegration under a hard surface was my own fate. I was taking a sabbatical term off teaching to stay in our flat at Montparnasse, when Marianne told me that she was in love with Deacon as well. She wanted to leave me in Paris and live with him for a while in his new house in north London. Curiously, I had forecast this very situation in my novel *The Raker*, a triangle between the Deacon figure and a brash writer of obituaries and a young woman, while Denis Brogan had long before told me of *l'ami de famille*, the accepted lover in French triangular relationships. I first knew of the affair when Marianne suddenly dropped her opposition to my going on my Gog walk over the Borders from Edinburgh to York without any money, sleeping rough. She no longer cared quite enough to prevent me. There was now an alternative.

Influenced by irrealism and anarchism, I had long intended to write the whole mythical history of Albion, the visionary Britain of William Blake, within the body and mind of a single amnesiac figure, walking to London at the end of the Second World War. He would be called Gog and represent the never-ending revolt of the people and the provinces against the power and the rule of London, represented by his half-brother Magog – the two names of the traditional giants of ancient England. Gog would conjure up the historical unconsciousness of the island as well as his own past life, although his recollections and impulses would be questioned by the attacks of his wife Maire. A cartoon of Albion, drawn in the eighteenth century and in my possession, already showed England and Wales and part of Scotland as a giant drinking a mug of ale astride a dragon fish. As in irrealism, the whole history of a nation might be contained in the form of one body walking at one time – past and present and future all occurring to his mind in the *now*, in the eternal struggle between the country and the city.

At any rate, that had been my vast idea ever since we returned from our mystical experience in Arizona and Colorado and New Mexico. I had not dared do it; but in my pride, confronting the news that Marianne wanted to leave me for Deacon, I told her that it would release me to act out and write my grand design alone on the open moors and in the urban wilderness of Limehouse. In the last analysis my trade was solitary and could not admit the close love of a woman; we had hardly been separated for the past five years, day and night. In my cold anger, I did not count the cost to my heart, the amputation of my emotions. Vainly I believed I should and could sacrifice my love to my art. And in a way, I was escaping from outward commitment and politics into an interior journey to the very essence and matter of my heritage, cutting free from present ties to explore the violence of the past in paranoia and ancient myth. We are what we were, I thought. I was, therefore I am, and so I will be.

8

WALKING LONG

So what – nothing like a little disaster for sorting things out.

Blow-Up, MICHELANGELO ANTONIONI

We had to play a film to change the sets at the Hampstead Theatre between the various scenes in *Adventures in the Skin Trade*. The shooting had to be done for next to nothing, and I was happy to do it in a surrealist or irrealist mode in the old black-and-white and silent manner. So there I was, filming a weathered Limehouse lady against the brick wall of my riverside house as a street vision of a whore in the mind of young Dylan Thomas, when a mysterious and beautiful woman I knew called Claire came in with a handsome elder Italian, saying that they were looking for locations. 'I'll see you when I've finished filming,' I said, returning to the view-finder of my tiny camera. And then I went upstairs to discover that Claire was with Michelangelo Antonioni, who was about to film *Blow-Up*, which would turn out to be the definitive statement of how young life in London appeared to be right then. I felt a fool when I found out who he was, and it was evident that I would lose Claire to him.

She would emerge in his film as the enigmatic girl, played by Vanessa Redgrave, who lured an unknown man to his death beneath a bush in a park, discovered by the young photographer enlarging his pictures. Antonioni saw himself as the victim, but, as he said in a preface to his screenplay which I was later to publish, even in the pursuit of perfection on screen, artists' private lives did not break off during the process. 'They acquire new point and bite, giving our work a function that is sometimes stimulating, sometimes debilitating, sometimes calming . . .' As Vanessa Redgrave was made to say in *Blow-Up* to David Hemmings, playing Thomas with his camera, 'My private life's already in a mess. It would be a disaster if . . .' Only to hear his reply, 'So what – nothing like a little disaster for sorting things out.'

We had already cast David Hemmings to play the young Dylan

figure in *Adventures in the Skin Trade*. Mercurial and reckless and uninhibited, he was dazzling in the stage version of the unfinished novel, which the poet himself had called 'a mixture of Oliver Twist, Little Dorrit, Kafka, Beachcomber and good old three-adjectives-a-penny, belly-churning Thomas, the Rimbaud of Cwmdonkin Drive'. Tennessee Williams was in town and saw the play and pronounced it to be the best on the London stage – which was to change my life once his opinion had reached America. But I suspect that he liked Hemmings's wicked beauty more than my words in that cherubic mouth. And we were not able to transfer the piece to the West End: we lost our star to Antonioni for his film, once Claire had taken him to see my play the night after I had taken her. For Hemmings was the quintessence of what Antonioni sought, the drifting photographer who exemplified the social revolution in 'swinging' London, although he actually led a life as regulated as a ceremony while claiming to know no other law but anarchy. Antonioni was already fascinated by 'a kind of sweet immorality' in British women and the chase after an aimless liberty by the young. For he thought that the pursuit of freedom mattered, not its conquest. Once it was achieved, all discipline was discarded, and decadence resulted without any visible future.

Claire would remain the enigmatic woman in Antonioni's life, when he proceeded to try to film American rebellion and violence in *Zabriskie Point*. I had myself reached Hollywood by that time and was highly amused to read of Antonioni leaving a host of film executives to trudge up to the top of a salt hill in Death Valley, where an unidentified British girl stood alone, to ask for her opinion of his apocalyptic climax, the blowing up of a whole ranch-house filmed by fifteen cameras. 'Did you tell him you were happy with that, Claire?' I was to ask her when I saw her again. 'No,' she replied with her mocking smile and blue commas of eyes, 'I told him that I wanted him to blow up all America.'

We did have grand designs then. And with the partial loss of Marianne as well, I felt both driven and free to try and accomplish my long walk. Until I launched upon my first major novel, *Gog*, I had thought that experience was something that happened casually to me. The material for my fiction would come from my normal life. But gradually, as I felt more in command of my style in the novel, and as I grew more to recognize my obsessions, I realized that I did not have to wait around for experience to occur. I could go out and find the experience I wished for themes that I needed. *Gog* took three years in gestation and another two to write. It demanded a great deal of research into the byways of mythology and the details of popular revolt in Britain; it also demanded a huge grubbing into the facts of being alive in 1945, something which I had largely forgotten. But it made me do another thing, which I began in terror and ended in gratitude. It made me tramp some four hundred miles without any money along the old right-of-ways in England and Scotland.

This experience of tramping, which gave me all the details I needed about season and sight and hunger and cold and just moving, was not a *real* experience of being a tramp, as George Orwell's was, when he described his years of poverty in *Down and Out in Paris and London.* I was tramping towards a perfectly good house in the London docks and a perfectly secure income from academia and writing. I was only playing at being the tramp, with my shorn hair and assumed accent. Yet the sensations which I experienced were all true enough. An empty belly is no forgery; sleeping on a moor, soaked to the skin, is no lie. Lying out in a gale all night on the site of an old Roman camp by Hadrian's Wall gave me a better picture of the feelings of a Roman sentry on guard duty nineteen hundred years ago than I could ever have reached in my imaginings or researches in London.

Approaching somewhere with the same physical sensations as one's hero makes all the difference in the description of a place. York Minster does not look the same to a fat man after a good night as it looks to a hungry man after a week out. People do not behave the same towards a dirty stubbled hiker as they do towards a car driver with a crease in his trousers. These are all simple observations, but vital ones. Until I had condemned

myself out of my own mouth to a host of friends, and until shame
drove me out to plod along as I had boasted that I would, I was
one of the complacent authors who claimed that memory or
plagiarism or inspiration could provide a far better description
of a thing than the thing itself. It would be convenient if this
were true, and far more comfortable, but it is not true.

In a true sense, the difficulty of writing a strange work such as
Gog forced even more circumstance from the experience. I had
actually met a gaggle of deformed children shepherded by their
Catholic nurses below Edinburgh on my walk, although I was
always accused of stealing the scene from one of my favourite
film-makers, Tod Browning in *Freaks*. The *chosen* experience which
led to the unexpected encounter also led to the difference in
this novel of mine from earlier and lighter sights. For the first
time the will to write did dominate my life for two years at the
cost of my feelings and a reasonable existence. Hardness was all,
and it produced a vision as blinkered as the old Blackwall Tunnel
under the Thames. The long, slow sharing of my wife with my
old friend seemed to have no ending and no turning. She said
she loved us both. I used to say that every woman needed two
men to give her enough time and conversation, while every
author needed half a woman to give himself enough time to
write alone. My statement was only a defence, which did not
even convince me. For company, I had an Abyssinian cat called
Mishkin, which used to sit on my lap while I typed until it decided
to join in with its paws, making my manuscript even more irreal,
or it would sleep in my bed with its head on my pillow, waking
me in the small hours by walking across my face as it left on its
nightly errands and me to my solitude.

I was offered three professorships in American history – in
England, the United States, and the Antipodes; but they all meant
running a department and gave me no time for my double life
as a historian and a novelist. I had no reason to choose security
with half a wife and no child. I had written a couple of plays for
Armchair Theatre on television, both based on family memories of

Africa. In *The Chocolate Tree*, a black grandson returned from West Africa to take over an English trading company. In *Old Soldiers*, I used my father's bitterness in finding no employment back in Britain after his forced retirement from the Colonial Service, once Tanganyika had received its independence. The play had a happy ending with Kenneth More as a parking meter attendant inspecting the rows of tall-standing machines as meticulously as he had the ranks of the Colonial Police. Such a lucky irony had not happened to my poor father, who had remarried a hospital matron out in East Africa after his divorce from my mother. Both of them had found that the Wind of Change that Harold Macmillan had loosed to blow across the dark continent had exposed them to penury and living on a reluctant pension and ingratitude and oblivion on their return to the motherland. The proverb once was that old soldiers never died, they simply went to China. But the old soldiers from Africa returned here to a living death from neglect.

The faint far whiff of writing screenplays in Hollywood began to change my solitary choices. It had long been the temptation and ruin of writers – Scott Fitzgerald and William Faulkner, Christopher Isherwood and even Bertolt Brecht. I was also from a generation weaned on the screen. Our very language was made spare by one-liners from the stars, John Wayne saying 'That'll be the day,' or the last line of *Some Like It Hot*, 'Nobody's perfect.' Above all, we had learned to write without blatant motivation; the dialogue and the acting and the background had to express all. While scribbling for the cinema meant an almost inevitable corruption in the process, a refinement of a gross of words into a residue of action led to the *reductio ad absurdum* of Hemingway, a sort of grace under producer pressure.

Of one hundred scripts commissioned for the cinema, ten reach some stage of pre-production, and one is finally filmed, usually after rewriting by many hands. My first screenplay for Columbia Pictures, *Before Winter Comes*, was blessed as my first novel had been, by an improbable instant acceptance. I was the sole screenwriter and the stars who were offered the roles instantly took them – David Niven as the British Army officer who was handed back to the Russians, the refugee Topol, an admirable administrator of an intractable camp, with Godard's girl Anna Karina playing the love interest and the young John Hurt in his first screen role as the good lieutenant. This story of loyalty and treachery, duty and betrayal, was set in the occupied zones of Austria at the end of the Second World War and it described the crimes of the British in handing whole divisions of Ukrainians, who had fought for the Germans, back to the untender mercies of Stalin. It was also an echo of the Allies' behaviour over failing to save the Jews from the concentration camps, sticking to the letter of the military law rather than reading the book of justice.

Because of an incident at Limehouse, I found I was already known in Hollywood. In a rare stint as a film producer, Frank Sinatra had come to Britain to make a picture. One scene was set on the Rhine; but opposite my river house on the Thames was a factory sign, ENTHOVEN. By cheating a shot from my balcony, a small fortune could be saved from the budget. I was insanely writing *Gog* when a front man hammered on my door, interrupting me. Would I accept a hundred pounds from Sinatra to shoot from my house? I swore, and said I was writing. Never taking no for an answer and presuming that my poverty was greater than my pride, the Sinatra gang returned a week later with several movie vans and set up shop in the nearby pub, the Black Horse. Again the front man hammered at my door. 'Would *two* hundred pounds . . .?' 'Get out, I'm writing!' The landlord of the pub later told me a furious discussion broke out in the Black Horse about what to do. Teach me a lesson? Or go to the Rhine? That would be at least another hundred thousand pounds on the budget. There was only one solution. Protesting and livid with anger, Frank Sinatra himself walked across Narrow Street and banged on my dusty door. Furious at a second intervention that morning, I ran down the stairs to open up. Hardly noticing the small shape in front of me and barely hearing his words, 'I'm Frank Sinatra, and I would like to . . .', I screamed at him, 'I'm writing. I never heard of you.'

So I arrived in Hollywood as the man who had never heard of Frank Sinatra. Where celebrity was all, this ignorance had amused them. I was to go to Tinseltown a dozen times a year over the next two years as a leading script doctor for Columbia and C.B.S. Films, and in whatever palace I stayed, at the Beverly-Wilshire or the Beverly Hills Hotel or on Malibu Beach, I would always feel an enervating mixture of excitement and envy, isolation and degradation. There was no question that screenwriters were the serfs of the industry. But in the beginning was the Word, and without the right words in the script, the stars would not come down from their Bel Air mansions and play. So the writers were pampered and overpaid, abused and ignored once all the relevant phrases had been squeezed from their fingernails by the torture of the Hollywood writing process, treatment after treatment and draft after draft, the mutilation of the original plot by a thousand cuts until only a twitching corpse was left with the right reflex actions for the great names of the business. It was little fun while it lasted, but it was fabulously profitable. I certainly could write faster than the Hollywood moguls could read.

I arrived at the time that the hippies were being incorporated, as I was, into the mass merchandising of the American way of life, although the high feeling against the Vietnamese War was briefly bringing together all the protest movements in the land, however much they disapproved of each other. Trawling through the underground press that had suddenly broken surface in a pullulation of rainbow bubbles, I found that the youth rebellion was also aware of its own disintegration and coming corruption. Timothy Leary might be declaring in *Open City* that 'you are a God, act like one,' and that if everyone in Manhattan were to 'turn on' and 'tune in', grass would grow on First Avenue, shoeless divinities would dance down the car-less streets, and deer would graze along St. Mark's Place. Your body had to become a sacred temple, but you should not 'drop out' until you had 'tuned in' and 'turned on'. Bad trips on drugs were only caused by the failure to 'tune in'. And the reason why? 'When you "tune in" you trigger off energy. Pot flicks on sensory energy. Hashish to somatic energy. L.S.D. to cellular energy. High dose L.S.D. to molecular energy.' Later on in the issue, *Open City* printed part of Andy Warhol's Velvet Underground and Nico Band, singing 'Heroin':

> Heroin . . .
> Be the death of me
> Heroin . . .
> It's my wife . . .
> And it's my life . . .
> Because a main up to my vein leads to a center in my
>   head . . .
> And then I'm better off than dead.
> Because when the smack begins to flow . . .
> Ah, I really don't care any more . . .
> About all the jim-joms in this town . . .
> And all the politicians making busy sound . . .
> And everybody putting everybody else down . . .
> And the dead bodies piled up in mounds . . .

Yet the same issue of *Open City* published the forthcoming V.D. or Vietnam Day, when tens of thousands of hippies were called to disrupt an appearance by President Lyndon Johnson in Los Angeles, not with the usual cries of 'Hey, Hey, L. B. J., How Many Kids Did You Kill Today?', but with positive peace signs such as 'Welcome Hanoi to the Great Society'. It was time for aesthetic rebellion, for creative anarchy. 'We must realise that numbers and time are on our side and that the Establishment needs us to fight this non-existent war . . . Hippies of the world unite; you have nothing to lose but your paranoia.'

Looking for hippie support against Vietnam and racism were the organizing abilities of the Students for Democratic Society, led by the charismatic Tom Hayden, later the husband of Jane Fonda who would be doomed to join rather than radicalize Hollywood. Hayden drafted the Port Huron statement of the movement; it tried to create a socialist student power on the back of the Free Speech turmoils at Berkeley, which culminated in a sit-in round the U.S. Navy's recruitment table on campus in December 1966, and intervention by the police. This was a declaration of independence of a new American revolution: 'We, the people . . .' became 'We are people of this generation, bred in at least modest comfort, housed now in universities, looking uncomfortably at the world we inherit. As we grew, however, our comfort was penetrated by events too troubling to dismiss. First, the permeating and victimising fear of human degradation, symbolised by the Southern struggle against racial bigotry, compelled most of us from silence to activism. Secondly, the enclosing fact of the Cold War, symbolised by the presence of the Bomb, brought awareness that we ourselves, and our friends, and millions . . . might die at any time. We might deliberately ignore, or avoid, or fail to feel all other human problems, but not these two, for these were too immediate and crushing in their impact.' The S.D.S. had begun by organizing students to fight for a broad coalition of issues to attract all the young rebels with different causes. They were for the Vietnamese and the blacks in the south, for the poor and the workers and even women's causes. But at their convention in 1967, the correspondent for *Indian Head* noticed that the anarchists now controlled the society, which was moving away from fighting other people's battles 'to fighting our own – "Student Power" and "We Won't Go". We took Stokeley Carmichael's advice to "organize where you're at" – we left an essentially liberal-reformist concern with minority group problems and took an introspective look at the deficiencies of our own lives. A genuine radical consciousness came with the realisation that this society oppresses people in many different ways in different situations, and that what is needed is not piecemeal material improvements for one segment of the population, but a revolutionary transformation of all parts of the social structure.'

The Black Power movement was already refusing all help from whites and turning from the politics of integration towards revolution. It was the same with women activists, now more con-

cerned with their own rights than those of oppressed blacks or
colonial people. It would also be the turn of the gay movements,
which would come out of the closet door, kicked open by the
hippie emphasis on open sexuality. And the millions of hippies,
whose support most of the radicals sought in order to give their
movements the mass backing of the younger generation, were
already at the peak of their self-contained alternative way of life.
They were being lured gently towards the scene that they
rejected, as *Indian Head* already saw. They were drifting slowly
into the smiling arms of Madison Avenue. 'The realisation that
they will not be able to continue putting down the plastic American values, while they are in fact enjoying them, will come too
late. Because the hippie is like a naive Pinocchio, there will always
be the danger of the cigar-smoking carnival barker ready to take
him for a ride. Once he gets on the carousel it will be going too
fast for him to jump off.' One aspect of the hippie movement
was its similarity to a lonely hearts club. For a while the hippies
shared the common bond of rejection. There was an ease of
mobility among hippie circles and a permissive atmosphere that
allowed them to search for whatever each one wanted. 'The free
structure of the hippie scene was its greatest attribute, but also
will be the source of its downfall. Either the hippies will be
assimilated into large semi-hippie situations or they will resort
to non-hippie tactics which will make them something entirely
different.'

Although *Indian Head* conceded that the tribalism and sexual
morals and drug culture of the hippies could not be assimilated
into the law-abiding masses, it foresaw the eventual incorporation
of the trend into society, until it would be stood on its head and
become what it had abhorred, the thought-police of the politically correct academics and politicians, who would rise to govern
America. And the hippie entry into political protest through the
Yippies was to create a good deal of sound and fury, signifying
not very much. Those who could organize protest, chiefly the
apostles of student power and Black Power, discovered that an
association with a permissive or a drug culture did their hard

causes little good. Vietnam was the only banner to wave that could unite all those who might be drafted, but burning the American flag was not a recruiting card. Even the underground magazine *Avatar*, based in Boston and courted in an interview by the aspiring president, Robert Kennedy, turned fiercely on the San Francisco paper, the *Oracle*, to condemn it for lauding the mind-blowing savagery that afflicted the flower children in 'Haight (Hate)-Ashbury', where rape was as common as bullshit and the love generation never slept. 'Tune in, turn on, drop dead? One wonders. Are Leary and the *Oracle* all in the same greedy place? Does acid still have to be sold as hard as Madison Avenue still sells sex? What do these nice people mean by "Love"?'

I also wondered and fled Hollywood, my job with Columbia over for the time being. I felt compelled to wash the gold dust off my feet with my second Gog walk along the lost sacred trail from Glastonbury to Canterbury. Except for one night off the hard way, spent in a prehistoric hill fort, I experienced no trip through time. But I turned off during a pelting thunderstorm to drop in and see the English writer I venerated, the bard and soothsayer of good and evil. William Golding lived in an elegant cottage on the edge of the watercress beds at Bower Chalke, half-way between – as he liked to say – the spire of Salisbury Cathedral and pagan Stonehenge. He took me in like the good Samaritan that he was; he wined and dined and dried me; and he told me a story of moral choice and deception that informed my novel and my life. Drafted into the navy during the Second World War, he had risen to become the captain of a rocket ship on D-Day. I had read what he had written about it in an essay called 'The English Channel'. He had seen seven (or was it eleven?) thousand ships at anchor. They oozed out like a stream of dark oil, milling about in a rising wind. Golding himself turned in at night, leaving his first mate on watch. When he woke, he discovered that they had become separated from the whole of the vast armada . . .

Indeed the Channel was big that night, oceanic and covered with a swarm of red stars from planes and gliders moving south. I found that we were miles west of our position. So we turned south-east and steamed at full speed all night over jet black waves that were showered with sparks of phosphorescence and possibly loaded with mines.

I stood there all night catching up and felt history in my hands as hard and heavy as a brick. I was frightened – not immediately of the mines we might set off at any moment, nor of the batteries ashore, nor of the thousands of enemy aircraft we had been promised. I was frightened, of all things, of being late and jeered at.

Golding arrived in time to take up his position with the other rocket ships off the Normandy beaches. One of the Allied planes dived into the fatal geometry of the curve of the first salvo of rockets. There, Golding's written account of D-Day ended, but he had not written all of the history of that night and day. The time that I turned off the hard way to see him, he told of his fear of his ship, the nagging knowledge that one spark, one tracer-bullet would blow up his floating fireworks factory to blazes. He told me of the moral doubt of choosing to risk his men's lives by sailing over a minefield in order not to be mocked for arriving late for the greatest sea invasion there ever was. Only later did he discover that the minefield marked on the chart was a decoy to deter the enemy; there had been no risk at all, no real moral choice – any more than there had been for me when I had decided not to go to Suez.

Golding also told me that evening what he meant by the phrase, 'history in my hands as hard and heavy as a brick'. The rockets he fired from his ship were called 'bricks'. His job was twice to lay seven hundred and fifty 'bricks' over a hellish half-acre, obliterating it in fire. At the invasion of Walcheren he had to do his duty again, creating his little infernos before the troops landed. That grey morning, the Royal Air Force did not appear to cover the landing, so that most of the other rocket ships were destroyed by shells and phosphorus and bombs, his own ship one of the few to be spared. Yet he watched their explosive fate as dispassionately as if he were viewing a war movie. Since then he has written about grace and mercy, chance and fate, struggle and survival for those who live upon the sea.

He also said that he was fascinated by Marianne, when they had met. He saw her as the lizard who ran over the back of his hand to sit on the sunny wall of the Tomb of Posidippa at Ravenna. She was the glittering, ageless, primordial reptile, half a million years old, knowing everything by looking at it through her third eye. I was the hot wall, while he saw himself in her. She was a mirror. He knew how lethal she was, an immemorial being trapped within the body of a young woman, a fatal attraction.

I resumed my walk and spent the eve of the summer solstice sleeping above Stonehenge, the towers and huts of the military camp on Larkhill squatting above the ancient ring of standing stones. I watched the modern druids at their dawn ceremonies and talked to their Grand Master afterwards. The sly certainty of the ages, the ambiguity of faith, the sophistry of mysticism, all of these given to me by Golding and the druids were suggestions that I tried to incorporate into *Gog*, which I finished writing that summer in a desperate isolation and a paranoiac confusion. I identified myself with my seven-foot amnesiac hero, rediscovering in his body the whole mythical and irreal history of his country, while being persecuted to the limits of sanity by Maire, *alias* Marianne. When she was to read the book, she said with her harsh laugh that she never knew I knew her so well, and that she did not know me at all. I was still obsessed by her, while she was disintegrating herself between the love of Deacon and myself, strong feelings which she could not resolve. I decided to remove her to reach a solution, although I knew there were no solutions in her life, only recurrent compromises. She could never give up anyone close to her.

With an advance of five thousand dollars for *Gog* in America and a borrowed car, I took a sabbatical winter term and Marianne to try and see every old stone beneath the Rio Grande. The

Mayan and Aztec and Inca civilizations had always fascinated me since my experience with irrealism among the Hopi and Navajo Indians. We sailed into New York on the Queen Elizabeth under the vast steel skeletal wings of the new Verrazano Narrows Bridge: 'ravished meridians left behind', my diary read. It went on to say that most of American pop art and op art was already doomed, but the things being done in metal and wood and plastic and kinetic sculpture were a renaissance of those forms. All around us and between ourselves, we sensed disintegration – the growing revolution of the young, anarchy and arson. Drawings and paintings of Manhattan burning spotted my journal, also my poem to the resolution of the American dream of liberty and equality of opportunity.

> Rockefeller sat in his Plaza
> And he drank his lemon tea
> And he cried: 'O my workers,
> How good you've been to me.'
>
> 'For you've laboured in your millions
> To set me here on high
> So I may sit and bless you –
> Yet you're as good as I.
>
> 'Each man can build his Plaza
> And sit by the side of me.
> Just take the elevator
> Till you reach equality.'
>
> Rockefeller sat in his Plaza,
> But he never finished his tea,
> For the fires burned his tower down,
> And his ashes they were never found,
> They came to be just dirt on the ground –
> Equally. Equally.

We drove to Monterrey, that ugly Mexican Birmingham, which was briefly under snow, the children building *gringos* which melted away, and the Indians waiting without expectation under their blankets and this heavenly calamity. We began a Mexican divorce, which might reflect our partial separation, our drift apart as we drifted along. I went on trying to convince myself that I had chosen 'my own emotional and mental solitariness, an urge to drop all responsibility for any other being and force myself further and deeper along the path of learning and creation.' Perhaps *Gog* was good enough to make it worth it. Certainly, reading the proofs of that gargantuan novel in the ruined earthquake city of Antigua in Guatemala gave me the gall to resign my second lectureship in American history in the knowledge that I would never work in academia again, after leaving two safe jobs. I would have to live as a freelance now in modern guerrilla jousts, by my wits and my pen. 'Poor Marianne,' I wrote, 'she deserved a better deal than a Scot bent on his savage streak, pursuing action to its ultimate end, perhaps without the talent to do well.' I called her Malinche, the Mexican princess whom Cortés had exploited and betrayed in order to win his Spanish empire from the Aztecs.

Wherever we travelled to see the ancient ruins, to Palenque, Sayil and Tulum, to Uzmal and Chitchen-Itza, to Mitla and Monte Alban, to Malinalco and San Cristobal de las Casas, to Antigua and Tikal, there were memories and echoes and present incidents of guerrilla war. The Mayans had always resisted the Spanish *conquistadores* and then the Mexican Revolution: outside the zoo of Guatemala City we saw a weird procession of Indians dressed as the 'liberating' French grenadiers of the doomed Mexican Emperor Maximilian, parading with the blond-bearded corpse of the conqueror Alvarado in a glass coffin. When we were flying into that city, the army and the police and a lone helicopter were fighting some guerrillas who had infiltrated the university, the sports stadium and an infants' school. When we flew on to the incredible steep-stepped pyramids of Tikal, with temples at their peaks higher than control towers over the rebel-held jungle, we found half the Guatemalan Council of State had come in that afternoon under armed escort. The Minister of Nothing kneeled to kiss Marianne's silver boots, murmuring, '*A sus piedes, señora*',

and warning us not to stay after dark for the guerrillas held all
the Peten around, the rainforest with the jaguars lying on its
branches. 'Musketry rattled this morning,' my diary read in Antigua. 'The exciting thing about Guatemala is that you never know
if the eruption is natural or artificial, a real volcano or a revolution or an execution going on, or merely thunder or a fiesta. All
are equally possible. The newspapers are full of executions,
arrests, murders: really, a most smiling and villainous land.'

Scottish and French in descent, we were generally excluded
from the loathing of the *gringos*, the Spanish and the Americans.
The oppressed Indians in the *altiplano* had not yet started their
revolt led by the urban Shining Path guerrillas, and it was difficult
to weep too much over the monumental masonry of the Incas at
Cuzco and Sacsayhuamun and Ollantatambo, where that heavy
civilization had crushed the marvellous and metaphysical Nazcas
with their desert geometry and fine weave-cloth, as well as the
Moche pottery that laughed at love and death, with skeleton jars
sporting an enormous phallus or fingering women with their
knuckle-bones, seducing them or sodomizing them. Eros and
thanatos had been more developed in that culture than in any
permissive modern society.

We took the *altiplano* railway to Machu-Picchu, bucking and
swaying by the brown and boiling rapids of the Urubamba, furi-
ously racing past the rainforests with red orchids spiky on the
high forks of the trees, and the sheer gorges occasionally terraced
by vain toil to gain a yard's strip of earth on each yard's fall.
Again I had a mystical trip at sunrise, standing on the sacrificial
stone facing the peaks of the Andes, watching a white wax ball
trying to clear its way through the swaddle of the mists rising
from the crevasse made by the angry brown worm of the river
below. When the sun was red at last, it was dead in line with the
flat rock shaped into a heart with a tunnel for sacrificial blood
ending in a point towards the source of the light of the world.
Around me, stones were hewn to correspond exactly with the
shapes of the surrounding mountains, points of alignment for
observing the solstices and the stars, as at Stonehenge and in the

Vale of the White Horse at Avebury and Silbury Hill, the writing of astronomy and geometry in stone and shape of earth, a vast vocabulary we had lost and would not recover.

The day we rode the interminable train from Cuzco to Puno past the high herds of llamas and vicunas growing their wool for sweaters was the day that Che Guevara was reported to have entered Bolivia on a bicycle, disguised as a priest. We took a Victorian steamer across Lake Titicaca, all brass and copper and cast-iron swivel chairs and red plush, and we managed to have a little rebellion on the train at Tiahuanaco so that we could all descend to see this battered square Stonehenge, the origin of the Inca religion, before we were driven down into the cold cauldron of La Paz, shivering with dread at the coming insurrection of the Cuban *commandante* with his thirty followers. After all, Cortés and his few men had brought down the Aztecs, Pizarro with even fewer had destroyed the Incas, so what might Che not achieve with his tiny band? It was not a hopeless cause or case. The start of that uprising certainly changed our personal lives and proved deadly on our passports. How could we ever explain that we were not one of the infiltrators like the French intellectual Régis Debray, who had come to join Guevara on his Bolivian campaign?

We flew back to Mexico to recover our car, and we drove north to New York through Monterrey, where we found our Mexican divorce was waiting for us. For once, the paperwork there had gone through on time for a few hundred dollars more. There was cold comfort in this legal document that confirmed our increasing separation. 'The circle has closed,' my diary read. 'We have travelled and we have arrived. A new life we begin. The old rules are dead, long live the new rules.' On our return to London we gave a bizarre interview to Drusilla Beyfus, who was writing on *The English Marriage*. The truth of our situation lay in our silences, because the other man Deacon was never mentioned, nor our disintegration behind our coolness and our pride. I appeared to say: 'Marianne is a glowing centre and a lot of heads roll for her. We have fantastic meetings. Everything becomes new and odd, suddenly she is a stranger wandering in again. This meeting makes things much better and extraordinary. Separation makes sex much more exciting. This is the thing. It is better to worry a bit and feel a little jealous and just not be too sure. It is better than a week or two of boredom, when life is just so dead . . . We do travel together and that's the most difficult accomplishment in the world. We travel very hard, great distances. People intrude too much at home, but the moment you get off in a bubble, it's fine. Travel is the best bubble of all, particularly in a country where you don't know the language. You are totally enclosed.'

And Marianne appeared to say: 'The side of Andrew that discards me is the part of him I have always respected. I have always admired him most as a writer and as a serious dedicated person, and I want him to evolve in that direction. Also, my acceptance of the situation gave me a chance to feel gratitude to him when he said, "Oh God, you are probably the only girl who would stand this." I would think, perhaps I am. No mistress would stand suddenly being ditched for three months . . . I think that the difference between Andrew and I is that Andrew has never put happiness at a premium. But I would choose happiness every time.'

9

A TRADE RISK

Assassination is a trade risk, which every prominent
public man ought to accept as a matter of course.

THEODORE ROOSEVELT

Finishing his book *Bomb Culture* in 1967, Jeff Nuttall also discerned the failure of the British peace movement, which had degenerated to a sort of sickness, while the protest movement had succumbed to the inwardness of psychedelic drugs. His own idealism had ended in mounting a show of rotting meat and decay in the basement of Better Books in the Charing Cross Road in London, and he considered the terrible child killings by Ian Brady and Myra Hindley to be the result of the cult of the working-class libertine, eulogized by Genet and the counter-culture. The disembowellings of dead animals at London happenings had culminated in the Sadean savagery of the Moors Murders. 'Moral shame, moral absurdity, moral abuse, moral paradox and moral outrage had frozen us at a point of almost total negativity.' The way out was the numbing of the moral sense. Sensation and pain and anger had to be used as propulsion. And yet, 'in the perilous adventure towards movement and construction, there was the possibility of terrible catastrophe.'

Talking of the youth music culture in the underground paper *Albion*, the performing poet Pete Brown also saw a big reaction following the advent of Dylan and the Beatles, and the emergence of folk musicians like the Incredible String Band, who had together produced a 'Vietnam summer'. The lyrics were full of references to drugs, as they had been in the 'twenties. Then it had been reefers and opium and cocaine, but now it was acid and pot and speed. 'What it did, as always, was to kill a few people, make a lot of bread for some very hidden people, get a lot of people stoned, make a lot of people make love who would have made love eventually, and make a lot of people wear bright clothes.' The good thing was that musicians did not ply their trade just for money or women. They began to communicate

actual experiences in their own words and music and fantasies.
A liberty of the imagination had been born again.

From the point of view of popular political philosophy, Mar-
shall McLuhan had risen to challenge Marcuse, who himself was
shifting towards a more violent solution. McLuhan's theory of
the global village, the world linked by electronics, gave hope
to the spawning underground press and the Liberation News
Service from New York, which aimed to be the Reuters of the
alternative culture. But his chief dictum, that the medium was
the message, that television and cinema would massage away the
protest of the masses, was soothing to the authorities, and turned
out to be true. In the future revolutions of South America and
eastern Europe, the first object of the rebels would be to capture
the television station in the capital. Marcuse, however, was becoming the apostle of the new Left, which was seeking aggressive
action against the modern state. His changing views were
summed up in 'An Essay on Liberation', where he now welcomed
the hippie youth culture as an agency of change. He saw in that
style of life a revolutionary potential. Its negativity and obscenity
were weapons against the Establishment. Like a reborn Walt
Whitman praising the American savage, Marcuse even enthused
over 'the exotic belligerency in the songs of protest; the seriousness of long hair, of the body unsoiled by plastic cleanliness'.

The old Left of European social democracy seemed worse than
the Establishment to the new Left: its ageing members were
apostates to Engels and Marx, traitors to Chairman Mao and
Fidel Castro. They did not campaign against the horrors of the
Vietnamese War, they supported the Labour government of
Harold Wilson which also supported American policy in South
Asia. As my old friend David (John) Caute stated in his acute
Sixty-Eight: The Year of the Barricades:

> The new growth was fertilized by a powerful chemical, a
> sense of betrayal . . . the Marxian critique of capitalism
> had yielded to the revisionism of social democrats who
> redefined socialism as a 'welfare state' founded in a

capitalist 'mixed economy' in which the public sector
served as a kind of hospital for sick or non-profitable
industries and services. This final period of the new Left,
the *Götterdämmerung*, was intensely ideological,
confrontational, and violent; waves of protest swept across
the advanced countries, each intensely conscious of its
solidarity with the others; indeed a new 'International'
was born among students. It is by the street scenes and
campus occupations of 1967–69 that the new Left is
remembered – and rejected – by the population at large.

Two methods were being advocated of unseating governments –
by outrage and fun or by sabotage and gun. The Situationists
and the Yippies supported revolution by spectacle, while the
black and student power movements preferred guerrilla war. The
Situationist revolution was through psychological and cultural
overthrow rather than by street or factory violence. The radical
poet Alexander Trocchi put its aims in subverting the whole
world more emphatically than its leader Guy Debord did. The
attack had to be cultural. With his thousand technicians, Trotsky
had seized the bridges, telephone exchanges and the power stations. The police had guarded the government in the Kremlin,
effectively blocking it from the real levers of power. 'So the
cultural revolt must seize the grids of expression and the power-
houses of the mind.' Intelligence had to realize its own power on
the global scale. Traditional authorities would be outflanked.
What had to be seized had no physical dimensions. 'It's not an
arsenal, not a capital city, not an island, nor an isthmus visible
from a peak in Darien.' It was these things too, but only by the
way, and inevitably. We must seize ourselves, the creative people,
the millions of potential technicians. There was no permanence
in human institutions or nature. 'There is only *becoming*.' By
modifying, correcting, polluting, deflecting, corrupting, eroding
and outflanking, what could be inspired was the *invisible insurrection.*

That insurrection had become visible at the University of Stras-
bourg in 1966, when some of the young Situationists followed

Debord's tactics, expounded in his *The Society of the Spectacle*, and took over and bankrupted the student union there by printing a pamphlet on *The Poverty of Student Life*, claiming that art was dead, while the student was a necrophiliac and a conspicuous consumer. This example of subversion by the economic means of capitalism itself would be a path-finder for the revolt in Paris two years later, when Debord would find himself briefly in charge at the Sorbonne before losing his power through ignorance about how to exercise it. No Trotsky he, and certainly no Lenin.

Such spectacles of the absurdity and contradictions of capitalism would also be played out at the Democratic Convention in Chicago by the American Yippies, but they seemed equally absurd and contradictory to the leaders of the black and student power activists. The moderate and charismatic Martin Luther King finally had turned against the Vietnam War as a killing ground for blacks, and he had described the American government as 'the greatest purveyor of violence in the world today'. The Black Panthers, in their dark berets and glasses and leather, were armed and rising in the ghettos of Oakland across the Bay Bridge from San Francisco. The words of Stokely Carmichael and Huey Newton and Eldridge Cleaver and H. Rap Brown were widely reported and feared, particularly the notorious phrase that 'Violence is as American as apple pie.' The opening of the Free School in New York, where courses were offered in Mao and Black Power and 'Latin America – the next Vietnams?' was showing how the winds of radical change were beginning to blow across the campus and the university yard.

The powers that were became frightened. L.S.D. was banned in California and Leary was busted for its use, eventually fleeing into exile. On police evidence Huey Newton was also put in jail as was Eldridge Cleaver for the second time, although it prompted the publication of his *Soul on Ice*, which seemed to favour the rape of white culture and a coalition with white radicalism in opposition to the separatist Black Power advocated by Stokely Carmichael. And in Britain, Mick Jagger and Keith Richard of the Rolling Stones were sentenced to prison for possessing minor drugs, then later released after a leader in *The Times*, 'Who Breaks a Butterfly on a Wheel?' This 'case of social revenge,' as *The Sunday Times* called it, led to letters in the press calling for the legalization of cannabis, signed by a hundred of the leading performers and intellectuals and even physicians in the country. Although the forces of law and order were gearing themselves for future confrontations, their governments were still trying to placate and divide and contain the rebellion of the young before repressing it. In England, indeed, the Sexual Offences Bill was passed at last, based on the Wolfenden Report; adult consenting homosexuals – except for members of the armed forces and merchant seamen – were at last free to come out of the locker room and give up hiding in the public lavatories which they called 'cottages'. The hippie doctrine of love and sexual acceptance had even persuaded the government to correct a long-standing abuse.

As if to shroud the growing miasma of violence, a new series of killings of great men thwarted history and affected many of us personally. Andy Warhol's cliché about everybody being a celebrity for a quarter of an hour held a grain of missing truth. In point of fact, we are all intermittently a part of history, when we feel ourselves to be involved. Particularly, the murders of our heroes can provoke street and private rebellions, and for seconds or hours, for days or weeks, we may threaten the security of governments. In Bolivia the army, helped by American C.I.A. agents and detector helicopters, killed Che Guevara. In certain radical circles, it was equivalent to the killing of Christ, and the iconography of the posters of the student world treated Che's death in that way. His beret as a halo round his head, his beard as an aureole, sometimes clutching the rifle of revolution in his hand, Che's martyred countenance was displayed on the walls of a million university rooms. Although the authorities required his body to be burned and his ashes scattered so that there could be no shrine to him, Marianne later learned that his two fore-arms were severed and these holy relics of the liberation struggle were returned to Cuba. Herself torn between Deacon and myself,

seeking a cause to resolve the divisions of her life, she begged
me to send her to Cuba to do a book for my new cinema press
– *Viva Che* – in tribute to the fallen hero. Her faith and need
and conviction were so great that I sent her away. Her absence,
at least, postponed a conclusion at home.

Cuba had become the darling of the new Left, an island that
could cock a snook, if not a missile, at the almighty Uncle Sam
only a hundred sea miles away. It was the model contemporary
revolution, where a small band of guerrillas operating from the
countryside had destroyed an urban dictator in Havana and had
brought equality and literacy to an oppressed people. The tens
of thousands of political prisoners, held by Castro and his ubiquitous informers on every block and in each village, were as invisible to the foreign radicals as the *Gulag* had been to the fellow-
travellers in Stalin's heyday. Marianne arrived in Cuba to be met
by what she called a wave of love, a baptism into revolution.
Politically naive, she never saw that she was the consenting victim
of an intelligent secret service, which wished to extend its influence and its sources of information. She went to the Havana
Cultural Congress in the January of 1968, which attracted nearly
four hundred intellectuals from Latin and North America and
Europe. Many of them were members of the Fair Play for Cuba
Committee, which had been formed eight years previously, and
which boasted leading authorities such as Sartre with his strident
and blinkered anti-Americanism and C. Wright Mills, who put
aside his examination of *The Power Elite* to tell his country to
Listen, Yankee and follow the Cuban path in emancipating blacks
and women and poor agricultural workers. A feeling of hope and
urgency in changing human society as well as the *possibility of
doing it* was a potent brew for the new radicals – even more
exciting than John F. Kennedy's inauguration had been for my
generation. The rhetoric seemed much the same, although the
disaster of the invasion at the Bay of Pigs and the continuing
American blockade still lay between the two countries. Ask not
what Cuba can do for you, ask what you can do for Cuba. So

asked, the decadent, romantic Marianne was converted into a fanatic.

The shame of American foreign policy became a brighter blush with the Tet offensive in Vietnam, where the Vietcong and the Northern regular army launched a campaign in the South on their New Year's Day. Nearly all the provincial cities were attacked; the American embassy in Saigon was penetrated; within four days the Americans lost nearly fifteen hundred dead and wounded, their South Vietnamese allies three times as many combatants. Although the attacks were repelled and the American forces were boosted to half a million men, it was the beginning of the end of Lyndon Johnson and his crusade against the Communists. Revulsion spread everywhere, particularly in the Caribbean and Central and South America. The evil, murdering *gringo* was the universal object of hate. In a mock war tribunal convened in Stockholm later that spring, Sartre would equate Lyndon Johnson with Adolf Hitler. 'He killed the Jews because they were Jews. The armed forces of the United States torture and kill men, women and children in Vietnam because they are Vietnamese . . . This is their way of enduring the genocidal situation in which their government has put them.'

My increasing involvement in writing screenplays in Hollywood, the huge income I was earning from acting as a script doctor on a dozen films, and my development of Lorrimer Publishing into printing the illustrated classic screenplays of Renoir and Carné, Bergman and Wajda, Kurosawa and Welles, all colluded to divide me from radical activities, even though I was earning the funds to support them. I had sent Marianne to Cuba to commemorate Che, I had not gone. I used to justify myself by saying that I was rewriting bad screenplays in order to publish good ones. And indeed, the half million copies of the eighty classic screenplays which Lorrimer was to publish over the next twenty years was to teach a whole generation the grammar of the cinema, as it taught me. I also had the privilege of meeting and working with many of the world's leading directors and writers. Perhaps my most rewarding encounters were settling on the true script of *The Third Man* with Graham Greene and working personally with Josef von Sternberg on *The Blue Angel*, when he showed me a caricature that he had kept of himself as a puppet-master manipulating the strings by which Marlene Dietrich jerked below him. To match the prevailing mood among the young, we went on publishing Godard as he moved towards revolution in *Pierrot le Fou* and Lindsay Anderson's and David Sherwin's *If*, the most anarchic attack on the public school as a microcosm of oppression since Jean Vigo's assault on the *lycée* in *Zéro de Conduite*, which we also published. Anderson stressed that the coincidence of making and releasing the film with the world-wide student revolt was fortuitous. The basic tensions between hierarchy and freedom, independence and tradition, liberty and law, did not alter. His schoolboys were old-fashioned, not anti-heroes or drop-outs or followers of Marx or Lenin or Mao or Marcuse. 'Their revolt is inevitable, not because of what they *think*, but because of what they *are*.' Their leader, performed by Malcolm McDowell, might play at being an intellectual and quote, 'Violence and revolution are the only pure acts,' but he acted by instinct from passion and energy and outrage, even when gunning down the masters and the parents at the end of the speech day.

Those feelings, indeed, lay behind the bad temper of the times, which were high on sporadic violence and low on an agreed ideology. The further killings of Robert Kennedy and of Martin Luther King appeared to be the apogee of the reign of personal terror instead of political persuasion. The rules of the game were reversed. Bullets and not ballots, assassinations and not armies, were the preferred instruments of change. Paradoxically the killing of the younger Kennedy, as he was running successfully for the White House in an effort to unseat Lyndon Johnson, defused the rising revolt against the Vietnamese War, particularly when Johnson himself refused to run again. The shooting down of both of the Kennedy brothers showed that nobody was safer in Dallas or San Francisco than in Hanoi or Saigon. When you met murder on the way, it did not wear the mask of L. B. J., but that of an anonymous gunman, famous only for a brutal and almost pointless act – its only purpose to make a celebrity out of obscurity. What my teacher Richard Hofstadter had found most despairing about his own society was its inability to come to terms with guns. They remained the 'equalizers' in a polyglot continental people, who were given unequal opportunities, yet were dedicated to the liberty to possess a weapon. 'Guns are neat little things, aren't they?' the attempted assassin of the actor and future president, Ronald Reagan, would say. 'They can kill extraordinary people with very little effort.'

In an article on 'Assassination: The Ultimate Public Theatre', reprinted in the programme for Stephen Sondheim's brilliant and ineluctable musical *Assassins*, Robert Jay Lifton affirmed that the pistol or rifle was the appropriate technology 'for annihilating king, leader and father, for becoming immortal by absorbing the power of all three. The "equalizer" presides over a grotesque caricature of American Egalitarianism.' In an article of my own on the killing of the great, I noted ex-President Theodore Roosevelt's courage in continuing a public speech while pouring with blood after being shot in the heart and only saved by his spectacle-case. He reckoned that assassination was 'a trade risk, which every prominent public man ought to accept as a matter of course'. But it seemed a paradox to me, because political assassination was justified in a sense by its success:

> The questions posed at the murder of Thomas à Becket
> or of Guevara have never been solved. Does the safety
> of the state demand that a rebel should be butchered in
> cold blood, even if he happens to be a brave man half-
> way to sainthood? And if that sort of state exists, which
> can use murder as a weapon, then does not each man
> have the right to pick up a gun and assassinate the agents
> of the government in order to create a better one? In a
> police state which denies human rights, who is the
> political assassin – the tyrannical policeman who
> murders the innocent citizen, or the armed citizen who
> murders the soldier obeying orders? The answer is brutal
> in history. All assassinations which succeed in changing
> governments for long periods of time are accepted by

their societies, and thus justified. All political
assassinations which fail are condemned as treason. As
in so many walks of life, in the murder of the great,
success is justification.

The assassination of Martin Luther King in Memphis, however,
was conspicuous by its failure. It killed the man, but it won his
cause, where it was not delivered by the white murderer into the
hands of the advocates of black power. There were riots in
the ghettos of one hundred and ten American cities, the National
Guard was called to quell the disturbances, and twenty-five
hundred people were killed or injured. Yet this was not a political
explosion, but an orgy of arson and looting and aimless counter-
violence. It was not what the leaders of the Black Muslims and
the Black Panthers had threatened, a race war in the streets
unless all the demands for black emancipation and equality were
immediately granted. It was the explosion of mass outrage at the
death of a hero, who would later be doomed by the saliva of
biographers to sexual innuendo and denigration, as the Kennedy
brothers were to be. But at the time he and the Kennedys had
been the messengers of a new hope in a new society: no historical
retrospective could change those facts. H. Rap Brown was wrong
in hailing the widespread ghetto riots as 'a rehearsal for revolution', and Tom Hayden in seeing them as an American form of
slum guerrilla warfare. They represented an enraged process
of the deprived laying hands on what they could not get and
destroying what they could not possess.

I was a spectator through the television screen in the great
hotels of Los Angeles during these murders and spoilings. I was
not only cut off from my own country and the radicalism there,
but also from my wife's pilgrimage to Cuba. This triple divorce
from the burnings and killings in America made me feel even
more intensely the corruption I had chosen in working in Hollywood. To screenwrite badly in order to publish well was no
excuse. To sprawl beside a small luminous box was hardly the
same as fighting in the streets. For the first time, I was conscious

that my age – and I was only thirty-three years old – had separated me from a younger and more committed generation, and from the few of my contemporaries who had still preserved some belief in the power of protest and political action to balance the scales of justice and the lot of mankind. When I was asked to write a simple piece for a newspaper on my opinion of what was going on, I chose to pen a polemic about how the generations were divided, and about how entrenched my own contemporaries had become. What we had gained, we now might wish to keep. I already knew, or thought I knew, that it was the fate of all revolutions as well as generations to conserve the fruits of the revolution and to become the keepers of the old faith, not the torchbearers of the new:

> The young will find it hard to get rid of us, the war children, with a national youth and a young manhood clamped between the end of austerity and the end of Empire. We had twenty years and more of hard times. Not much food, not much light, not much freedom, not much happening, too much family, too much government, too much drabness, too much . . .
>
> The war children were inventive and adaptable and took to the new media techniques like sparrows to a dust-bath. They were used to risk and improvisation, skilled in the daily survival that war imposes on children. They were contemptuous of the mistakes of the past that had given them such a harsh childhood and adolescence; but that same harshness had schooled their take-over and had whetted their greed. So the 'sixties were a ball for them, and the war children looted and sneered and carved out their own positions of power. As they attacked the Establishment, they replaced it.
>
> What of those younger than them, the war babies and the post-war infants? These were brought up in a belief in security, in peace, in pretty comfortable times. Their assumptions were a rising Gross National Product (however lethargic), full employment, no bombing short of an atomic holocaust, and a revolution or war merely a passionate unreality. They climbed over the crumbled

walls which the war gang had knocked down, and they
inherited a liberated city of girls and music and
opportunities, and a culture that had more to do with
love than war, with sharing than greed. They made their
own culture of clothes and music, and their own
entrepreneurs took the loot from that. But it was only a
culture of youth and entertainment, while the war gang,
now in its thirties, held the communications system and
began to entrench . . .

As I look at myself and my peer group, and as I watch
ourselves constructing the redoubts and piling up the
earthworks of our easily-won positions, I reckon it will be
a hard attack for our young despoilers. You see, we were
actually trained in war. We know how to use a real
machine-gun and lob a grenade, something which the
few serious Third World revolutionaries I have met find
quaintly impressive for a honky. And when I add I grew up
in burning cities and liked the instant slum clearance,
they laugh. I mean, hard early times take a man half-
way to pardon.

The war gang is going to be very difficult to dislodge.
They haven't 'had it' like the generation before them,
who fought the depression and the Second World War.
In fact, they haven't had enough, as they weren't ever
young and easy under the Apple labels. If circumstance
takes away the first twenty years of having and getting,
then those deprived of their youth are going to have and
get and hold onto too much in their middle age, as
compensation for the lean early years. The war gang
knows how to man the stockade, it is quick to improvise
and contain and even include. The young are going to
have to be dandy guerillas.

There's a faint hope that the seats of power won't be
warmed by the bums of the war gang for too long. Power
is essentially boring after a while and even greed has its
limits, especially for war children whom rationing made
to feel that conspicuous consumption à la Jagger is
somehow immoral. So, as their guts grow soft and
spread, they may give up as easily as their predecessors.
But just as arms have never been piled up in human
history and not used, so very few men have ever given up
power voluntarily. I speak as a war child, expecting

disaster nightly, and living many a day as if it were my last. As I said, the young will find it hard to get rid of us.

10

REVOLT AND REACTION

When the last of the sociologists will be strangled with the tripes of the last bureaucrat, will we still have problems?

Graffito on a wall of
the Sorbonne in Paris,
May 1968

Philosophers and physicists contributed to the disintegration of our days. At Cambridge, I was taught that philosophers no longer sought to change the world as they had in the past, from Plato to Marx. They simply wanted to provide us with sharper tools for our thinking. How we used these was our own affair. And the introduction by Planck of the quantum of energy into physics had upset Newton's apple-cart, invented at my old college of Trinity along with crème brulée, so that we could only calculate where a particle *probably* was in a given place at a given time. Although Einstein had hoped to restore determinism to science even with his theory of relativity, Eddington had found indeterminism at the heart of things. So I had learned at Churchill College among the Nobel Prize-winners. Where previously we had one thing existing in a state and changing that state predictably, now we had to consider aggregates of processes. We could only quantify them, as Richard Neville did in his *Play Power* when analysing the content of the underground press – so much space for Vietnam and the draft, for Black Power and the new politics, for police brutality and student unrest, for hippies and drugs and pop music, for new society ideology and cinema and comic strips, and for advertising. But the underground press itself was to be ephemeral; except for *Rolling Stone* and the *Village Voice* and *Time Out*, it was as indeterminate and fleeting as any quantum of energy. As in philosophy and physics, so in history and the youth revolt: all was a process, in which we might plunge deep or dip our big toe or stay outside on the shore. Impermanence was our necessity.

Through Carrie – I will give her the name of the Carrington of our post-Bloomsbury generation of writers and artists and musicians – I found that I was again part of the human disintegration of the times. No sooner did I think that I had seized

Carrie than she was gone, as elusive as an electron. Speaking seven languages including Japanese, excellent at chess and mathematics, as witty as quicksilver and as far-ranging as lasers, she spread passion and havoc wherever she chose to glance with her sharp and taunting grace. We were together for five years, or rather apart for most of them. She liked to return to me and would leave a closet full of her clothes hanging in my bedroom to deter all competitors. When I asked her why she had to go off with the few good friends that I had kept, she replied with her deflecting laughter that my few friends were so much nicer than hers. I was to have none left by the time that she finally left me for a leading conductor, but the last of them did say that he hoped a time would come when he no longer thought with his loins. Carrie even drew for me the proof that the shortest distance between two points was an arc. And so it was on the surface of the sphere of her life. There were no straight lines in that, no constancy and no direct progress.

Marianne returned from Cuba and stayed briefly in my house on the river; we were still, in our fashion, together. She spoke phrases that I had never heard and could hardly understand. It was the jargon of late street socialism, even more meaningless than the sloppy slang of flower power. When she said of the civil war in Nigeria, 'Biafra is a bastion of Portuguese-Rothschild imperialism,' I replied that the statement was in an incomprehensible language. Nigeria was in the British Commonwealth, neither the Portuguese nor the Jews had anything to do with what was essentially mere tribal strife, and the whole vocabulary of Marxism would have to be rewritten or Russia would collapse, because its rhetoric was stuck in the nineteenth century and no longer applied to the modern age. Russia itself held the last great empire in eastern Europe, after the colonial powers had given up their possessions overseas. The imperialism which it saw in others was its own practice. And it would collapse inevitably from its own colonialism over Catholic Slavs and Muslim Central Asians, if it did not adapt as capitalism had, and speak in terms that had some relevance and sense. My prophecy proved correct, but at the time, I appeared to be a ghastly reactionary. Marianne left for Paris to work for the Cubans in soliciting eulogies from great names for *Viva Che*, as well as for the student revolt that would swell to bursting point that May of 1968.

I was to learn more about the truth of the divisions in the Black Power movement and of colonialism when I tried to stage a *Black Beowulf* in the Roundhouse. I brought over from Ghana a diplomat called Desmond Tay, who was also the leading hand drummer in West Africa. When I confessed to him that my father had served in the Gold Coast Police, Tay recalled being one of his constables and said he was the best officer they ever had, fair and just and true. So much for my guilt about the old Empire. Tay and his troupe beat their drums for our recording for eight hours until blood came out of their fingernails, while a motley work-bag of actors from Africa and the Caribbean chanted my Anglo-Saxon lyrics to the beat of the tom-toms. This ill-starred venture collapsed when the Africans in the cast went to war against those from the West Indies, calling them slaves and Uncle Toms, while the West Indians called the Africans tribesmen and savages. I called it a day when three large gentlemen from Jamaica and Trinidad demanded all the money I had, to make a film of their oppression in fascist Britain by the Grendels of the fuzz, as the police were then known. I never again thought that the blacks would combine better than the Scottish clans had, and so present a united front to English power before they were ground down.

In America, the Black Power movement was also splitting from the student activists. It was evident at the occupation of Columbia, sparked off by a faculty decision to build a new gymnasium in Morningside Park for use mainly by the university and not the Harlem community. When the students, led by the local S.D.S. chief Mark Rudd, took over Hamilton Hall, the blacks refused to occupy the buildings with the whites, who had to leave en masse to occupy the Low Library and the president's office with a Rembrandt on its wall. Three other campus buildings were seized, and Stokely Carmichael and H. Rap Brown dropped in to bolster

black resolve, while Tom Hayden arrived to organize white strategy after failing to persuade the striking students to accept black
hegemony. Hayden invented the slogan, 'Two, Three, Many Col-
umbias', echoing Che Guevara's exhortation to create two, three,
many Vietnams in Latin America. He believed that the occupation was a prototype of future guerrilla tactics on every American campus. Curiously enough, Hayden had mourned the death
of Robert Kennedy, whom he had found was detached and very
fair-minded, but the assassination of Martin Luther King was the
real fuse for the powder-keg of the revolt, which rapidly became
a radical chic event, attracting Norman Mailer and even Stephen
Spender. When he visited Low Library, he visited it as an observer
and a writer, not as a participant or even a sympathizer. Asked if
it was like Spain during the Civil War, he remembered the University of Madrid thirty years before. The difference was that, unlike
the students at Columbia, the young Spaniards had used their
university as a university; they had continued to study while
making their revolution.

I had driven to Austria to stay on the lake at Hallstadt because
the director of *Before Winter Comes*, the old terrier J. Lee Thomson,
had wanted me available for rewriting during the shooting of the
film. So I could not be present at the student insurrection in
New York any more than in Paris at the beginning of that May.
Yet my partner at Lorrimer Publishing, Peter Whitehead, was
shooting one of his *Ciné Vérité* pieces at Columbia, while my wife
Marianne was fighting daily on the streets from the Sorbonne.
Whitehead wrote to me of his film, which he thought in his
euphoria would make Godard's *Weekend* and Antonioni's *Blow-Up*
both look like fantasies; his had the makings of a classic. He had
been within one of the first communes of the revolution, and
when the police smashed their way in with their battle-cry, 'Up
against the wall, mother-fuckers,' he was the only one of the
seven hundred protestors who was not beaten and dragged off
to the cop-shops:

I was only allowed to film because of a miracle – the
appointed chief of the Mathematics Building knew my
films and begged the students to let me in. Anyone with
a camera is from Axel Springer and Co. and worth
murdering as far as the kids are concerned. I became one
of them, sleeping on the floor (hardly) for five nights,
filming the meetings, election of their parliament –
microcosm of democracy in action with Che and Castro
et al all over the world! – defence lectures, parties,
barricades, spontaneous happenings . . . the whole story.
I have the proof – if my instinct is right – of the first truly
great act of violence against the regime – which was
ultimately put down by fascist intervention. I sat in the
window and looked at a thousand police standing in
lines outside with their guns and their axes . . . while we
were threatened with violence if we didn't get out. I am
so exhilarated – and so filled with hate that the gun is
now in the hand . . . nothing at all will ever make me
doubt now. What is marvellous is to have shared a
commune with a hundred *revolutionaries*, all of whom feel
as I do . . . my film these last five months, *The Fall*, has
been my instinctive solitary revolution . . . now I have
found there are others. Fantastic. The end of *Weekend* . . .
except without the guns. Just the fear and the hate . . .
the young in rebellion. Next time it will be guns.

As Marianne had done in Cuba and was rediscovering at the
Sorbonne and at Nanterre, where the French student revolt had
begun, Peter Whitehead was finding a community of rebellion
at Columbia University, and he was recording it.

My screenplay for Columbia Pictures was also being recorded
– with all the compromises of commercial considerations. The
script was not allowed to say that a Jew was returned to the
Russians by the British, so Topol had to become a gypsy, rather
reducing the impact of the film. David Niven had me banned
from the set because he always changed his lines and did not
like the author present when he did so. A gift of two trout he
had caught was meant to mollify me. The high moment was
Topol's Sedah, given in a Salzburg hotel, with bald neo-Nazi

waiters bringing in the unleavened bread, all the lamentations irrelevant because Israel had just recaptured Jerusalem, and myself assigned to read the role of the Wicked or Sceptical Man. I made my peace with Topol by coaching his English for his best speech, about fleas living for only twenty-four hours as they were performing tricks in a flea circus; under the brute lights, they only lived an hour. This minimalist concentration camp was compounded by my one day's role as an American military policeman asking for official papers, a caricature of my father's life. I was desperately worried about Marianne as the news of the ferocious street fighting in Paris spread, with the tear gas and the batons and the mass arrests; so was Anna Karina with her broken connection with Godard, whose chief action was to put an end to the Cannes Film Festival, along with François Truffaut, in support of the national strikes in France. Later at the première of the film in London, Anna Karina would say to me, 'Andrew, you look sad.' And I would say, 'Yes, I was also married to a French revolutionary for too long. She has gone to Cuba.' And she would say, 'I know, the revolution is good, it is good to feel for it – but not a hundred and fifty times a day.'

I drove to Paris before the shooting finished, at the end of May. I had four jerry-cans of petrol on my roof-rack because there was none to be had in France. On the roads outside the provincial towns, the gates of the factories were barred and red flags flew from the machine shops, while men stood idle, peering through the wire and the grilles at the future. They shouted 'profiteer' at me because of the cans of gasoline on the car roof. On television Prime Minister Pompidou appeared beaten, giving huge concessions to the workers – more than nine of twenty million were on strike. President Charles de Gaulle had flown to Germany to check on the loyalty of the seventy thousand troops in the French Zone; their tanks were said to be rolling towards the embattled capital.

When I reached our apartment in Paris, Marianne was lost in the Sorbonne, so I went to the Theatre of the Revolution at l'Odéon, which had been taken over as a night-and-day debating chamber by the rebels. Drama had become real, the *Marat/Sade* play was a street event, the halls being made into parliaments. Stephen Spender was there, and he found it like the sixth act in a Theatre of Cruelty. Although the performances were chaotic, they seemed to the audience more entertaining than Ionesco or Beckett. Spender noted that the Paris students were like hippies without a drug culture; they wished to live the life of the revolution even while they were taking action to bring it to be. They did not wish to hear of the downfall of the anarchists in the Spanish Republic, who had also wanted democracy. Their revolution was thought to be new and unprecedented. The others might have failed, but theirs would succeed. As three of their slogans went: I TAKE WHAT I WANT AS REALITY BECAUSE I BELIEVE IN THE REALITY OF WHAT I WANT, and: BE REALISTS, DEMAND THE IMPOSSIBLE, and: RUN, COMRADE, THE OLD WORLD IS BEHIND YOU.

Although I thought I knew that the failure of the student revolt was certain, there was a contagion of hope at the barricaded Sorbonne, where more slogans were scrawled on the walls: HERE ALIENATION BEGINS – RATHER LIFE! and: YOUTH IS ETERNAL DRUNKENNESS, IT IS THE FEVER OF REASON, a phrase that Rimbaud could have written. Already new authoritarian groups were taking over from the free-style fighting students, hurling their cobblestones at the riot police, the fearsome C.R.S. with black helmets and plastic shields. Ex-mercenaries from the troubles in Africa, the Katangais, were introducing the methods of their opponents into the revolutionary cause: extortion and beating and rape. As another graffito read: LIBERTY IS THE CRIME THAT CONTAINS ALL CRIMES. IT IS OUR ABSOLUTE WEAPON. While the forces of repression and the state grouped for a showdown, the students seemed to shift from demands for reform to the desire for an apocalypse. Sinister scrawls on the walls such as: AND IF WE BURNED THE SORBONNE? caused a shift of Parisian feeling from favouring the rebel cause to vilifying it. Too many cars had been torched or made into barricades, private property was under threat. Noam Chomsky had told the occupation squads at Columbia that they would rather Karl Marx had burned down the

British Museum than worked on *Das Kapital* in it, and Stephen Spender echoed the thoughts, coming to the conclusion that however much the university needed a revolution, and the society needed a revolution, these were separate issues for the Sorbonne activists, who might still use the weapons of the trained mind. 'For the university, even if it does not conform to their wishes, is an arsenal from which they can draw the arms which can change society.'

Marianne, too, saw the change in conditions in the Sorbonne, although she would not come back with me to England. She would fight on to the bitter end. Her worst experience had been when she was swept to the front of a mob trying to storm the Senate. Two iron barriers secured by a chain held back the press, and through the chink between them, she saw machine-gunners waiting behind their weapons for the charge and the inevitable massacre. But government *agents déprovocateurs* dressed in students' clothing had shouted to the crowd to attack another government target, the *doppelgängers* of Dany Cohn-Bendit who had started the whole revolt in the concrete jungle of isolated Nanterre, one of the new French universities like the concrete ziggurats which I had visited in England.

Marianne also saw the writing on the wall with the reaction of the right wing to de Gaulle's deal with the Communists, who hated this explosion of anarchism and radicalism outside their Stalinist control of the faithful in France. The president promised general elections and gave the unions great concessions, their leaders could return to the workers with more wages and less factory hours, the students were now isolated. The Champs Élysées was packed with the cars of the bourgeoisie hooting the five-note slogan, '*Al-gé-rie Fran-çaise*', for the Algerian war had divided French society as the Vietnam one had America. It was 'the triumphant bacchanal of the Social World of Conspicuous Consumption, shameless, crowing, and more vulgar' than any crowd that Spender had ever seen on Broadway or in Chicago.

For it was the consumer and manipulative society that the revolt had attacked – and the workers and their leaders had now sold out and adopted it. Most of the slogans on the walls bore the same message:

THE MORE YOU CONSUME, THE LESS YOU LIVE

SOCIETY IS A CARNIVOROUS FLOWER

MAN MAKES LOVE WITH THINGS

MERCHANDISE IS THE OPIUM OF THE PEOPLE

HIDE YOURSELF, OBJECT!

HAPPINESS IS BOUGHT — STEAL IT

THE IMAGINATION TO POWER

DOWN WITH ACCOUNTS, LONG LIVE THE EPHEMERAL

UNIONS ARE BROTHELS

NO BARRACKS FOR THE SPIRIT

ART IS DEAD — DO NOT EAT ITS CORPSE

CULTURE IS THE INVERSION OF LIFE

DON'T CHANGE MASTERS, BECOME THE MASTER OF YOUR LIFE

NO MORE, GRAND PATRON!

And on one of the dozens of street posters manufactured at the occupied École des Beaux Arts, a radical conjugation:

I PARTICIPATE
YOU PARTICIPATE
HE PARTICIPATES
WE PARTICIPATE
YOU PARTICIPATE
THEY PROFIT

The Beaux Arts was almost the last of the occupied buildings to fall, and under attack Marianne was given the original of its most famous poster to take away to safety, the blue-black shape of a riot policeman looking like a space terminator with his truncheon raised, and C.R.S. = S.S. blazoned on his shield. She gave it to me to carry away to England to commemorate the failing rebellion, along with two other significant posters, one of de Gaulle's shadow holding a hand over a young man's mouth: BE YOUNG AND SHUT UP, and the other of the radicals' defiance of anodyne democracy, de Gaulle hitting France with a tricoloured baton and saying: KEEP VOTING – I'LL DO THE REST. As I left Paris for Calais and the ferry, I picked up three battered students from Rouen and Boulogne, who had come into the capital to protest, and now were going home, because they were frightened and beaten. They were very young and had no ideology; they had joined in the struggle for the excitement and for the attack on all authority, particularly their *lycées* and their parents and the dreaded *bac*, the universal examination. If there was any slogan that took their fancy, it was: THE MORE I MAKE LOVE, THE MORE I WANT TO MAKE A REVOLUTION. THE MORE I WANT TO MAKE A REVOLUTION, THE MORE I WANT TO MAKE LOVE.

Marianne and I had always tried to spend the Fourteenth of July together, Bastille Day, dancing in the streets at the end of the Île Saint-Louis, where she had been born. She had agreed to give up the lost struggle and come back to England, if I came and got her. The fight against the war in Vietnam was now taking place mostly in London, with more marches planned on the American embassy, and she had to get *Viva Che* to press. After we had waltzed to the accordions on the Île Saint-Louis, we were walking back across Saint-Germain, when we ran into a trap set by the riot police, bored that they had no big demonstrations to break up. I had stopped Marianne wearing red and black, the insignia of the anarchists and a rag of incitement to the bulls in their dark uniforms. Tear gas made us cry on the Boulevard Saint-Michel. 'Don't run,' I said. 'Walk. We'll take the back streets to Montparnasse.' As we walked along a narrow road, forty C.R.S. storm-troopers stood in a wall in front of us, fingering their batons. 'Don't run,' I said again to Marianne. 'Walk towards them. Shut up. I'll talk. And don't laugh.' She always laughed nervously under stress, particularly from men in peaked hats, let alone helmets. I walked up to the largest of the special forces. 'Tourists,' I said in English, smiling amiably. 'Hotel. Montparnasse.' He growled, '*Vous êtes étudiants.*' 'Don't speak French,' I said. 'Hotel. Is Montparnasse there?' I pointed over his shoulder. Marianne did not speak or laugh. The ranks of the troopers parted like the Red Sea in front of Moses and the Israelites. We walked between the plastic shields as if protected by still waves.

The defeat of the students in Paris did not lose their war across the world, although it was an unsettling example, as the defeat of the Commune had been in 1848, when most of the cities of Europe had exploded in rebellion before they were repressed. A map of contemporary outbreaks of urban violence printed in *L'Événement* with its graffito on the cover: WHY IT ISN'T FINISHED YET, showed six revolts in Japan, one in South Korea, one each in Indonesia and Malaya, regular uprisings in China, two outbursts in India, five in the Middle East and another five in Africa, five again in eastern Europe and five in Italy, many in Germany where the Berlin student leader Rudi Deutschke had been shot in the head, some in Spain and the Low Countries and Scandinavia and Britain, eleven in South America and two only in the United States. The examples of Columbia and Paris had ignited the students of the globe, who had nothing to lose but their final examinations. Massively repressed in every country, the scattered fires still spluttered in England, as always a little behind the times and never knowing when it was beaten.

The analysis of why the students had lost was already under way in Paris, where the intellectuals such as Sartre would always rather diagnose a failure than support a fragmented rebellion. He had begun by praising the young, saying, 'Your movement is interesting because it puts imagination in power.' Something which astonished, something which jolted, something which repudiated all that had made French society what it was then, had come out of the revolt. But it could not work, because anarchists and fragmentary Trotskyite groups could not organize the mass of the workers. The rebellion could only pave the way with cobblestones for the Marxist revolution and the dictatorship of the proletariat, which was not yet ready to happen. There was no chance of Dany Cohn-Bendit's vision of a federation of workers' councils and soviets and strikers running the country in a classless society. The angry older men, indeed, like John Osborne, vehemently repudiated such a vision, saying to Ken Tynan: 'Student power is a very factitious thing. It always seems to me that, "What am I?" is a much more interesting question than, "What are we?" ... What happened at the Sorbonne seemed more animal than human to me ... The prospect of rule by instant rabble doesn't appeal to me either.'

The failure of the urban revolts led by students referred the attention of the new Left to the example of Mao and Castro and currently the Vietcong. Régis Debray, put in prison for a while during Guevara's campaign in Bolivia, but soon released, had come out in 1967 in his *Revolution in the Revolution?* with the *foco* theory, using Cuba particularly as an example. The establishment and uninterrupted development of a guerrilla *foco* in the country-side was the key to the revolutionary process. First, it attracted peasants to the cause; secondly, it defeated scattered government forces; thirdly, it drew support from the towns; finally, it took over the capital by infiltration as well as attack. The book was written before Guevara's disastrous attempt to create a *foco* in Bolivia, but the successful Cuban example under Castro and the struggle of the Vietcong from the jungle towards Saigon were magnets for those radical activists, moving more and more towards guerrilla acts of sporadic violence from motivated cells or *groupuscules* set against the power of the capitalist state.

For, as in Hungary at the time of Suez, which had started my personal rebellion, Russia again was forfeiting all pretence to be the backer of socialist revolutions across the world by intervening in Czechoslovakia to conserve its eastern European empire. The Prague Spring had been the only successful urban revolution in 1968, but the rise of the Dubček régime to power was a middle-class uprising of the intelligentsia, resenting Soviet and socialist control over economic activity and political life. At the end of August, a quarter of a million troops crossed the frontiers to crush the reforms. Russian tanks surrounded Wenceslas Square and united the Czech nation by their act of aggression. Although the Czech leadership was summoned to Moscow and bullied into submission, Soviet power was revealed as a gun barrel behind a brazen mask. Two thousand workers at the C.K.D. factory in Prague described the Russia of Chairman Brezhnev as it was, 'an imperialist state with all its characteristic attributes ... neither the homeland of socialism nor a shield of socialism'. The Tsars had put out the last lights of rebellion in 1848, and now, one hundred and twenty years later, that final extinction was the act of a politburo in the Kremlin. Refusing to adapt, the Communist leaders doomed the Union of Soviet Socialist Republics to future disintegration.

Lyndon Johnson had already dug the grave of his political career during the Vietnamese War and his refusal to run again led to the Democratic Convention ending in sad farce and despair rather than street drama and hope. His fall and the preoccupation of most of the western nations with their own domestic riots had made Brezhnev feel secure enough to invade Czechoslovakia, just as the involvement of the West in the Suez affair had permitted the Hungarian invasion. But the foregone conclusion of the Democratic Convention – the nomination of the good grey man of liberal reform politics, Hubert Humphrey, against the ex-member of the House Un-American Activities Committee and backer of Senator McCarthy, Richard Nixon – vitiated the plans to disrupt it. Uselessly, Tom Hayden tried to set up a socialist and anti-imperialist demonstration against a party leader, clean of policy in Vietnam and preferable to the tricky Republican candidate, who had made his name in a crusade against reds under the beds.

So the power of protest was delivered to the Yippies, led by Jerry Rubin, once a leader of the Free Speech Movement in Berkeley, who defined his strategy and tactics as 'happenings, community, youth power, dignity, underground media, music, legends, marijuana, action, myth, excitement, a new style'. Another bright light among the Yippies was Abbie Hoffman, who had left the civil rights movement for the alternative culture, claiming that 'long hair makes us the new niggers', as a symbol of rejection of the old order. The Chicago police and the National Guard were mobilized by the tough and reactionary Mayor Daley to see that the Convention was not disrupted by the tens of thousands of drop-outs and several hundred radicals who gathered in Grant Park to hear the rants of their leaders and of some of the greater rebels of western literature, Burroughs and Genet and Mailer. The clashes between the police supported by the guardsmen and the Yippie rioters in the park and later in Michigan Avenue were more violent than those in Paris, the clubbings and the tear gas, the curses and the stomping. Even the convention delegates and the news commentators were beaten. The only black elected to the Georgia State Legislature, Julian Bond, said in a speech that he had never seen the police behave with more brutality in Mississippi or Alabama or his own state. Unfortunately, the mass of the American people approved of this assault on the long-haired and wayward 'children' of the new age: their antics were orgies that provoked violence, their picnics in the park were plots to subvert the American way of life – they were, indeed, in the Yippie manifesto, which called for the legalization of all psychedelic drugs, the abolition of all laws relating to crimes without victims, the total disarmament of all the people beginning with the police, the abolition of money, full unemployment and fucking anywhere, anyone at any time.

So *Homo Ludens* and Play Power were changing into *Homo Violens* and the power of the club – as Lenin had defined the state. A British observer for *Oz*, Peter Buckman, was visiting the United States that long hot summer, and his analysis of radicalism there was masterly and sinister. He found that two months after the events in Chicago, most of the people who were supposed to be outraged by the brutality of the Chicago police now supported the repression. Government allegations about Communist and foreign involvement in the student and black militant movements were believed. When a group called the Up Against The Wall, Motherfuckers, shot at some cops from the

centre of a crowd in Berkeley, the university was declared 'a state
of civil disaster'. The American Left was preparing for a long
exile, 'that will make the bad old McCarthy days seem like a
childish dream'.

There was no dialogue between the radicals and the liberals,
Trotskyites and Maoists, young and old, or black and white. And
much worse was the gap between rhetoric and reality. The Black
Panthers, now led by Eldridge Cleaver, wanted guns and a war
of liberation before there was genocide. But few of the radicals
thought a revolution was possible while the Left was so divided
and isolated from the rest of the community. They were split,
anyway, between those who believed in organization and those
who trusted in spontaneity. The first group wanted limited action,
the second daring protests that might spark off wider action, as
at Columbia University and in Paris. But no reliance could be
placed on the 'masses' to support a revolution, as they were
mainly getting what they wanted from the system.

These ripples of spontaneous action did widen to some of the
British universities, particularly the newer ones. Although there
had been turmoils at the London School of Economics two years
previously and also at the Regent Street Polytechnic and the
Holborn College of Law and Commerce in the capital, the contagion of student revolt demanding representation on governing
bodies spread to Birmingham and Leicester and Hull and chiefly
to Essex, the new university where I had been offered the Department of American Studies. There a strike supporting three sus-
pended students and demands for places in the Senate led to
the founding of an alternative university on the site and to Situationist pranks against the authorities. Had I been teaching there,
I would have probably followed the reaction of most of the other
professors, an initial sympathy with the wishes of the students,
ending in anger at disruptive tactics that effectively put an end
to the possibility of education or examination. The problem of
a 'free' university was that every undergraduate was free to learn
nothing much and occupy a place. Personal liberty could mean
a deliberate choice of continuing ignorance. As the Chairman of

the Board of Governors, Lord Robbins, said after another student
occupation of the London School of Economics, 'You can't have
a democracy paying the money for youngsters to do what they
like.'

For the first time since the General Strike, the authorities in
London feared an insurrection in the capital, when the Vietnam
Solidarity Campaign announced another march on the American
embassy in Grosvenor Square. Previous marches had led to running battles between demonstrators and mounted policemen,
and to scenes of violence in the green garden of the square
that could have been played on the Boulevard Saint-Germain or
Michigan Avenue. *The Times* lost its nerve, claimed there was a
plot to seize vital installations and television stations, and advised
all major offices and shops to put up steel shutters for the day.
Reduced to watching rather than participating, I joined Mary
McCarthy as an observer for the National Council for Civil Liberties on that day of conflict, in which the divided radicals and
splintered Left threw away any chance of changing British politics
by defiance in the streets. The anarchists and Maoists and Stalin-
ists wanted a direct attack on the American embassy, but the
main organizers of the march, Tariq Ali and his helpers on
the Trotskyite radical magazine *The Black Dwarf*, decided to avoid
a confrontation and march their hundred thousand supporters
to Hyde Park for peaceful dispersal. 'This was the largest explicitly
revolutionary demonstration since the 'twenties,' Ali wrote in his
autobiography, *Street Fighting Years*. 'We were not crazed utopians
and the ruling classes in Western Europe did not see us as such,
but as the advance guard of a new order. We wished to transform
Western civilization because we regarded it as politically, morally
and culturally bankrupt.'

Whatever his beliefs and strategy, Tariq Ali and his organizers
acted out the role of the *agents déprovocateurs*, who had turned
Marianne and the Paris mob away from the machine-gunners
outside the French Senate. Bullhorns and megaphones persuaded the vast majority of the marchers to progress peacefully
to disintegration in Hyde Park. Mary McCarthy and I watched a

few thousand anarchists and Maoists attack the American embassy and Ten Downing Street. On the last of the Aldermaston marches, I had fought with the anarchists and run with their red-and-black flag past Downing Street. Now I stood on the sidelines, watching the police horses stamp the assault on the embassy to shreds and later break up the anarchists in the Mall as they chanted, 'Wilson, we want you dead!' The whole mass protest seemed as futile and temporary as an electric storm, all that rage and fizzing and dislocated howling, achieving nothing.

Both *The Black Dwarf* and *Oz* had printed the lyrics of the Rolling Stones' song 'Street Fighting Man' before this last large demonstration against the war in Vietnam. Mick Jagger himself had appeared at the previous assault on the American embassy, intending to join in the attack; but when he was recognized by people in the crowd his participation ended in signing autographs. He had been ousted from activity by his trade. He was forced to become a by-stander, as many of us were now choosing to be, from age or from loss of hope of change. This poignancy of the outsider suffused the most inflammatory lyric of its time, banned by the British Broadcasting Corporation for inciting revolt:

> Everywhere I hear the sound
>   of marching charging people
> For summer's here and the time is right
>   for fighting in the street . . . boy.

> Yes I think the time is right
>   for violent revolution,
> From where I live the game they play
>   is compromised solution.

> *But what can a poor boy do*
> *'cept the same old rock roll thing.*
> *But sleepy London is just*
> *No place for a street fighting man . . .*

11

A CHILD FOR
THE REVOLUTION

Tear out this page
Warm your rage
Make it a ball
Burn it all
Fire, fire, fire, fire

London's burning, Prague is burning,
Paris burning, Chicago burns.
Call the engines, call the tanks in,
Call the bullets, it's your turn.
Pour on water, pour on slaughter.
Students all will rape your daughter.

Hear this name
Light a flame
The world's a ball
Burn it all
Che, Che, Che, Che

Buenos Aires, Rome are burning.
Saigon's burning, Tokyo burns.
Call the engines, call the troops in,
Call the truncheons, it's your turn.
Old men use fear to kill the new.
It is their love to murder you.
    Ho, ho, Mao.

ANDREW SINCLAIR, 1969

'The end of the 'sixties came as a kind of incredible collapse,' Jim Haynes wrote, 'a collapse of hope, and of the innocence and naïveté of the decade when everyone felt that we were changing the world, that we could change the world. Then maybe a few people began to realize that through the music, through the drugs, through long hair and colourful costumes, through our attitudes, hopes and fears, we weren't going to change the world. We could only maybe change ourselves a little bit. And I think this resulted in a depression for some people, a rush of cynicism.'

That may have been true for many of the members of the alternative culture at the time; but after the failure of the student risings of 1968, the political rebels took two opposed paths – either into extreme violence or into compromise and inclusion. It was the same for popular music in that last year of the decade, the ultimate communion of mass love preached by the Beatles at Woodstock, set against the aggression chanted by the Rolling Stones at Altamont. Urban guerrilla factions were starting to split from the radical student bodies, the Weathermen and the Revolutionary Youth Movement in America, the Red Brigades in Italy, the Red Army Faction or Baader-Meinhof gang in Germany, the Angry Brigade in Britain, and Action Directe in France. They supported John Lee Hooker singing 'Motor City is Burning': 'All the cities will burn . . . you are the people who will build up the ashes.' The Black Panthers were descending into paranoia and criminal acts. Eldridge Cleaver and other Panthers broke parole and jail, hijacking aircraft and descending on Cuba, the last hope of the revolutionaries. They had not won the backing of the black ghettos, terrified at their tactics of armed confrontation. 'We thought of ourselves as a vanguard,' Huey Newton was soon to confess. 'When we looked around we found we were not the vanguard for anything, we lost the favour of the black community and left it behind.'

The same collapse was evident in the disintegration of pop art. Even *Oz*, in a bitter article on the Institute of Contemporary Arts in London, 'Ho! Ho! Ho Chi Mall', accused it of being the worst and most insecure part of the old arts Establishment and cashing in on the doomed 'revolutionary rave-up'. Che Guevara and Paris and the occupation of the Hornsey College of Art had all occurred on cue, 'just as flower power began wilting, to give the same old magazines another set of slogans, of innovations, of trends . . . Increasingly the attack on art is also an attack on integrity in the name of the mass produced, easily consumed, throwaway, knick-knack objects. Consume faster! consume everything! don't think about anything! Buy art! Buy art's art! Buy non-art! You too can be a collector!' The revolutionary posters from the Beaux Arts were already hot collectors' items. 'Buy a History of Anti-Art! Buy an Anti-History of Anti-Art! Buy the Anti-Art Bulletin! Objects! Institutes! New! Revolutionary! Happenings!'

This disillusion with the consumption and decline of the alternative culture along with student and black protest in the old world did not extend to the Third World, where Cuba and the Vietcong remained examples of hope. Reviewing Jeff Nuttall's *Bomb Culture* favourably in *Oz*, David Widgery accepted its main thesis. In many ways the trough between the end of the Campaign for Nuclear Disarmament's fruitless non-conformity and the beginning of the Vietnamese Solidarity Campaign, 'between post-Hiroshima and Vietnam, between Hungary '56 and Paris '68, was a period of being stranded in the unbearable, especially politically. Looking back on it now, it would seem that it took craziness, illness, dope or political extremism to get through it.' But the metropolitan smugness and self-deceit of Swinging London was eroding along with the brisk merchandizing of the pop phenomenon. The problem with the radicals, as Nuttall had written, was that they held 'their role of opposition to a thoroughly secure establishment more important than the overthrow of that establishment.' This enthusiasm for apocalyptic rhetoric without any of the dangers attendant on revolutionary commitment was the prelude to inclusion within the Establishment. But Widgery still had hope, because a dissident intelligentsia had merged with a mass and rebellious youth movement. This temporary alliance of bohemians and revolutionaries had to disintegrate. All anarchic happenings had to fail. 'Where there is revolution there is anarchy, the first stirring, the first cry, the first position before organisation begins. We must greet and welcome anarchy. It is not the sword of the revolution, only its herald. But the herald performs a genuine service.'

Yet the hope of those who still could hope for political change no longer lay in the *focos* of urban guerrilla resistance in the major capitalist cities, although the Weathermen bombed seven major companies in New York in a year, causing more than forty deaths and twenty million dollars' worth of damage. The last hopes lay in Cuba and in Vietnam. These were the chief combatants against the evils of imperialism, which had now become the rallying cry among all other cries as it had been in the 'thirties, now that the majority of student and black activists were moving towards an accommodation with the powers that were in their own countries. Che Guevara was the apostle and the martyr of this last hope. As John Berger wrote in an article for Marianne's illustrated *Viva Che*, the photograph of his corpse reminded him of Mantegna's painting of the dead Christ that now hung in the Brera at Milan. 'Guevara was no Christ. If I see the Mantegna again in Milan, I shall see in it the body of Guevara. But this is only because in certain rare cases the tragedy of a man's death completes and exemplifies the meaning of his whole life. I am acutely aware of that about Guevara, and certain painters were once aware of it about Christ.' Guevara had found the condition of the world intolerable. Imperialism had demanded cheap raw materials, exploited labour and a controlled world market. Now it demanded a mankind that counted for nothing. Guevara had foreseen his own end in the revolutionary fight against this imperialism. At the news of his death, Berger had heard somebody say, ' "He was the world symbol of the possibilities of one

man." Why was this true? Because he recognized what was intolerable for man and acted accordingly.'

Rather like the end of the film of *Viva Zapata*, when his white
horse escapes after he has been killed and so a myth is created
that he lives on, many of the tributes in *Viva Che* refused to
recognize his death and saw his resurrection in all the revolutions
that would be sparked from his ashes. As the Cuban poet Nicholas
Guillen wrote:

> Not because you've fallen
> does your light shine less brightly.
> Your guerilla's silhouette
> sits astride a horse of fire
> between the wind and clouds of the Sierra.
> You are not silent although they've hushed you up.
> And although they burn you,
> although they hide you underground,
> although they conceal you
> in cemeteries, forests, mountains,
> they won't stop us from finding you,
> Che Commandante,
> friend.

And as Adrian Mitchell wrote in 'How to Kill Cuba':

> You must burn the people first.
> Then the grass and trees, then the stones.
> You must cut the island out of all the maps,
> The history books, out of the old newspapers,
> Even the newspapers which hated Cuba,
> And burn all these, and burn
> The paintings, poems and photographs and films
> And when you have burnt all these
> You must bury the ashes
> You must guard the grave
> And even then
> Cuba will only be dead like Che Guevara –
> Technically dead, that's all,
> Technically dead.

Although I did not believe that Che's example could succeed outside Latin America – and so I wrote in a short book on *Guevara* for the Modern Masters Series, which included Fanon along with Wittgenstein, and McLuhan along with Trotsky, as the teachers of our time – I was an admirer of his asthmatic courage in taking to the jungle to capture a continent, the ultimate in reckless commitment. When Marianne brought to me from the Cuban embassy in London his authentic *Bolivian Diary*, not the *ersatz* C.I.A. version published elsewhere, I was moved enough to translate it with an exiled Argentinian student and to publish it. This made Lorrimer seem to be a revolutionary as well as a cinematic press, and so the secret services of four countries put us under surveillance: those of America and Britain, France and Cuba. It was, however, invaluable in gaining me a Cuban visa, when I had to go there in 1969 to extricate Marianne from her revolutionary folly.

The style of the *Bolivian Diary* then seemed to me as flat and necessary as that of *Robinson Crusoe*, yet its cumulative effect was even more powerful and moving than Defoe's masterpiece, because the reader knew in advance that the hero would be captured and executed when the pages of the diary went blank following the entry that the army had claimed to have located his hide-out and the news seemed to be a red herring. I wrote of the *Bolivian Diary*:

> At the beginning, the war games of the guerrillas seem
> no more real than Boy Scouts at play; then real deaths
> begin, in torrents or in ambush. Bitter quarrels break out
> over a tin of condensed milk. All of living is stripped to
> the essence of survival, dominated only by the
> commitment of Guevara and his men. There is no need
> to talk of the reality of the book, for it is real. And the
> sparseness of its prose contains the dignity, humanity,
> and spirit of the only Garibaldi of our age. It is sad that
> our country, which took Garibaldi to its heart because
> then it backed the revolution of its time – the liberal and
> national revolution – should now react to Guevara with

fear because he has tried to be the new Bolívar and unite
Latin America in one whole against poverty and
oppression. The Old World has, indeed, aged when it
cannot appreciate the hope of the New.

The irony was that this radical publishing was being subsidized
by the major studios in Hollywood. I was still acting as a script-
doctor for them on rewriting screenplays that were never to be
made, a series of exercises in well-paid futility which sapped my
self-belief in my powers as a scribe. I seemed to be selling out,
as so many of the radicals were, to the seductions of the Mammon
of de Mille, although the rapturous reception of *Gog* on both
sides of the Atlantic still persuaded some people that I was a
good writer. But now I refused to reforge the Hollywood scripts
in Los Angeles; instead, I returned to type them in the best
suites in the old hotels of Mediterranean Europe, chiefly in Nice
and Venice. And there I took Marianne in the October of 1968
to the Grand Hotel on the anniversary of Guevara's death. Our
sitting-room was a vast cube on the Grand Canal opposite San
Salute, the church built in thanksgiving to God for saving the
lagoon city from the plague. Napoleon had slept in the suite, as
had Mussolini and Hitler and Pope John. The faded silk on the
walls, the greening gilt frames and the black glass of the wrinkled
mirrors that reflected the marble floor suggested that we were
in a mausoleum, not only of the famous dead who had been
there, but of those we mourned and of our buried ideals and
passion. On the anniversary of Guevara's murder, I had huge
candles brought in with the special dinner, and their flames
made fractured spirals of lights in the obscure reflections of the
ancient mirrors, as much ghosts as little funeral pyres. When
the feast was over, we made love in melancholy. But we did make
love, not revolution.

I did not know that Marianne was desperate to have a child.
She flew back from Venice to live again with Deacon. Within a
few weeks, she found herself pregnant. Torn between both of us,
remembering what had seemed to be the communal love of

revolutionary Cuba, she bought a single air ticket to the island and left. Two letters were sent to Deacon and myself, announcing that she intended to give the child to the revolution. If it was a boy, it would be called Che, if it was a girl, it would be called Tania, la Guerrillera. To my chagrin, she also sent a telegram to Deacon which stated: YOU FIRST, REVOLUTION SECOND. This left me a bad third, although she had always sworn to me that she loved me the best. I was still her legal husband and the only person who could get her out of Cuba, if her nerve failed and she wanted to leave. That would not be a facile matter, for the authorities took away passports when strangers entered. As usual, arriving was far easier than departing. Hot water is fine for a plunge, but it scalds after a dip.

My commitments in Hollywood took me back there. The strain was becoming intolerable for me, my disdain for the work I was doing, my worry over Marianne and the child. I could no longer hide my feelings from my various producers. The blacks were now burning down their slum ghetto in Watts: arson seemed now the only answer to their frustration. Faced with a demand for yet another re-write in words of one syllable, I burst out into manic laughter. As I had already discovered, returning money was the only thing which impressed the moguls, because nobody ever did it, and certainly not the serfs called writers. So I wrote out the right words: a cheque for twenty-five thousand dollars to include all fees to date and expenses, and I gave it to my producer of that day. I said I hoped the blacks burned down all the nineteen villages without a centre that constituted Los Angeles, strung out between its spaghetti highways. I then told him what I thought of Hollywood and himself as luridly as I could. He only smiled and stroked the cheque as if I were an imbecile, and then he told me that I would never work there again. Unfortunately I did, because this new idiocy of mine, the returning of the money, persuaded a few producers – those who called themselves independent, poor dears – that I could still turn an honest word as well as a tidy income.

Anyway, I could not get to Cuba, until Marianne asked me to

come. I insisted now on staying on the beach at Malibu to do my
work, and my disintegration was hastened by Carrie, dropping
by on a flight from Japan. If my life already seemed intolerable
her presence made it worse, although I always regretted her
absence – particularly in Hollywood, where I felt so discontented
and isolated. Yet I could not live with her any more than she
could live with me. I was merely her last port of call, the refuge
of final return. As if in *Les Liaisons Dangereuses* in the age of
modern communications and no letters, she lay across my body
to talk on the international telephone, telling the few of my
friends that she was on her way to them. We shared a complicity
in the betrayal of those who loved us. It was a perilous intimacy,
which made me feel more lonely and full of self-disgust than
ever. She said she loved me the best of all, too.

Later, both Carrie and Marianne would reproach me for my
greatest sin that was also a virtue, my tolerance. I hated scenes,
I allowed them to go off with other lovers, I would fight for my
right to scribble in solitude, I did not care enough, I was committed only to making money and my own choices. I would not
reveal my need or my heart. It was also the sin and the virtue of
the liberal 'sixties, a blanket of permission to do whatever you
wanted. No limits were left, the markers were moved beyond
the horizon towards Shangri-la. My only bedrock was an inner
strength, a self-sufficiency, and an undemanding acceptance, to
which Carrie and Marianne always believed that they could
return. To say, 'That is enough,' or 'Too much – it is over,' would
be my betrayal of each of them. Instead, my bolstering of each
of them involved the betrayal of my friends and, perhaps, my
country.

When Carrie flew back to London and my beloved rivals, I
wrote of her compulsion to remain a feminist on the loose –

> What is the heart of rootlessness? A wind, a rustle, an
> empty room, an open door, footfalls fading, a hole in
> the sand, a torn paper bag, a sycamore propeller, the
> echo in a drain, a crumpled envelope, a laddered

stocking, a ticket stub, mud dry on a shoe, a vapour trail,
a siren in the fog, or Carrie coming into a room as if she
were going, and leaving a room always for ever. Even if
she were only off to the bathroom, she would be washing
her hands of the man waiting for her with fine soap.
Other fields were not always greener for Carrie, but they
were *other* fields, not this field, where she knew the grass
and it was as boring as any lawn. Who knew if above the
field beyond the field beyond that, the sky was not three
times larger as the sky in the American West was three times
larger than the sky over England? Rootlessness might well
mean destruction on earth. As yet there are no branches
to space or roots to heaven. Discontent is divine,
vagabondage the free search for fulfilment. To settle at
all is to settle for the devil, and the devil is the deadly
dull.

So I wrote, in an effort to understand Carrie and her ways. Later,
I found her likeness, if anyone could be like her, was held out
to be the spirit of the age. The culture of the 'fifties and the
'sixties, Robert Nisbet declared in *Encounter*, was about the self.
'Whether in radicalism, in literature, in the performing arts, in
philosophy, psychology, music and art, not to mention
sociology . . . the self, the autonomous self, the performing self,
the contemplated self, *above all* the contemplated self – tri-
umphed.' Standards went to the winds, causes were vehicles for
the glory of the self or the maximum leader, as Fidel Castro was
called in Cuba. The fashionable philosophies of those decades
from logical positivism to semantics, from deconstruction to the
new criticism, were making art itself impossible for the artist,
who was continually catching himself in the act and disintegrating
the moment of creation. To be self-conscious was the watchword
of the ambitious, but the pursuit of the ego now resulted only in
celebrity and sterility.

Marx's dictum that history repeated itself first in tragedy and
then in farce seemed no longer true. Now history was repeating
itself first in egocentricity and then in force. The quest for personal fulfilment of the alternative culture and many of the acti-

vists was being repressed by the state. Personally, as at the time
of the Suez affair, I was becoming involved in history again, this
time unwillingly through the dramatic role that Marianne was
choosing to play in the world revolution. One telephone line still
operated between Hollywood and Havana, so heavily tapped that
it sounded like a chorus of cicadas. 'Hello, Marianne,' I would
say, 'how's the baby?' I was unaware that each time I said 'baby'
on the bugged telephone, the various secret servicemen listening
in presumed I really meant 'bomb'. The baby was growing all
the time, Marianne said, and she was being housed for free
by the government in the commandeered Hilton Hotel, now
called the Havana Libre. It was getting infernally hot, and she
was feeling very uncomfortable, particularly when getting to the
doctor for her weekly check-up on the crowded *wawas*, as
the antiquated Cuban buses were called. But Eldridge Cleaver
had turned up in town and had joined forces with a few other
black hijackers of American aeroplanes. The Black Panthers were
now her best friends, as were the *commandantes*, although she
had not met Fidel Castro yet. But she would soon, and the
revolution would win.

As she repeated this news over the line to Malibu, I could
detect a certain cracking in her voice as well as the chirping on
the line. She did feel most alone in spite of the hot springs
of socialist solidarity. My particular brand of comfort was three
thousand miles away, lodged in a hostile country. She still wanted
to give the child to the revolution, but she wanted to meet me
first. The problem was that the Cubans had taken her passport
and would not let her leave the island. And then, suddenly, all
was well. They had allowed her to go for a few days to Mexico
City, although she was now seven months' pregnant. Would I fly
down there to meet her? We could stay in the same hotel on the
huge central square, the Zocalo, our old base for our previous
explorations of Mexico. I could not refuse, and I booked my air
ticket south of the border.

I had not reckoned that the seats behind me would be filled
with an approximation of the Yale football squad. Although I

knew that the C.I.A. recruited most of its executives from that Ivy League College's secret society, Skull and Bones, I had expected their undercover agents to be rather more under cover, not sporting crew-cuts and blue blazers. And when I arrived at the hotel in Mexico City to find Marianne, I almost anticipated the news that we were having breakfast the next day with two important people, whom she happened to have met on the aeroplane from Havana: an ex-president from Bolivia, where Guevara had been killed, and an ex-finance minister from the Dominican Republic. The next morning, we were grilled more than the toast. Of course, both of them supported Cuba against American imperialism, but what exactly was Marianne doing on the island, and why had I flown down from California to see her? The answer was obvious enough. Marianne had a big belly. There was a baby in it. Not even friends of an intelligence agency could mistake it for a bomb.

Marianne had been sent to Mexico City not apparently with a mission for the Cuban secret service, but to buy revolutionary supplies for the exiled Black Panthers. The nature of the desired goods revealed that the Black Panthers were as much slaves to the consumer society as their predators. They had not taken in the slogans of the Paris student revolt: THE MORE YOU CONSUME, THE LESS YOU LIVE, and: MERCHANDISE IS THE OPIUM OF THE PEOPLE. They wanted bright headscarves for their mistresses, varicose-vein stockings for somebody's daughter's mother, a tape-recorder with the latest pop albums, and indeed, notebooks and pencils to write a *Cuban Diary*. Eldridge Cleaver particularly wanted some lurid boxer-shorts, the antsy-pants made famous by the conservative Senator Barry Goldwater – 'something cool and sweet for my nigger ass'. And a last urgent telegram arrived at our hotel: FORGOT MY BATHROBE. Trailing and choking though the smoggy and broiling streets of Mexico City on these radical errands, I could not feel I was on a revolutionary mission. Yet the various large operatives who followed me and accosted me at cafés were not yet persuaded. Marianne rarely managed to leave her room and display her coming motherhood, so her baby still meant a bomb to some of my retinue of spies.

Our room was also bugged, so that the truth did out – for those prepared to believe it. I begged Marianne to fly back to England with me and have the child there. She said that the Cubans had still kept her passport, that they had only issued her with a four-day permit to stop over in Mexico before returning to Havana. I told her the French embassy would issue her with papers, and, at the worst, we would fight the notorious English immigration officials. She was, after all, still married to me, except in Mexico. She insisted that she had to go back to Cuba. She had taken a revolutionary oath to return. She could not break it. Anyway, she had to take the Panthers the revolutionary supplies which I had bought for them. I told her that if the baby was born in Cuba, it would be a Cuban citizen, and that she would be pressured – and so would I – into doing intelligence work for Raúl Castro until the end of our days; we would pay the price of seeing this child of the revolution.

'I still have to return,' Marianne said, 'but you must come to Cuba and get me out. You are the only person who can. You will be the guest of the government. They already expect you.'

'But you will be eight months' pregnant,' I said. 'Nobody will be allowed to fly you out. It's against all air regulations.'

'For Cuban Airlines,' she said, 'anything is possible, if the government says.'

'And for Murphys like me,' I said, 'the law is still – only the impossible ever happens.'

She returned to Havana. I agreed to fly back to London, order my affairs, take an aeroplane to Madrid and then on to Havana, from where I might never leave. She would arrange that my Cuban visa was quickly granted. I was awaited. I saw that I had fallen into a trap, but there was nothing else I could do. I could not let us both become the servants of the revolution against the blackmail of visiting the child. And I loved her still, and her nerve had broken at last. She did not tell me yet of the rift between Cleaver and the *commandantes*. These were the unnamed perils to come.

On my flight back to London, it was a Frenchman's turn to sit next to me. My interrogator was absolutely charming. He gave me a friendly grin and offered me a *cognac*. So I smiled back and accepted and said how bored I was at being followed by members of the secret services, when they were so bloody obvious. What was *his* cover story?

'First, I was Che Guevara's astrologer in Havana,' he told me most seriously. 'And then I was his acupuncturist in Pyongyang in North Korea.'

I laughed until I choked. An intelligence agent with wit. Incredible.

'I will tell you all you want to know,' I said. 'The truth. We'll drink a bottle of brandy, and I will tell you the whole truth.'

As the truth was that the affair was about a baby and not a bomb, I had the chance, at the very least, of getting the French secret service off Marianne's back. I could also excuse her revolutionary actions and Intelligence work for Cuba as a matter of self-drama, the old sin of my English generation of the 'fifties, and now the aberration of her Parisian one at the end of the 'sixties. I told the French agent that she came from a family of the Left, which had been present during the Spanish Civil War, and that her attachment to the Cuban Revolution was romantic rather than reasoned. She had told Deacon that her vision was of dying on the barricades, waving the red flag like a new and true symbol of Marianne. I told this to the agent without mentioning Deacon's name, but I added that I had assured Marianne she was more likely to end up serving twenty years' time in an unspeakable Latin-American jail. I also told him that I was going to get her out of Havana within a few weeks so the child would be born in Paris and be a good citizen of the next French revolution. This made him laugh, we drank a lot and played chess, he filled his dossier on us, and the French secret service bothered Marianne no more.

Our little personal tragedy was becoming a farce. Perhaps Marx had been right about history, and certainly Graham Greene was in *Our Man in Havana*, where a vacuum-cleaner drawing, rather than a baby, meant an atom bomb. Yet I also felt that our egocentricity and self-dramatics would lead to a display of force, if anything were to be solved. Indeed, in the pop world in America that year, the mass pursuit of inwardness at the Woodstock Music and Art Fair would contrast with actual murder and repression at Altamont. These were the themes of the 'sixties for me, love and self-love set against force and anger. Our lives may only be a wrinkled and black mirror to our times, in which we see our reflections occasionally as we pass by; yet willy-nilly, we must catch and give a glimpse of our ephemeral history.

The Woodstock fair at Bethel in New York State attracted quarter of a million of the stoned young, who drifted around the various booths and events in a beatific trance of being, a tractable mob in pursuit of private peace. This was the apogee of the youth culture of love sung by the Beatles. Its lack of disturbances prompted *Time* magazine to call it 'history's largest happening', which would become 'one of the significant political and social events of the age'.

It was not so during that December at Altamont, a disused race track near Berkeley on the west coast, where the Rolling Stones decided to give a free rock concert. Warned of possible violence from the aggressive drug factions at Haight-Ashbury in San Francisco and from the splintered Panther groups in Oakland, the manager of the Stones took bad advice from an old leader of the drop-out Diggers, who had now joined the Hell's Angels in their black leather and metal studs, on their Harley-Davidson motorbikes. These dark angels would be the guards of the performers and the platform. Some four hundred thousand people arrived and packed the stadium. Free medical teams had to treat nearly a thousand of the audience for bad acid or related drug trips. The Rolling Stones descended on the site by helicopter ninety minutes late, to face an aggrieved and chanting riot. Naked and mind-blasted girls tried to crawl on stage near to Mick

Jagger and were savagely beaten by the Hell's Angels. Finally, a black man in the audience pointed a gun at Jagger and was beset by the Angels, who stabbed him to death. Jagger appealed for a kind of truce, asking for everybody 'to cool out and groove' but three more people died and hundreds were injured in the *mêlée*. And so the love generation ended in the abattoir and on the sacrificial slab.

But also in China, where Chairman and Madame Mao had loosed the Red Guards, people were being harassed and humiliated in their tens and hundreds of thousands for the mere crime of having independent minds. The flowers of the new cultures were bursting into flames.

In his history of the new Left, *An Infantile Disorder?*, Nigel Young found that the last two years of the 'sixties were, for youth culture, a period of songs such as the softcore 'Revolution' of the Beatles and the harder 'Street Fighting Man' of the Stones. Physical action was a more expressive experience than political strategy. It was an outlet for desperate discontent, an imitation of the dramatic gestures of the Tet offensive in Vietnam or the cobble-chucking in Paris. It was really a 'theatre of resistance', which was metamorphosed into much rock music, but reached a climax in the actual killings at the Altamont music festival.

I did not know that I was flying on that aeroplane from Mexico City towards England to meet two of the greater recognitions and resolutions of my life. My father had suffered his first stroke and my mother thought I was becoming a revolutionary idiot. I went to see my father in the little bungalow which he had bought near Hastings and called the Matchbox. In spite of his age and his condition, he retained all of that stern immaturity that gave him the nicknames of 'Zinc' and 'Boy' throughout his life. I learned how much I had hurt him and my stepmother by playing out my mother's wars against them, respecting her commands and refusing to see them. In the face of dying, all prohibitions are irrelevant. And so I began to make it up with my father before his end, and I am forever thankful that I did.

In their last little place in the twilight of the British Empire, among the carved Ashanti stools and Arab teak chests from Zanzibar, these two old Africa hands had found a private peace, and I was allowed a little understanding and forgiveness from the straightjacket of my radical prejudices and hardness of heart.

My mother, in her house at Falmouth, was furious at my visit to my father, although she did concede that a stroke might make a difference. She still venerated my dead step-father and took any deviation by me from her side as a betrayal. And then occurred the only time that I have ever lifted a hand against a woman, a scene from a minimal *Hedda Gabler*, which was also a laying to rest of the imperial past. We had never referred for fourteen years to what had happened at my crisis of conscience over Suez. That day, I happened to say to my mother that she had changed my life and had caused me great embarrassment among my friends by making me turn back from going to Hungary, after sending me a letter praising my desire to leave Cambridge and telling me to follow my convictions at all costs.

'I never wrote you that letter,' she said.

'You did,' I said. 'I have kept it in a box in the attic.'

I left her sitting by the Aga cooker in the large kitchen of the Cornish house, as I went up to the loft to retrieve the letter. I knew that it was an occasion. Until then, I had presumed that my mother, like a little Mussolini, was always right. I had followed her dictates without question or in silence. But I had crossed her by seeing my father, and now this second proof of her error was upon us. We loved each other dearly, but here I had questioned her veracity as well as her authority.

I found her old letter to me, the beginning of my career as a writer. And I brought it down to her, sitting in the kitchen, and I put it into her hand. She read the first of the five pages of notepaper, opened the door of the Aga and pushed the letter towards the glowing coals. I caught her wrist and took the letter from her fingers.

'You can't burn the truth,' I said.

We never talked of the matter again. But there was something broken between us. She knew that I knew that she was not always correct. The code of the Empire had a fallacy in its righteousness. But it made for more humanity. Although she had hardly touched me since the age of four – contact was bad for boys, especially kissing, in case they became cissies – now we began to embrace and hug, until we ended in that power of love that was the message of the day.

12

AND IT STILL IS NEWS

Them that's got shall get
Them that's not shall lose
So the Bible says
And it still is news.

'God Bless The Child That's Got His Own'
sung by BILLIE HOLIDAY

There is a tiredness in the affairs of men that is the grimace of governments. By the year of 1969, Harold Wilson and his cabinet were stumbling in office; and as the nonsense poem noticed, the gunpowder was running out of the heels of his shoes. His puff of a 'classless, dynamic new Britain' merely blew smoke over a long industrial and imperial decline. He postured on a world stage where the house lights were being killed one by one. His long combat against the Establishment and the mandarins of Whitehall was a sapping series of skirmishes. Through experience rather than disillusion, he was losing, like the rest of us, the belief in being able to change things very much. The bright hope of the 'sixties was turning to the long evening of the next decade. Wilson would not win the next election that heralded the inconsiderable ten years to come. Even his return, five years later, would only be to resign at the bitter end.

His slow sinking was posted by the plots of the security services against him. His authority was ended by their actions and their innuendoes. Those who live by conspiracy, alas, can only see the lives of others as conspiracies. With his realistic view of the economics of Britain, if not its global politics, Wilson was falling foul of the War Office and the Pentagon. To President Lyndon Johnson, and Richard Nixon with his Communist-baiting past, Wilson and his country were becoming suspect in the 'special relationship' with the United States. They would not send troops to Vietnam or maintain all their military and intelligence bases in the Near and Far East. They would not supply arms to South Africa or break-away Rhodesia, both fighting black 'socialist' rebellions. A vital police station for oil and the Persian Gulf was abandoned in Aden, although the unsinkable aircraft-carrier islands of Diego Garcia were being handed over to American

control. The Central Intelligence Agency was making allegations
to M.I.5 that Wilson was a paid Soviet agent, and so strong were
the slanders that a proud and perfidious newspaper baron, Cecil
King, even plotted a coup with some military support in order
to replace the Labour government with one of 'national unity'.
Such then was the absurdity of conspiracy theory, which
approached insanity in the crevices of power.

With my own minimal involvement through Marianne in the
anticipated world revolution, I found myself burgled and the telephone tapped during my brief return to London before setting
out for Cuba. But all was bungled: far more Groucho than Karl
Marx, or Charlie Chaplin booting the globe in *The Great Dictator.*
The loft rented by two women next door to me in Narrow Street
was pillaged with every paper taken, even from the wastepaper
baskets, but the whisky and the television set were ignored. The
Limehouse police were puzzled: it was not a local crime. I knew
the solution. The spycatchers had merely struck at the wrong
terrace house. So I decided to save them the trouble of playing
the next act of the farce. I picked up my telephone and asked
for the security services to telephone me back. I wished to
denounce a foreign agent. When the call was duly returned from
the unknown, I accused myself of earning all the money used to
finance the revolutionary books of Lorrimer Publishing – such
as *Viva Che* and Guevara's *Bolivian Diary* – from major American
studios rather than Cuban slush funds. There was no need to
steal my bank accounts from my home. The accounts were at the
Midland Bank in Great Portland Street, and doubtless they would
be available to spooks with credentials. My paymasters were
known radical organizations such as Columbia Pictures and
C.B.S. Films, which would be glad to hear that they were supporting a dangerous fellow of my calibre. But really, Hollywood was
my nipple, not Havana.

My confession had two good results. My house was not burgled
and Hollywood stopped employing me. While my case was not
comparable to the Hollywood Ten standing up to the House
Un-American Activities Committee in the bad times of Senator

McCarthy, certainly the C.I.A. would inform Tinseltown to stop using someone who might turn the profit of his pen into bombs against capitalism. I was never asked again to write for a major studio, a resolution that was best for all of us.

I was, however, left with a cabin on Malibu Lake, where I was to find myself on that night of the supremacy of American endeavour and imagination. The clouds covered the whole earth, except over California. And to a Euripidean croaking of bull-frogs, I could walk out from the television pictures of an astronaut taking a first great step for mankind to watching the diffuse orange of the moon in the night sky, signalling that it was there, and the human had arrived on those far volcanic rocks, and it was not mere science fiction from the sprawling city of dream manufacture, which I would hardly visit again.

There was no sacrifice in giving up the rich source of my self-despair. And as I submerged in an emotional slough of despond in London and tried to think how to extricate Marianne and the unborn child from Havana, this parody of international con-spiracy became a skid onto a squeaky series of banana-skins. The telephone men, who appeared to set their bugs on the Lorrimer Publishing telephones, grinned about their entrapment; they would be called 'plumbers' in the Watergate affair which would bring down President Nixon. The right term scuppers each wrong time.

'The telephones are not out of order,' I said.

'They will be soon,' they cried, 'just fitting new equipment, squire.'

'Will you have bugs on *every* telephone?' I asked. 'Everyone here is innocent except for me. You'll just be wasting your time listening to calls about meeting boyfriends and office supplies.'

'We'll hear only what we want to hear,' the chief plumber said, tapping his nose. 'Modern technology.'

That modern technology consisted of a *bel canto* of whistles and flat notes every time that a particular name was mentioned. The actual contact and spy I was forced to use at the Cuban embassy in the negotiations to rejoin Marianne was called Guido.

My old friend from Cambridge, Michael Frayn, rang me to say
that he was going to Cuba to write a play called by the ambiguous
name of *Clouds* – rather a better assignment than extracting a
pregnant wife. Did I have any advice? Little to say at the moment,
I said, but I would probably reach the Havana Libre before
him. I did, however, tell him about the trilling telephones and
warn him that his system would now be tapped because he had
called me. He laughed, thinking he was still talking to the young
paranoiac he had known from his Cambridge days.

   A week later, Frayn dialled again in a wild panic. He was
hearing strange noises every time that he picked up his receiver.
I could not be right, could I? They were bugging his telephone,
too. It contravened all his liberal rights, and he had really
believed he was living in a Blackheath or Hampstead *in excelsis*,
as most of my old friends believed, where our democratic rights
and freedom were respected. I asked if I might play him a minor
aria, using only one name from the Cuban embassy. With his
permission, I sang in my tuneless but variable fashion the name
of Guido *presto* and *molto lento*. In whistles and squeaks, the telephone wires delivered the performance of a Tito Gobbi with
flatulence. 'They don't have enough surveillance men,' I said.
'There's a budget cut even on eavesdroppers. So they automati-
cally record the conversation on our tapped machines only when
a key name is mentioned. Guido, Guido, Guido, Guido, Guido,
Guido,' I sang, murdering the scale in an impromptu *arpeggio*.
His eardrum smarting, Frayn hung up, almost persuaded that I
was not the victim of a delusion of persecution.

Future risks seem to call up past alternatives. In this testing time,
I had accepted an invitation to a feast at Churchill College to
commemorate its founding. I drove up to Cambridge in trepi-
dation and with a sense of separation. The college was mostly
built now in a comfortable redbrick style, distinguished only by
the quality of its scientific fellows, who seemed to treat the Nobel
as an in-house prize. A historian there, who researched into the
unsinkable history of the British Navy, could not understand my

decision to quit a lifelong appointment at Cambridge and the teaching involved. He had read that my old books were deferentially mentioned in works of American scholarship. 'But you had a *niche* in history,' he protested. 'Ah,' I replied, 'but never a pedestal to stand on.' He would not understand that even tenure is no anchor for a wanderer.

More telling to me was meeting the old Charles Snow again, now a life peer, but still trying to be the sage before mortality finally called the shots. Ten years after his lectures on the 'Two Cultures' and the scientific revolution, he was now speaking and writing on the state of siege of the western nations. 'The world closes in. We are bombarded with communications, but again those don't set us free.' Television deluged us with knowledge about what was happening in other cities and countries. We knew all about immediate human suffering. 'We see people starving before they have died: we know that they are going to die.' We knew of the famine in Biafra, one of a series of famines in Central Africa. 'We know so much: and we can do so little. We turn away.' This shutting ourselves off showed our unease. The great strata of the young were also making their enclaves against those of other ages and countries. 'They too have turned inwards: into their own customs, and often their own private language,' where structures did not exist, merely barriers. 'For once you try to dismiss structures, you are dismissing society, any kind of society, including primitive, advanced, or anarchist, and you are huddling into a private refuge of your own.' The hope in changing ourselves was being lost. 'We are behaving as though we were in a state of siege.'

Snow now regretted not dealing with the population explosion in his previous lectures on the scientific revolution. Population growth was the greatest of the crises in the world and led to the withdrawal symptoms of the West from the problems of Central America and Africa and Asia. He did not predict the rich nations and the great powers breaking out of their state of siege nor the young from their self-serving trenches. Once again, he seemed to me to have diagnosed the temper of his times, as he had at

Cambridge when he was attacked by Leavis and his pack of hounds. This time, however, he was not derided so much as ignored. His wisdom seemed an irrelevance faced with the she-nanigans of the agencies of the western governments, which appeared merely to wish to perpetuate themselves in their accus-tomed power and machinate the destruction of any alternative.

My chief concern, however, was how to reach Cuba and return with Marianne before she gave birth to a child given to the system of Cuban Intelligence. My rival and friend Deacon was also disturbed. Every night he railed at me about the faithlessness of women, or a woman, while I wallowed in a grandiose self-pity. He swore the child was mine and ranted at her deception and broken promises to return to him. He slung down two suitcases of her clothes in my Limehouse garage and said he would marry a Guinness lady. I wrote in my diary:

> Both Deacon and I are thin and nervous as Marianne
> takes our lost weight upon her. Deacon has run from
> responsibility, refusing to admit it. Marianne has played
> both men against the Cuban Revolution and threatens
> to lose all three – unless I heed her need, play *macho* to
> the Cubans, say the child is mine, and whisk her away
> to give birth in my country. Do I only exist in the needs
> of others or do I have my own? Will I become the
> misanthrope I fear, Count Frankenstein or Timon of
> Athens, only moved to betray my feeling when the cry
> of one of the few I love wrenches the armour aside and
> makes me lumber near? Must I be present as the formal
> priest or witness, as Deacon and Marianne slice each other
> with their knives of revenge, only succeeding in sinking
> both blades into my gut?

I carried a small copy of *Timon of Athens* round in my pocket for a year, until its covers fell off. I identified wholly with the mis-judged man, ostracized for his reckless generosity and turned into a human animal. I was to give his name to my film company and my son. The Greek Senator had been right about him, as my old friends were right about me:

> Still in motion
> Of raging waste? It cannot hold; it will not.

It had not in my own case, as I wasted all I had painstakingly earned, particularly the intimacy of love. I had always quoted Reverdy, that I did not need liberty so much, but only to be chained by what I loved. But I had broken my chain with Marianne and had allowed the affair with Deacon, in order to regain my liberty to write. And now I was wasted in heart and deed, I could only agree with the savage Timon in his isolation:

> Timon will to the woods, where he shall find
> The unkindest beast more kinder than mankind.
> The gods confound – hear me, you good gods all! –
> The Athenians both within and without that wall!
> And grant, as Timon grows, his hate may grow
> To the whole race of mankind, high and low!
> Amen.

And then I also liked Shakespeare's hero throwing back the gold he had rediscovered in the faces of his flatterers and refusing to save his city from the wrath of the avenging Alcibiades. His pronouncement upon his life seemed sweet to me:

> Rogue, rogue, rogue!
> I am sick of this false world, and will love nought
> But even the mere necessities upon't.
> Then, Timon, presently prepare thy grave;
> Lie where the light foam of the sea may beat
> Thy grave-stone daily: make thine epitaph,
> That death in me at other's lives might laugh.

My rantings at deception and the ingratitude of others would not match those of Timon, but I suppose that I did feel what my diary recorded of my temporary misogyny.

How strange that only some men have honour and no
women. Men indeed have honour as women have
children. There are decent men and women in fair
proportion. But women fight honour in men as their
greatest enemy. They operate on the advantage and
commitment of the moment, and honour is their worst
enemy, for it involves fair play to the absent and the
fulfilling of past obligations even at the expense of
present happiness.

I have now been permanently sick in the stomach for
weeks. The heart does lie in the guts of a man. *Enfin
quelque chose m'arrive*, as Giacometti said smiling when he
broke his leg in a Roman gutter. But is there no
conclusion to this confusion and pain? Love ends with
neither a bang nor a whimper, just a tight mouth to
hide the knife in the belly. Are the only alternatives either
to be inhuman or suffer pain?

I decided I had to write *Magog*, the sequel to *Gog*, about the
suffering of *l'homme raisonnable de pouvoir*, whose logical exercise
of power led inexorably to the decline of Britain through wrong
choice. 'There is a third alternative to pain or inhumanity – work,
good work.'

Now Deacon changed his mind and begged to go to Cuba in
my place. I laughed at him. I had my plan, I said. Only Marianne's
official husband could get her out, and I was still that. I no longer
knew whether I was betraying my friend or he was betraying me.
I might be betraying my country to excise Marianne from Cuban
Intelligence. And through my other relationship, with Carrie, I
was certainly betraying the few friends I might still have left. If
my behaviour was not already offensive and ruinous enough, my
lies on Carrie's behalf had to merit their hatred, as Timon's
reckless generosity had done with the Athenians. One of my last
and better friends invited me to dinner and asked me the hard
question about Carrie's double life. Was she continuing with me
as well as beginning with him? I had sworn to her never to tell
the truth. So I said that the question was irrelevant. What
mattered was the commitment that he secured from her in the

future. I was going to Cuba, anyway, and might not return for some time. But I could not give up Carrie any more than he could, and so I evaded his question and earned another enemy.

In Shakespeare's plays, at the moment that the great matter is of treachery to court or country or companions, the fool enters. But in this case, a Great Dane strode into my soliloquies, as if Limehouse were the Elsinore of the Thames, and he were the ignorant Fortinbras, who entered with the blood and guts of Hamlet's family all over the castle floor, so he could sum up the whole mess that had taken many festering years to achieve, with his supreme and crass righteousness.

> Take up the bodies – such a sight as this
> Becomes the field, but here shows much amiss . . .

He had met Marianne playing the revolutionary St. Joan of Arc in Havana, and he now inflicted his homilies on me on his return journey to Copenhagen. Knowing nothing of the situation, he advised me to go to her and surrender and tell her that I loved her. He then added that he hated the spoiled wives of rich men, who played at revolution. He also declared that he was writing a story called *Rocket and Nib*, about a Canadian friend of his who had met Marianne preaching the revolution on the street-corners of Havana, pregnant in her white leather mini-skirt. Rocket's message was a failure to the few surviving Cuban street-corner boys, while Nib's was a huge success. He could not imagine why. Her parting gift to Rocket had been two hundred dollars with the inspired phrase, 'From each according to his means, to each according to his needs.' 'Christ, I need this,' Rocket had said and had bought four ice-creams; there was one more flavour in Havana than in Howard Johnson's, as Fidel Castro was always pointing out to prove Cuban superiority. I did tell the Great Dane why Marianne called herself Nib – it was Deacon's name for her from a Lautrec drawing we both had – meaning Nothing, Nada, Nil, as well as the pen point.

'How do you have the *shame* to go on writing?', a girl had

asked the Great Dane, and now he asked me. I could hardly reply, I had done it all my life; it was my trade. I did rather agree with the Dane, when he protested, 'I am not a runaway, I am a throwaway.' We parted company after I had knocked him down when hearing screams from one of the women who lived the other end of the terrace. I felt that revolution had gone to his loins, as it so often did in those days when free expression meant asserting one's manhood. Life was such a mess, there was no purpose, disintegration was all. In fear and exhilaration, I planned to fly to Cuba. I lived in recklessness and the hope of destruction, feeling the liberation from all responsibility which so many millions of my countrymen had felt when drafted into the armed forces in the last world war.

It was not a good time for hope or planning a future. President Nixon was escalating the horror in Vietnam, the bombing and the pollution of the forests by chemical weapons. The huge protests in America were being suppressed even by the media. There was no television coverage of the half million people who would demonstrate against the new mobilization in Washington at the Monument there. And the New Year would see the Ohio National Guard firing on the demonstrators at Kent State University, killing four students and wounding another nine, while two more would be shot at the black Jackson State College in Mississippi. There was no question that the forces of repression were putting out the embers of the student revolt.

When the commentator Christopher Booker turned to praising the importance as well as the nostalgia of the 'seventies, he lauded the unravelling of three central strands of the modern dream. The first was the belief that science and technology would enable us to unlock the secrets of the universe and to master nature for the material benefit of all mankind. The second was the utopian creed that political and social planning could create justice and equality and comradeship in society. The third was the hope that the change of the laws of repression would liberate the people into the pursuit of their personal happiness and

fulfilment. The trio were the figments of traditional social imagination. Booker thought that all three were scotched in the 'seventies, but the truth was that they were threadbare in their rags
and tatters by the time the decade had begun. Materialism as a
doctrine had been weakened by the threat of nuclear pollution
and the counter-culture of flower power; social planning had
been doomed by the draconian, yet chaotic, despotisms of Russia
and China and the emergent African countries that called themselves 'socialist'; and the freeing of the people and the young
had led to the avid pursuit of things rather than happiness, and
where happiness was the shifting goal, it was an inward score that
spurned all social responsibility.

In the years before he became a member of the literary Establishment which he had mocked along with the rest of us, my
fellow American scholar Malcolm Bradbury wrote his most acute
pieces about his society, particularly about the students whom
he taught. 'The Pubertoids' expressed the view of our ageing
generation that something was amiss with the younger lot. We
had become the traditionalists of the 'fifties, which we had
attacked in our own time. The most important difference
between the traditional and the consumer society was the question of teenagers. In traditional society, teenagers were 'persons
between twelve and twenty, who are not yet fully grown, whose
judgements are apt to be fallible, whose tastes incline towards
immaturity'. There had been teenagers throughout history, but
nobody until recently had recognized what they were. In fact,
teenagers had no age, they had a state of mind, which was valued
by a society that did not believe in growing up. Anyone could be
a teenager at heart. 'In fact, in a consumer society, to be a juvenile
delinquent shows a conspicuous adjustment to the moderm world
– one has found a *modus vivendi*.' Youth had become a form of
protest in an era where deviance was smart. Protest was 'the most
pressing of fashions'. At least the protestors believed in *something*.

13

TO TRAVEL
WITHOUT HOPE

But pheasant is the ration this week for *all* Cubans.

CARLOS

Sometimes, to arrive is to travel without hope. I suffered a long flight from Madrid but I did have the time to prepare my lines. The secret policeman who met me off the aeroplane in Havana was charming, black and experienced. His declared name was Carlos.

'We are so glad that you are giving your son to the Revolution, Doctor Sinclair.'

'If it is a son.'

'He will be. And he will fight for the Revolution.'

'Yes,' I said. 'For the revolution. The revolution in my country, which needs it even more than yours. We are still capitalists, you see.'

Carlos looked at me with some amusement.

'Let us take your passport,' he said. 'I will attend to all the formalities. You are our honoured guest for all the time you will stay here.'

Surrendering my passport, I was taken by black limousine to the Havana Libre. The sense of imprisonment within a socialist experiment pervaded throughout. Propaganda posters for bringing in the *zafra* or sugar harvest dominated the hoardings – huge red numbers in the shape of a train, 10,000,000, that tonnage pulling along coaches marked VAN VAN VAN, presumably for the vanguard of the proletariat. There was even an element of play in the state effort to get office workers back to farm production – a pair of cows on their hind legs juggling with hearts. A line of Havana women in green fatigues fired their rifles vainly out to sea, where only Russian freighters lay, and no Yankee battleships such as the *Maine* to start another American invasion of the island. Yet an American spy ship was monitoring everything and lying just outside territorial waters, giving rise to the jingle, 'On a clear day, you can see Pueblo Two.' The luxury shops in the old Hilton arcade of the Havana Libre had empty shelves except for coloured water in strange bottles and some wooden toys. 'No tips, *compañero*,' I was told in the lobby seething with agents and undercover men and the swelling Marianne, surprised that I had reached her. She was very friendly with Carlos and told me that he was only a guide and host to visitors. All was open and free here, although we could not leave Cuba, of course.

We were already in trouble, because of her friendship with the Black Panthers. Whenever one of them hijacked an aeroplane from the United States and forced it to land in Havana, the Cuban police put the kidnapper into a work camp for six months to interrogate him and evaluate whether he was a planted American agent or a genuine black radical as well as a criminal. One of these Panthers had broken out and reached Cleaver's apartment in Havana. When the authorities demanded his surrender, they were met by wild black revolutionaries flourishing automatics and accusing them of racism and exploitation and treating their fellow freedom fighters like slaves. In return, the Panthers were now being threatened with deportation. What a good way out of Cuba, I thought, saying nothing to Marianne. Deportation might be the only solution, if we could provoke the government into it. Yet Marianne was confident that she could solve the immediate problem, moving heavily between the Panthers and the *commandantes* and Carlos with the birth of the child only weeks away.

In the chipped *chic* of our decaying suite without charge, I told Marianne that if we ever left Cuba, she must give up Deacon or the Revolution. I could only tolerate one rival, not two. She could not give up the Revolution, she said. I would know why when I toured Cuba and saw what was being done for the people. But she swore that she hated Deacon. She never wanted to see him again. If I could get her back to Paris, she would have the child there, and as I had told Carlos, both of them could fight for socialism in their motherland. As Carlos was probably listening to what we were saying through some device, he should have been satisfied with our revolutionary honesty.

In matters of the heart, however, agreements lie in telephone receivers. Deacon reached the Havana Libre and our bedroom line. He would meet us at the airport if and when we flew back to London. He must see her one last time, and it would be final. The very last time, Marianne insisted, and she had to pick up the last of her things that were not left in my garage before she went to Paris to give birth. Weakly I agreed, as I always had, although I still saw little prospect of our return. I should have known that there is never a last time in the affairs of women and men. All ultimatums are merely postponed to the next instalment.

Marianne took me to meet the Black Panthers in their barricaded rooms. Their leader, Eldridge Cleaver, was a natural in his role as an urban guerrilla. He contained the extremes of behaviour without achieving the golden mean. The internal wars needed to overthrow American society had polarized his contradictions. Cool and explosive, large and light on his feet, slow-moving and quick in riposte, deadly serious and very funny, lucid and fantastical, sympathetic and lethal, he dominated without diplomacy. His misunderstandings with the Cubans were more a matter of street wit than substance. They understood his asides as true statements. Given an old crone to act as a cook and a spy on the apartment, he said, 'If I got to have a cook, make her young, white and willing.' This was reported as, WANTS A YOUNG WHITE SLAVE. When he saw a black Cadillac in the street, he observed, 'I want to get me a big black Caddie for this big black ass.' This was reported as, WANTS BIG AMERICAN CAR. When he bought some grass to smoke in Oriente province and was asked his source, he said, 'Fidel gave it to me.' This was put down as, SAYS HE GOT MARIJUANA FROM CASTRO. And when he sang in the lobby of the Havana Libre, 'I guess I'll have a ball with Haydeé Santamaria,' his dossier read, WANTS ALSO TO RAPE CUBAN OFFICIAL WOMEN.

The wisecrack taken too seriously is the end of understanding, particularly in a socialist society given to spying on each other. But there were serious differences between the Panthers and their revolutionary hosts, which derived from their backgrounds and their expectations. The black hero in the Cuban revolt against Spanish imperialism at the end of the nineteenth century was Antonio Maceo, not the white Martí and Maximo Gomez. It was Maceo who had led the long march from Oriente to surround Havana over sixty years before Castro had repeated his tactics in his Revolution. Maceo had been killed at the moment of victory, perhaps by his own side. To the Panthers, he was their forerunner, and his death was like that of Martin Luther King, a white conspiracy against black power. Maceo had freed the exploited cane-cutters, and now Castro was forcing them back to harvest the *zafra* and pay off huge Russian loans. Castro had only one black Cuban high in his administration. Racism was still as endemic in Cuba as in South Africa.

Trying to broker a peace with the Panthers, Marianne and I had dinner with Carlos in the Havana Libre, where the huge menus now had only a lack of choice to offer. Through the windows, summer lightning flickered over the peeling stucco colonnades of the Malecon facing the scimitar of the bay. Carlos was indignant and accused the Panthers of being counter-revolutionary. He was black, he had risen from the cane-fields, he was the living proof that there was no racism in modern Cuba. 'All the Panthers want from the whites', he declared, 'is their women.' Cleaver had, indeed, called Carlos a white nigger, and perhaps that remark had been reported to him as well. Sexual jealousy about the Panthers had been compounded by one of them taking a radical French journalist off a *commandante*. This was no way to respect rank and the Revolution on the island.

Failing in our peace efforts, but accepting a grand tour of socialist triumph from coast to coast, we returned to visit the beleaguered Panthers. They were adamant that the Cubans were bigots. They just wanted to stay long enough on Cuba to arm themselves and invade Mississippi in a rubber boat, five of them to conquer a continent, rather fewer than even Cortés or Castro had used. Their attitude put me finally face to face with reverse racism. While I was younger, I had believed in biting the hand that fed me, in case it might pat me on the head. But this was ridiculous. To flee the homeland of America and condemn it as a racist, to arrive in socialist Cuba and assert it was more racist, what did this say about the accusers? Perhaps it was better to go back to Wittgenstein and ask who was the target. Were the Panthers accusing themselves? Might even I be freed from being a necessary racist by virtue of my heredity? I wrote in my diary:

> What to do with ex-criminals so thin-skinned that every failure or frustration or disappointment is interpreted as racism? What to do with those who want to perpetuate and exaggerate the divisions of race, who wish to falsify history in order to prove that racism always was and will be paramount, who interpret their every paranoia as a just view, who think that each demand is a fair recompense for the past suffering of their people? The trouble is not that the Panthers are black-skinned, but also dark-skinned. They see through their dark glasses obscurely. They make racism the only reason for every action, despising all other explanation. They spread the cult of the race war, where it only exists partially and poorly enough. Worst of all, they confuse the good cause of black pride and dignity and opportunity into the howl for division and partition and hate.
>
> Cleaver is a brave man, usually brilliant, sometimes an irrational ranter. I had to tell Carlos that the Panther leader was more a *bandelero* than a *guerrilla*. For the Panthers are individual and instinctive fighters from a Pavlovian reflex to anything fancied as racialism. They are not a disciplined political group obeying orders to overrun a country. They are bandits playing as revolutionaries, albeit from an oppressed and exploited minority. RESTITUTION NOW! Yet how can you promote people by skin rather than merit? Of course, we must have equal opportunity, but there can be no favouritism for white or black. Yes. I confess. I am a privileged bleached male, and this point of view suits me. But I did earn my own way from the age of thirteen. And even if I was born in the right place at the right time – if those are the words for the Depression and the Second World

War in Europe – yet birth is no baby's choice. It is the
lottery of the genes, whatever society may do later to
redress the balance.

Actually, the behaviour of the Black Muslims and the Panthers
to their women was worse than that of any White Male Pig. With
his dangerous wit, Cleaver was hilarious about their efforts as
Muslims to reduce women to kitchen slaves behind a veil. He
told of a time in Oakland where the men had gone out with their
black berets and truncheons on the streets, and their women had
taken over their armoury in their absence. When they returned,
they found their wives and lovers with their Sten-guns and hunt-
ing-rifles, yelling that they would blow the men apart unless they
got their equality. Women's rights before black male dominance.
'Honey, honey,' Cleaver begged his wife, who had actually followed him to Havana, 'don't shoot me! You'll be free and equal.
Just take your pretty finger off that there trigger!' And so she
did, and most of the Muslims left the faith and became socialist
Panthers instead. One of Cleaver's Cuban guards was still a Black
Muslim, but this failing was dismissed lightly. 'You see, Andrew,
he only eats pork *between* meals.'

Leaving the Panthers surrounded by the police with no truce
in sight, Marianne and I set off in that envied black Cadillac for
our grand tour. But as so often, the successes of the Revolution
were the failures, and defeat was snatched out of the jaws of
ideology. The crèches were the most disillusioning, and the
mental asylums. So much progress, so much loss of love. In
the aimless rooms where the children were abandoned so that the
mothers could go to work, thirty small ones to each nurse, they
loved the coming of large people. They would rush up and want
to be swung round and round by their arms. '*Cuidado,*' I was
told. 'If you swing one, you must swing all.' This was the terrible
law of the equality of children, let alone socialism. I swung them
all until I felt my arms might drop off. The mental asylum was
presented as the escape from Bedlam. In the bad old days under
the dictator Batista, the insane had been tortured and put on

show in the Casa de Dementes for the amusement of the rich. Now they were doped into tranquillity. Some of them, though, ceased to be political prisoners, sedated into a sort of acceptance. I bought with dollars a picture by one of them of a lighthouse. He was said to be a schizophrenic, but the drawn frieze was an infinite series of mazes and entanglements, the perfect execution of the caged mind. As a psychiatrist told me there, it was the responsibility of the patients to rehabilitate themselves. 'You cannot separate psychiatric hospitals from politics. A hospital *is* a mental patient.' And as for us, the patients were thrown into a panic by visitors. 'This is what kills them.'

The temple of the island was the ejaculation block of the breeding bulls. There the great Rosafé Signet had given his life to Cuba, so that his progeny would pull the cane carts and provide the beef and the milk of his adopted country. Bought at the age of nine from Canada, he had died in service at twelve years old, jerked off electrically into the false vagina of a cow while straddling his wooden mount in his last throes, his semen frozen into insemination pills that might produce another three hundred calves from those departed loins. 'The Revolution does not sacrifice unnecessarily,' the farm manager said about his bovine hero. 'All cattle are sacrificed in the end.' He caressed the spunk-slick wood of the terminal block and told me that his obsession with breeding bulls was shared by Fidel Castro. They had brought the best of all sorts to the island, Charrollais and Hereford, Shorthorn and Zebu, Holstein and South Devon and Criollo, Brown Swiss and Red Pollard. So proud was Castro of his bulls that he had an art exhibition given to a Cuban expatriate in Havana on one condition: between each hanging masterpiece stood a stall and a bull, the true work of art and regeneration. In comparison to these philoprogenetive studs, I felt a hell of a failure, with one child perhaps to my credit, even if Cuba might also prove to be my last exit.

Such macho thinking on the island derived from Spanish times. Many of the political leaders were, indeed, the descendants of the *conquistadores*, not of the imported African slaves. This was the complaint of the refugee Black Panthers, that even the Revolution could not outgrow inherited racism. The other enduring bogey on the island was the Catholic Church, hated by the régime for its supposed intolerance, and hating the régime for its idolatry. The churches were still there on the whole and were pointed out as demonstrations of socialist good faith. But they were hardly attended and the saints' holidays were all given new names, Che Day rather than Good Friday, or Fiestas of the Heroic Patriots of Vietnam or the Workers of the Sugar Cane. I was reminded of that great moment in René Clair's *À Nous La Liberté*, which we had also published at Lorrimer, where the children sing at their desks, 'Freedom is work. And work is freedom.' And so it can be, for those that believe it so.

The queues for everything brought me back to my childhood during the last world war. Let alone queues for the buses and the thirty varieties of ice-cream and the few kinds of food off the ration, there were queues for books as well as the *posadas*. There was a huge line outside an empty store for a new book about to appear – it seemed an author's paradise to me, if the work passed the censor. The queues for the *posadas*, the legal places of assignation because of the housing shortage, had bushes growing around them. There the shy young women hid until their husband or beau reached the head of the human snake and paid for his six hours in a cubicle with his beloved. 'Every so often,' my diary reads, 'the man breaks ranks with his place kept, and he rushes off to the thickets to love up his girl, so her resolve for sex won't desert her by the time he reaches the front of the queue. The *posada* is the one refuge from the eyes of parents, who have the only places to live. Privacy has nothing to do with comradeship.'

The worst thing, and this George Orwell had noted in *1984*, was having to exist in a permanent state of war, fomented by incessant propaganda. There is a truth in everything, and there was a cold war and a blockade between the United States and Cuba, but to keep a whole population on daily alert over a decade had induced a certain lassitude. The blaring and lurid references every day to the Bay of Pigs invasion and the wicked war in Vietnam were used as incentives for voluntary work in agriculture, the short cut to promotion in the state system. Work was not freedom, but fighting for more freedom meant more work. The trouble was that the sound of the liberty bell on one note had induced scepticism. And when this was allied to actual physical exhaustion, because office workers are inefficient cane-cutters and produce more blisters than sheaves, a general doldrums governed the land, where nothing much ever seemed to mean anything. The economic waste of the queuing and the bad communications could never be contradicted by the persuasion of volunteers to hack down the sugar stalks. With all possible strength and faith in a new world, as the old horse Boxer had discovered in Orwell's *Animal Farm*, working for a wrong system only left one as dead meat.

As personal experience involves one in parts of history, so it necessarily changes one's view of history. Great and difficult changes in society had already been accomplished in Cuba by the Revolution. In my diary, I wrote:

> All are fed adequately, if rationed in a boring way. All are
> educated, wear shoes and have equal opportunities,
> whether white or black, whatever the Panthers say.
> Uniquely in Latin America, Castro has solved the worst
> problems. But equally there are the badnesses, the
> bureaucracy, the waste of time, the inefficiency, and
> above all, the militarism – pardonable, perhaps, in terms
> of fear of the United States. Yet Castro has too many
> guns and too little butter. He cannot keep his people
> waiting for ever under a permanent war psychology in
> spite of the great gift the Americans gave him at the Bay
> of Pigs. A national tiredness is succeeding a natural
> tropical indolence. How long, O state of war, how long?

The great nightclub of the old régime, the Tropicana, was still kept open. Carlos took us there to prove how tolerant the Revolution was. Eight overweight white naked marble nymphs still cavorted round a raised fountain bowl, from which water jets sprang into different colours of red and green, purple and blue. The restaurant was in a tropical garden and faced a floor-show on many levels, where dancers and singers and drummers and big bands were crammed into frills and tight pants, performed on rising and falling giant toadstools, and were illuminated by mad rainbows of violent spot-lights. The extravaganza had fossilized in a stale vulgarity as if it were a wake to Carmen Miranda and Busby Berkeley. 'You see how we keep places like this from before the Revolution,' Carlos said. 'But now all the people can come here.'

Looking around the other tables, I saw a noisy Italian baseball team, delegations of Russians and North Koreans, other party functionaries in dark suits like Carlos – those sort of people. And I glanced down at the roast pheasant on my dinner dish.

'I am sure all the people can come here now,' I said. 'But they do have to pay for it. And isn't this pheasant on my plate?'

Carlos was not put out, and said, 'But pheasant is the ration this week for *all* Cubans.'

His cold gaze told me this was no joke. Briefly, visions of factory pheasant farms flitted across my mind. Perhaps it was true in a country where, as Aaron Burr had once declared, truth was what was boldly presented and plausibly maintained.

'Lucky for you,' I said. 'When we had rationing even after the end of the Second World War, the best we got was corned beef.'

In spite of the entertainment, Carlos did not avoid the matter of our meeting at the Tropicana. His words were a threat and a warning to us as much as to the Black Panthers.

'We are such good internationalists,' Carlos said, 'the only true ones. So no one will blame us if we keep order here.'

'But keeping people here,' I said. 'Is that the same as keeping order?'

'Sometimes,' Carlos said. 'But you are happy here?'

'Very happy,' Marianne said.

'Until we go,' I said.

'Until you go,' Carlos said, 'after you have given your son to our Revolution.'

I went back to the Panther apartment, feeling that provocation was the only solution. The Cubans could kill us or deport us. Either was better than detention and later blackmail through the baby. Cleaver was compelling and paranoiac and under pressure from the other Panthers to storm into the streets and shoot it out with the militia. 'There'll be tanks coming down those avenues soon,' Cleaver said. 'I heard they're coming in from Oriente to get us.'

'You would be better off here,' I said. 'Do you mind if I join you? I know how to work those.' I was looking at the old Bren-guns and Sten-guns that littered the floor, out-of-date British army issue, which had somehow turned up here. 'I can strip and use them,' I said. 'I also know the right fire positions when the Cuban army comes to get us. I used to be an officer in the Coldstream Guards. I was very good at guarding Buckingham Palace. Though we didn't expect an attack from Fidel and the boys.'

Cleaver began to laugh, and his cackle set off his dour friends. They fell about to find the company they kept, and they thrust their weapons at me. It was far out for Cleaver, but as he said, he couldn't always choose his comrades. And as I knew, we were only in the same trench because we had a common enemy. There is nothing like shared hostility to bring East and West together, when never the twain shall meet.

'Marianne tells me you used to teach history too,' Cleaver said. 'American history. So tell this "convict" here—' his happy name for his soul brothers – 'just why he shouldn't have landed in Haiti on his way to Cuba. You know what he did? Get off that hijacked Boeing, kiss the runway and say, "This be a free black republic for two hundred years. This been free since the American Revolution, where we're going back to have a proper one." So those local cops, what do they call them?'

'*Tontons Macoutes*,' I said.

'They take him to a quiet place and they reckon to shoot him. But he says he's crazy, so they send him on here. I say he don't know any history. You tell him.'

So I found myself teaching American and African history in that apartment in Havana, while we waited for the attack of the *commandantes*. I explained, or I tried to explain, why Haiti had become a black dictatorship and why so many African republics had done the same, although Nkrumah in Ghana and Nyere in Tanzania were still heroes to them. And then we stripped the Bren-guns and put them together again. And I assigned fire-positions from the windows and the balcony, choosing one for myself. I might have been back in Cambridge with my old tutor Gallagher, working out deep into the night where we would put the mortars and the Maxims when they came to get us. And I might have been teaching my students there about imperialism, what a bad thing it may well have been, but worse could take its place. As it was, such youthful fantasies and concepts had become the realities and the concrete rooms of this dead end in a city, where I found myself against my will.

News of our preparations for armed resistance; a personal letter from Cleaver to Castro, carried by Marianne; the fact that we were more trouble than we were worth; the fear by Castro of provoking another Bay of Pigs if the Panthers were allowed to invade Mississippi in their rubber boat; the damage to the Cuban image if a few foreigners were eliminated in a fire-fight: all or none of these may have produced a repetition of my *dénouement* over Suez, a drama that ended not in a bang, but a damp squib. Instead our passports were restored to us. Places were found on the Cuban airline to Madrid for Marianne and myself, although she was only a couple of weeks from giving birth; and also the Panthers were booked to Algeria, which had agreed to take them in, rather too far away for them to mount any invasion of the United States overnight. We were all taken for a last day on the beach at Santa Maria del Mar, the perfect finale to our Cuban holiday.

Eldridge Cleaver joked as usual as he looked towards distant

Miami beyond the horizon. 'Guess I'll swim across,' he said. He spoke of the last Panther to join him. 'There he was in jail, breaks out at eight at night, hijacks a plane at twelve, and at three he's back in jail again in Cuba. It's like travelling from Folsom to San Quentin.' He also told of how a clever warder had broken a strike by some of the harder prisoners when he had been inside. The 'girls' among the men were separated from their dissident lovers and were put on the grass outside where they could pair off with other prisoners under the eyes of their regular guys, who could not stand the sight and surrendered. Cleaver himself had found solitary confinement very peaceful, as long as he did not feel persecuted about it. The Bible was the only reading there, and he read the good book, 'so I could preach better later'. That was a curious prophecy of what he was to do, in the end.

Not having to invade America was, I suspect, a relief for him. He was no longer condemned by his own declarations. Deportation by Cuba was the answer to his commitments as it was to my prayers. Yet Marianne and I were not able to leave without a final obligatory visit to a cigar factory. We knew the history. The last Havanas rolled by hand were still made for the plutocrats of the western world, although officially interdicted by the United States. The luxury market of London brought in necessary hard currency. England was the only country that would not accept a machine-rolled product, yet the irony was that American cigarettes were the drugs of the poor in Britain and Cuban cigars the symbols of the rich.

We saw nothing of the myth that Havanas were shaped on the bare thighs of beautiful maidens. Old women sat at weathered school desks listening to a reader, no longer intoning the works of the Saints and the Christian Fathers, but those of Engels and Latin-American Liberation. They selected from the different forms of dried leaf, the inner ones called 'tripes' and the outer ones as crushable as silk; whiffs of the acrid dust of the tobacco coated the lungs with snuff. They pulled out the central spines, then they wrapped the selected layers into tiny tight torpedoes against the hard wood of their desks. 'Roomfuls of earnest scholars,' I recorded, 'making their Churchills or other brands, finishing the ends with an axe-bladed knife and natural gum, all cropped to pointed cylinders like fat pencils. These are checked, sorted for colour, and put into the old-fashioned wooden boxes with the expected labels dating from Victorian lithography. An artisan profession and an art.' The box of cigars that we bought had Mr. Punch and his dog Toby surrounded by the tobacco workers at their trade, and stamped upon it, HECHOS A MANO – HAND MADE.

Before our permitted flight, I affirmed to Carlos that we would continue the Revolution in our own countries. Lorrimer Publishing would print the trials of Fidel Castro and Régis Debray and a book against the American war in Vietnam. And Marianne's revolutionary fervour did not abate: a few weeks after the birth of her boy, she would leave for Pyongyang in North Korea and demonstrate on the edge of the Demilitarized Zone with Cleaver against the American troops standing with the South Koreans on the far side. We kept our bargains. My small experience with secret policemen is that they do not do you in, as long as you refuse to take their money. There was no question of a Cuban subsidy for what we did, and my Hollywood one had almost ended.

Marianne did not go into labour on the turbulent journey across the air currents above the Atlantic. Deacon was to meet us for the last time at London airport. She would then proceed to Paris to have the child in France with her mother to help her. She made one concession to my feelings. If it were a boy, it would not be called Che or Inti, one of Guevara's lieutenants. He would be called Timon, the character from Shakespeare who obsessed me now. Yet Timon had become a recluse because of the faithlessness of those he trusted. I saw no moral in that play in my present case. Yet I should have remembered his words:

> All is oblique;
> There's nothing level in our cursed natures
> But direct villany . . . Destruction fang mankind!

14

I LOVE YOU BEST

Don't you know that you can count me out.

JOHN LENNON, 'Revolution'

'The reason for all the pain, passion and conversation in the world is our irremedial urge to justify ourselves.' That is what I wrote to finish my Cuban diary, before I went back to my office at Lorrimer Publishing and found two lines in pencil in the round handwriting of Marianne, scrawled on the back of a brown envelope: *Gone to Oxford for weekend with Deacon. I love YOU best, you silly boy.*

It was hardly a justification, but it was the destruction of my life. I went back to Limehouse, took all the suitcases returned by Deacon, packed the things which she had from me, and I sent them by carrier to his house in London. I added a brief note to the effects, quoting Timon of Athens in his view of the human race and of the value of words. Then I telephoned two people who desperately wanted my house on the river and told them that they could have it. I wanted no roots, no love, no ties. I wanted hardly to live, but then, life does go on, as they say.

I was still at Limehouse, when I felt a burning pain in my vitals. I thought I was dying, but I was not. A clot of blood passed through my penis. It had not happened before, and I felt gutted. I telephoned the good doctor next door, and he told me not to worry. 'It's only a gallstone, Andrew,' he said. 'But go along to St. Thomas's in the morning, have an X-ray, they'll find you're fine.' And so I was, except for one fact. At the time that I passed the clot, a baby was born in Paris who was to bear the name of Timon. These two issues of blood happened simultaneously. Of course, a man cannot give birth. But goodness only knows what inducement of the mind can create such a painful reproduction of the act of giving life to another being. I cannot explain it, I can only recount the fact. To this day, I believe in the strange correspondence of mind and body, and I do not know to what extremity that influence will extend.

France is a legal society, as England is, even if the Code Napo-
léon and case law compound the differences. A birth certificate
had to be signed by the father. I had a telephone call from my
French mother-in-law. The baby was certainly mine and would be
called Timon. He had blue eyes, while the eyes of Deacon were
brown. I should not doubt, I must come to Paris and sign. And
so I flew over and signed the certificate, and I am always glad
that I did. As he was a wonderful baby, so he turned out a
wonderful boy and young man. I have consistently believed that
all children are innocent: only their parents are guilty. And the
fact which I did not then know and discovered later – that *all*
European babies are born with blue eyes – did not shake my
belief in him, when he turned out to have brown eyes.

This is not an account of my feelings, but rather of the excesses
of the times. Within a month of Timon's birth, Marianne flew
out on a free ticket to Pyongyang, where Eldridge Cleaver and
the Black Panthers were also invited. In a way, we were all
paying the price of our deportation from Cuba. We were being
honourable revolutionaries, if that is no contradiction in terms.
It was to depress my political future as Cleaver was now travelling
under my name; Algeria was soon to deport him to France,
finding him as unwelcome a guest as Cuba had. But briefly, as
Andy Sinclair, he was roaming with Marianne to Pyongyang,
which I termed the Acapulco of the revolutionary classes. Certainly, a spectacular was laid on for all the gypsy revolutionaries.
As Marianne's article on her experiences began:

> The Russian limousine was scented with jasmine. It was
> sunset and I had just arrived in North Korea. I sat in
> the car with three Koreans: my guide, my interpreter
> and the chauffeur. As we drove down the flower-lined
> road that led from the airport to Pyongyang, I admired
> the fields of yellow Indian corn, of golden-green rice, of
> trees loaded with pink apples. 'Yes,' my interpreter replied
> proudly, 'Thanks to the wisdom of our leader, Comrade
> Kim Il Sung, we have produced a bumper crop this year.'
> His expression then grew mournful as he added, 'But it

is not like that in the Southern part of our country. There, under the yoke of the U.S. imperialist aggressors, our people groan with hunger and the land is barren.' He paused for effect, then went on resolutely, 'This is why we can not rest until the U.S. Beast is driven from our country and Korea is reunified. Then we can share our happiness with our brothers in the South.'

So the propaganda was believed, so the words were wrapped in luxurious welcome. In vast demonstrations in natural stadia as in the gladiatorial combats of the Roman circuses, the Magnificent Leader was depicted on screen and in the patterns of ten thousand costumes as personally breaking the tanks and bayonets of the American bogeyman. 'The terms used to describe the Americans, even in official publications, would make up an entire bestiary: they are "vampires," "hyenas," "wolves," "crocodiles" and every other sort of monster. Children are systematically indoctrinated in anti-Americanism from the earliest age. In a kindergarten I visited, lines of four-to-six-year-old children were waiting for their turn to go and stab a cardboard image of an American soldier with toy guns.' Marianne even went and demonstrated with Cleaver at Panmunjon, confronting the 'fascist beasts' to the south – and she was photographed fully while doing this. 'The North Koreans feel that, after Vietnam, it will be their turn to fight. They are, naturally, very encouraged by what they call the "crushing victory" of the North Vietnamese, and they have the unshakeable conviction that, as one of their generals put it not long ago, "Should the U.S.–South Korean forces launch another aggression, their presence on our soil would be ended for all times".'

Thus the jargon of the war in Asia spilled into our private lives. The Americans were, indeed, doing very badly in Vietnam. Although President Nixon had authorized the bombing of Cambodia as well as North Vietnam, the forces on the ground were not progressing. And so that wily politician was looking for a solution, and it lay with the Chinese, no friends of the Vietnamese on their border. It had always been true in history. Go to the

country behind the back of the country that is hostile. The enemy
of the enemy may be a friend. The dicta of the past more and
more proved the difficulty of changing the present. President
Nixon could do a deal with Chairman Mao, the eagle could
lie down with the dragon, and the 'paper tiger' – as the
Chinese called American power – could fly as a kite above
the Great Wall. Only the lesser countries would lose, as they
always did.

I had to put paid to Hollywood as I had to the East End of
London. I sold the cabin on the Malibu Lake, where the sets for
the original film of King Kong still provided grottoes of fantasy
on the arid hills. It was a withdrawal, a coming home. The friends
I had known in California were also pulling back from the dream
of creating an alternative culture to conserving their different
way of life. It was a reverse route in American history, which had
always praised the conquest of the savage and the forests and the
mountains by the civilized and the frontier and the city. But as
early as the works of Jack London and Upton Sinclair, violence
had become the condition of the people of the urban abyss
and the industrial slums. And now, there were concurrent and
opposed popular visions of future disintegration. In one version,
world wars and the brutalization of life would reduce every
metropolis to a ruined nightmare, in which the thought police
of *1984* or the droog gangs of *A Clockwork Orange* would rule the
streets. Already in these dark prophecies, Calcutta was a prototype
of the ungovernable and starving slum of the future. The other
vision of the *Brave New World* by Aldous Huxley saw it as a society
controlled by eugenics and the pursuit of pleasure through a
drug called soma. Better in Huxley's Utopia to be a pig satisfied
than a savage dissatisfied.

The moralist of *Brave New World* was literally called the Savage.
At first fascinated by its scale and easy happiness, he then took
an emetic to purge himself of what he called civilization. In his
dialogue with his Grand Inquisitor, Mustapha Mond, he declared
that he liked discomfort and inconvenience; he even wanted the

right to be unhappy. 'I want God, I want poetry, I want real danger, I want freedom, I want goodness. I want sin.' He even desired disease and starvation and pain, if he could keep his liberty. When he finally retired to the solitude of the Hog's Back in Surrey to become a hermit and to flog his evil out of himself, the descending tourists with their drug-induced orgy-porgies drove him to a guilty suicide.

To Huxley, there had seemed no compromise between the Utopia promised by full technology and the savagery praised by that primary sociologist Malinowski in Melanesia. Future man must surrender to the control of mind and body by the state, or he must live in foul and diseased freedom on some reservation in the wilderness. Fifteen years later, however, Huxley wrote a new foreword to his book, in which he stated that he had found a serious defect in his story. His solitary Savage, brought into the genetic and tranquillized organization of the new society, had only been offered two alternatives, 'an insane life in Utopia, or the life of a primitive in an Indian village'. By the end of the Depression and the Second World War, Huxley felt that the Savage should have been offered a third alternative – the possibility of a sane existence with a group of exiles from the Brave New World, who would live within the borders of the Indian reservation. Their life would be anarchistic and run on the co-operative principles of Kropotkin. Science and technology would be man's servant, not his master; religion would be his goal. In the atomic and totalitarian age to come, only a large-scale movement towards decentralization and self-help could save the sanity of mankind. Without it, the world governments would condition their peoples by suggestion, drugs, eugenics and social status to love their servitude. The Brave New World was near, not six centuries away as in the novel.

This was the belief of the withdrawing hippies, who took with them into their rural communes the drugs which Huxley had espoused and feared. The pioneers had cleared the stones from the land; the hippies were stoned on the land. Compromising with Huxley's vision, the counter-culture also took its urban violence back into Arcadia. Weapons were stockpiled against the coming atomic Armageddon. The retreat became the redoubt, the escape was dug into a bunker, the dream evolved into a primer of existence. Instead of the probable nuclear holocaust of Thomas Pynchon's *V,* there was the psychedelic resistance in California of his later *Vineland.* As for Stewart Brand, he turned his *Whole Earth Catalog* into a success in the mass market. Yet its lists of how to live almost resembled advertisements of alternative stores of survival goods rather than wisdom. And in an incredible finale in the Cow Palace at San Francisco, when Brand wanted to give away his publishing profits to the best cause, the long night's debate went to the loudest and the loot to the strongest. A young giant walked to the platform and removed the packet of thousands of dollars by brute force.

John Lennon of the Beatles had been the supreme poet and performer of this new age, already growing older. His marriage to Yoko Ono and his taking to his sheets with her appeared to be a paradigm for another decade that looked for privacy and peace rather than protest and conflict. Already in his most extreme lyric, 'Revolution', Lennon had signalled that he would not go all the way:

> When you talk about destruction,
> Don't you know that you can count me out.

Now he moved into hotel beds in Amsterdam and Montreal and gave interminable peace conferences in pyjamas with his wife. His song 'All we are saying is give peace a chance' was chanted by half a million demonstrators at Vietnam Moritorium Day in Washington in the November of 1969; but his return of his medal, the M.B.E., because of British support for American policies in Vietnam, was as irrelevant as it was out of date. His song 'Imagine' was a hippie dream of a peaceful global brotherhood of man, a utopia without the numerous possessions which he had himself. In spite of an erratic demonstration in favour of the I.R.A. and a song 'Power To The People', his pulling back into an exclusive zone of two people in the Dakota building of New York City was the swansong of this troubadour of his times.

I had always wanted to live in the parks of London, if I could not live in Soho or the docks. Bohemia and river and greenery, these were the attractions of this metropolis. Unfortunately, I discovered in Regent's Park a mansion with a separate mews for very little money down. That it was a short and full-repairing lease and a national monument did not deter my appreciation of the proportions of the Georgian rooms and the sheer size of it all. It was financial suicide, but I did not care. William Golding had always told me that I needed a great deal of space to write inside, and so I did not count the cost, although I should have known that the sublime Nash with his stucco fronts was a jerry-builder. At least, the place was suitable for Magog's residence. Now I was disillusioned with my radical past, I was freed to write the antithesis of *Gog*, that anarchist hero. This was now the story of the man of power, the civil servant who had led Britain into its irreversible decline after the end of the Second World War. His sin was his failure. As his epigraph to the book read: POWER CORRUPTS. POWERLESSNESS CORRUPTS ABSOLUTELY.

One of my neighbours in Hanover Terrace was the archetype and scribe of Magog's world. Noel Annan, now a life peer, had orchestrated King's College at Cambridge and then University College, London, and also many of the more important commissions appointed by the governments of Harold Wilson. Urbane and charming, intelligent without passion and wise without reach, he wrote the history of his kind of people in *Our Age: Portrait of a Generation*. He assumed that a few hundred like-minded Oxbridge graduates had run the country and its culture for the past twenty-five years. The arrogance of this mandarin élite was matched by its tolerance. It regarded itself as an Immoral Front. 'If someone said, "People should be stopped from doing that," the Immoral Front insisted that authority should justify its laws and conventions. If the young wanted to demonstrate, or utter absurd views, or do disgusting and disobliging things, or make love with their own sex or in heaps, we might think they were idiotic or ill-mannered; but, if they were entitled to do so, we saw no reason to stop them; or if a law did exist to stop them we asked: was it wise and humane and on what grounds did society issue this prohibition?'

What the Immoral Front never did was ask itself whether disgusting and disobliging young people cared at all about these elderly opinions. They did not. Their age was hardly Our Age. There was no communication between the generations. The professors and the civil servants knew next to nothing of the revolutionaries and the pop singers and the artists, who had tried and failed to change the powers of that time. Proudly, Lord Annan could write that no government had ever contained so many former dons and intellectuals as the Labour administrations of the 'sixties; but among them, there was no leader who could arrest the decline of Britain from the superpower of the 'fifties to the sick man of Europe twenty years on. And there were few or none among Our Age who might stop this, either. There was certainly no populist, who would understand the many alternative strategies of government propounded by those excluded from Our Age, that self-appointed group who never considered the old Roman question, *Quis custodiet custodes?*, 'Who shall guard the guardians?' They knew they were the right guardians. There could be no others. They did not see that it was not Our Age but another age, the years of the heedless young:

> Come mothers and fathers throughout the land
> Don't criticise what you can't understand
> Your sons and your daughters are beyond your command
> Your old road is rapidly ageing.
> Please get out of the new one if you can't lend a hand
> For the times they are a-changing.

So Bob Dylan used to sing, but the election of the Conservative government under Edward Heath in 1970 signalled an expected backlash against the extended tolerance of the post-war era.

Christie Davies' book on *Permissive Britain* had chronicled a long period of parliamentary relaxation. 'Activities which society had previously disapproved of and banned are now permitted and can be freely indulged in. Perhaps the most striking of these is the abolition of most of the laws prohibiting homosexual acts between consenting male adults. As regards other matters, it is now much easier than it was to get a divorce or an abortion, to place cash bets on the dogs or the horses, to indulge in tombola or bingo or to get a drink on a Sunday west of Offa's dyke. In addition censorship of the press, books and the theatre is much less severe than it was.'

Against the wide tolerance of the Immoral Front of Lord Annan and his friends, a moral minority began to form. The particular prosecution which led the counter-attack was on *Oz*, the Australian underground magazine, which used the language of the street and the young. The grounds of the prosecution were under the Obscene Publications Act. 'Will you lend a hand?', its editor Richard Neville asked the trial jury, quoting the song of Bob Dylan. 'Let it be a verdict which will confirm the values of tolerance, reason, freedom and compassion. Let it be a verdict which helps to remove the barriers between us all.'

The judge Michael Argyle had another opinion of the number of *Oz* which had been called to justice. He defined obscenity as 'loathsome, repulsive, filthy, loud' and made it clear to the jury that all these adjectives were to be found in the 'Schoolkids' issue. Most of the expert witnesses, who had appeared in court to defend *Oz*, might be thought 'to admit the magazine was obscene or else tell lies'. One of them had said that *Oz* was a window into the hippie culture. 'Well, ladies and gentlemen, sometimes that window needs cleaning.' The jury found *Oz* guilty on the obscenity charges. But by the astute compromises of British justice, when faced with a howl of derision from the Immoral Front, the judge was retired from other obscenity trials, the *Oz* defendants were released from jail and deportation, and their fines were mitigated. No longer did the Conservative prime minister have to consider motions in the House of Commons

that editors were being imprisoned 'for political and social attitudes rather than for criminal offences'. A fudge had averted a
confrontation.

What shrewd mercy had spared, economics condemned. The
underground press had too little capital and was losing its audience. Only when it became more commercial and appealed to
the consuming side of the young did it survive. As Peter York
noted in *Style Wars*, the minority cultures of the 'sixties were
merchandised and fragmented into the conflicting trends of the
'seventies. Protest movements and alternative ways of life were
analysed and serviced as a multitude of different markets with
even terrorism producing a fashion in heavy boots and army
surplus gear. Capitalism seemed to be stimulated by the attempts
to confound it. Wounds became voracious mouths. It swallowed
the spears that were stuck down its gullet. It grew and expanded
under attack, splitting like the amoeba to contain any intrusion
within a new cell. Supremely adaptable and inventive, it ingested
the barbs and hooks of its accusers and turned them into buttons
and bows for sale.

The short-changing of the times was never more apparent than
in the three pop festivals held on the Isle of Wight in successive
years after 1968. At the first two, some hundred and thirty thousand people had paid to enter, doubling the population of the
small island. The second gathering was, indeed, a British Woodstock, a happening at the same time that attracted Bob Dylan
himself to sing of the blowing wind and altering age. Yet the
third festival was a monitored and mercenary affair that attracted
half a million consumers to hear The Who and Jimi Hendrix
and Joan Baez, the piercing voice of former protest. Security
guards with Alsatian dogs patrolled the wired fences, causing
conflicts with 'White Panthers' who tried to tear down the palisades and let in the poor and the young for free. Dozens were
arrested for possession of drugs, litter and excrement soiled
the green fields, and the Hell's Angels turned from guarding the
event to attacking it, as at Altamont. The excluded watched
the loudspeakers from an adjoining hill and viewed the celebrity

marquee where the singing stars were entertained after their arrival by helicopter. At the end of the show, the broken ones were paid by the organizers ninepence per sack of garbage to clear the mess away.

I decided to end my novel of *Magog* there, with the ageing man of power politics from Regent's Park seduced into this attendance on a last crusade after a lost Jerusalem. He had helped to pollute the planet, allowing nuclear and toxic waste to be dumped in the English Channel and the North Sea, oil slicks to tar the beaches from underwater exploration, chemical weapon research to blight nature, and pollutants to foul the air. 'Nothing could stop the spread of the global cancer except a turning back to the old ways of earth,' Magog now thought, 'and even the young liked new things too much to stop the making of more and more things, which would mess up the land still further.' And all he might do in the twilight was to join the hired scavengers and pick a bit of litter from the grass. Personally, 'beginning to put the place right'.

Those who had done a little, such as Richard Neville, to mould the thinking of the 'sixties saw no future in protest or organization, uniforms or violence. They reverted back to a dream of an Eden and the Middle Ages. Once upon a time, Neville concluded in *Play Power*, culture had been fun and games. Then it had become anti-play, more earnest and drab and puritan. Now play was being revived in rock and fashions and happenings and street theatre. 'Purposeless play is creative. The most inventive scientists and researchers play. Many new inventions started out as play. Artists play.' The reason why was that play was an affirmation of life. It was not an attempt to bring order out of chaos or to try and improve things, merely a way of awakening to life as it was, and letting it be.

The politics of play was the plea. 'The strategy which converts the Underground to a brotherhood of clowns; the lifestyle which unites a generation in love and laughter.' It was hardly a philosophy that would change the world, but it was a fond illusion that would excuse the failure of youthful radicalism and pass the time of day in an adult future.

15

WON'T GET FOOLED AGAIN

'The question is,' said Alice, 'whether you can make words mean so many different things.'

'The question is,' said Humpty Dumpty, 'who is to be master. That is all.'

LEWIS CARROLL, *Through the Looking-Glass*

When we were young, at the time of the Suez crisis, we believed that government mattered. There was the Establishment that vitally affected our lives. We had to subvert it by satire and infiltrate and even try to replace it. Fifteen years on, the government seemed irrelevant. It was hardly worth altering because policies were much the same in the Labour and Conservative parties and had little effect on the life-styles which we were choosing for ourselves. A certain radical fatigue and consciousness of public impotence afflicted many of us. Even The Who's attack on the Tory victory in 1970, 'Won't Get Fooled Again', was later dismissed by the guitarist and composer Pete Townshend as stressing detachment rather than opposition. The song was stating, 'There's no point in having anything to do with politics, and revolution, because it's all a lot of nonsense.' Anger was not the expression any more, neither was love. Not to be involved or committed was the stance for the 'seventies. Townshend regarded the previous decade as ridiculous through its lack of sense of reality and its refusal to see how things might be changed within the existing system. And yet, among the young audiences, although not among the leading performers such as himself, there had been an incoherent belief in a kind of rebellion. 'I think that's the closest Britain ever came to having a potential for real revolution.'

Yet radicalism was now fragmented and on the wane. Among those few who were still dedicated Marxists, the debates raged over support for the I.R.A. or the socialists in Northern Ireland, for the Palestinians or the left-wing parties of Israel. The feminists split from their male colleagues in the underground press and divided among themselves into conflicting cells. The women's movement added to Richard Neville's sense of confusion after the *Oz* trial. 'It made enemies out of friends to some extent.'

The solidarity and harmony of the underground were breaking up like the fragments of a grenade. The leaders of Black Power were quarrelling among themselves for dominance, if they were not in jail or in exile. Their language was that of Humpty Dumpty, whom Stokely Carmichael was fond of quoting. 'When I use a word ... it means just what I choose it to mean. Neither more nor less ... The question is who is to be master. That is all.'

The killing of Malcolm X by his own people in the United States, and the descent of Michael X or Abdul Malik from his 'Black House' in the Holloway Road to the gallows in Trinidad, denounced by the revolutionary movement there, displayed the envy and self-mutilation that were tearing apart the aspirations of the earlier surges for racial equality. Eldridge Cleaver himself, pushed onto the margins in Paris, tried to market macho jeans with a codpiece – to be called 'cleavers' – and began to settle his differences with the American Justice Department. His Bible-reading in prison converted him into a Born Again Christian, ready to conduct mass baptisms in swimming pools. Without such extreme switching the radical gadflies of yesteryear, such as Malcolm Muggeridge, were becoming religious and rural sages, while the regress from Marx to Adam Smith of the ageing Angry Young Men was led by Kingsley Amis and John Osborne. Reversal was the state of the art.

Inclusion had always been the temptation of protest, and the early years of the 'seventies were the proof. The failure of the urban rebellions of 1968 had heralded the failure of the alternative and counter-cultures. Their programmes were always ambiguous. The protest against the economic and cultural imperialism of America was allied with the consumption of the mass-produced goods of the pop arts. The campaign against consumerism in capitalist societies, 'merchandise is the opium of the people', was not conducted by Maoist peasants or fundamentalist Islamic bedouin from the deserts, but by bourgeois intellectuals, who enjoyed the goods and used the methods of modern technology in the sophisticated urban centres of the West. And the engines of state repression feared by the counter-culture were already working to include the assault on their operations. Accommodation was to ingest the rebellion against authority. The spreading of patronage was to assuage the criticism of its existence.

Even those who criticized state institutions, as did the social historian Raymond Williams, were now serving on the Arts Council of Great Britain and finding it difficult to adapt to fresh purposes. He was conscious of the change in the policy of the Council, with its revised charter. He held 'the fine arts' to include theatre, opera, ballet, concert music, painting and sculpture, while 'the arts' now took in literature, film, photography, performance art and community arts. The increased scope of the Arts Council was yet another art or artfulness, the art of inclusion, which would digest the protest against state patronage as it digested Williams's own reservations – he offered his resignation twice during his term of office within the Council, but ended by serving out his time and praising the organization's work and careful balance between its duties.

Williams pointed out that the wireless was the major distributor of concert music and drama; as with the Arts Council, the British Broadcasting Corporation was a semi-autonomous body funded by tax money. Television, split between the B.B.C. and the independent companies, was becoming the major distributing channel of all the arts. There was no consultation between the B.B.C. and the television companies and the Arts Council about a common cultural policy. Literature was still largely excluded from any patronage except by commercial publishers: grants to individual authors or little magazines or poetry readings rarely exceeded one per cent of the Arts Council's budget. Whoever wrote that in the beginning was the word was not referring to the patronage of it in Britain.

Yet in the absence of alternative patrons, the very leaders of the alternative culture looked to conventional sources to subsidize their works and to the market to sell them. As the underground newspaper *International Times* warned, the standard London process was to seek change and to be trapped by finance and commerce, until the project was caught on its own terms. The commercialization of modern art also supported its manifestations for a while. But the leading galleries of contemporary painting, the Beaux Arts and Indica and Robert Fraser and Kasmin, were all forced to close because of falling sales. As *Studio International* reported, the unhappy fact was that 'London galleries – ostensibly dealing in Culture at the highest level – are heavily mortgaged to what is, in fact, a crushingly boring subculture.' The Arts Council itself was drawing back from its years of taking risks with the arts. During the chairmanship of Lord Goodman, its bureaucrats had followed the advice of its many panels, particularly on community arts and multi-media activities. As Goodman engagingly said, 'One of the most precious freedoms of the British people is freedom from culture.' Charles Osborne joined the Arts Council in 1966, and his unofficial memoirs, *Giving It Away*, showed the bureaucrats gradually taking back the grants from the control of the experimental advisers. In his first five years on the Council, Osborne thought that 'it had squandered large sums of money on "community arts", that perversion of the aesthetic urge invented by bored arts administrators yearning to become social workers.' The 'seventies would see that urge dampened down, and Osborne's view of the Experimental Projects Committee would prevail, that 'its job was to sort out the sense from the senseless'.

During its period of expansion, however, the Arts Council did do well to open the Hayward Gallery on the South Bank and the Serpentine Gallery in Kensington Gardens. American taste now began to tyrannize the British scene. Its most influential art critic, Clement Greenberg, was correct in saying that the main premises of western art had migrated to the United States, along with the centres of gravity of industrial production and political power. He condemned national schools of art. There was now an 'International Style' in which paintings and buildings and machines '*look* what they *do*'. It was a sophisticated version of materialism, but Greenberg was right in that the power of patronage had followed the domination of technology. The centre of the contemporary art market was shifting to New York, and its standards and canons were taken as gospels by the curators of the galleries in Britain. International, or more properly American, values were in vogue. So young British artists, stimulated originally by the Tate Gallery exhibition of modern American Art in 1956, started to follow their transatlantic cousins. Imitation became the sincerest form of recognizing cultural domination.

In analysing the significance of the pop culture of the 'sixties in Britain and why it ran out of steam, George Melly emphasized in 1970 that its split from 'high culture' was utter and led to its failure. It did weaken the class system without destroying it, but its exclusiveness and anti-intellectualism saw to its loss of influence except among the young. 'The result of each generation may differ in style and detail but is based on the same need: the escape from the family. Once this is achieved, and pop is a very successful way of making the break, it loses its impetus.' But the success of pop in making any change to society would push it to extremes, such as the Sex Pistols, where only the psychopathic and the disturbed would be influenced. It had another inherent difficulty. Its anti-intellectualism and rejection of a cultural heritage in favour of instant creativity meant that pop artists relied on their instincts. Most of them had hardly been educated. Improvisation could provide an initial spurt, but ended facing a brick wall, which could not be climbed. The reaction of pop artists at this point was 'to lose confidence, to turn desperately to unreal solutions'. John Lennon with Yoko Ono had tried to advance beyond pop and had reached desperate gestures, 'in the vocabulary of a clapped-out avant-garde'. Pop had turned pretentious or sour and 'become either an intellectual and exclusive concern, or been forced into an alliance with violence or the fat men in suits.'

Disillusion with the effect of pop music was matched by disintegration in pop art, under the influence of the United States. The object, whether Coca-Cola can or silk-screen portrait, was dematerialized, taken from the gallery and the museum to the streets and open spaces. The inflatable structures by Jeff Shaw and Graham Stevens at St. Katherine's Docks converted sculpture to baggy dirigibles in front of superannuated warehouses. Even the chief source of the received image, the television set, began to suffer from implosion by over-use. Like the black holes in space, the tubes reverted to a fireball and concentrated their energy on an internal blast. The 'sixties appeared to have liberated and destroyed the image. It might be replaced by Play Power as if art were a fairground where the living form could flop free. Spaceplanes were created and inflatable structures, again by Jeff Shaw. 'It was here, in this imaginary space of "Pneumatics", that the 'sixties' "free body" found its final apotheosis.' This was the verdict on the art scene in London during the decade. 'Tumbling, disoriented, buoyed up against gravity, discovering a second, sculptural skin . . .'

The American experience again broke up the film world in Britain and affected me, returning my career to where it had started, but from the new perspective of more than a decade later. The failure of several block-busters and the success of the low-budget *Easy Rider* revolutionized the expectations of the studio bosses. Cheap was good, small was beautiful, stars were unnecessary if they cost too much for their little light. It was the proof that the alternative culture of the hippies could be commercialized and another comet was born from it, Jack Nicholson. The musical of *Hair* would be yet further proof of how Wall Street might exploit Haight-Ashbury, and the dollar became the stem of flower power. Asked by Kenneth Tynan to do a sketch for the equally commercial *Oh! Calcutta!* with its simulated sex and nudity pretending to be codpiece art, I refused. I did not think that royalties should derive from the freedom of the love generation.

For my part, a programme of ten inexpensive films was announced to be made at Elstree under the guidance of Bryan Forbes. As a screenwriter become director himself, Forbes could accept me as the director of my own material, in this case *The Breaking of Bumbo*. But thinking like my past students, he did not want a *historical* novel or film. He wanted to reflect the protest of the 'sixties. And I was happy to oblige, as I thought I knew something about radical chic and what had gone wrong with the fourteen years after I had staged my first failed revolt against the system. I wrote in an introduction to a new edition of the novel:

> Since I wrote *Bumbo* after Suez, I never experienced another issue that split society as much nor another love affair that split me so much until 1968, when the middle-class students rampaged in the cities of the world. What is clear now is that 1968 was another 1848, whcn the students and sometimes the workers fought for urban victories and got temporarily beaten by the forces of reaction. But briefly there was my lady fighting in the streets of Paris, and it was Commune time, and the dead hero Che was still raging in his followers' cries of revolt and pain, and hope flew in red and black rags that lit the bombs that burned the parked cars, until the élites of left and right broke the young faith between them so that they could sag back in their seats of power once more – official enemies, but foulweather friends. The same old dirty collusion.
>
> So Bumbo was broken again. Not this time by the force of protesting against an unjust war at the last gurgle of Empire, but by the farce of struggling for a utopia against an unjust deal done by the powers that were and are, are, are amen. That these powers are radical or reactionary, socialist or capitalist, liberal or totalitarian, makes small change for the young. For the old men still rule in the same old ways. Did not Lenin have to re-employ the Tsarist bureaucracy to make the Bolshevik government work?
>
> The screenplay of *Bumbo* could now be rewritten and updated. Its morality was clear, Bumbo's cry before going down for the last time under the bottle of a skinhead, 'What did you bloody risk?' Those who incite a soldier to mutiny will be sentenced to decades in prison in time of peace and to death in time of war. The reservists who mutinied at the time of Suez were put away for many years – as long as they were not officers. Soldiers who mutiny against Vietnam really serve time. The worth of a

revolutionary action lies more in the danger of its doing than the manner of its speaking. Che spoke of Bolivia, but also went . . .

Bumbo is finally *included* in the film as in the novel. He is received into a wealthy marriage. He joins the class from which his efforts to escape have seemed to be mere youthful high spirits. As they say here, you had better be a radical when you're young to escape from being too reactionary when you're old, for age you will. The ruling class of England – that most anti-revolutionary of all countries – has always included the brilliant rebels battering at its gates. It admires and contains a successful attack upon itself. The peers and the powerful have always been ready to marry their daughters to the rich or the coming, and they have always accepted the company of the pushing and the arrived. Castes may fall by exclusion; but classes can endure by acceptance of new blood. Bumbo falls to the temptation of inclusion. How easy to fight a mailed fist, how hard to resist an open hand.

Above all the film makes clear what is only implicit in the novel, the total lack of communication between class and class, group and group, trade and profession, young and old in London. The young radical students don't trust the middle-aged radical professor any more than the self-made Sergeants in the Guards trust young officers or young soldiers. As Bumbo says in the screenplay, when he drunkenly tries the impossible of making the Guardsmen seek a common cause with the students:

'Soldiers and students, they're the scum of the earth. Pushed around, lousy pay, do this, damn that! The trouble is they hate each other. I mean, can you imagine having a student for a friend? . . . But if soldiers and students get together, they could change the scene. Demos with guns! Nothing could stop them . . . Nothing!'

Of course, because an officer is speaking from a different class the men all reply 'Yessir', meaning nothing. And Bumbo finds himself leading his strike alone, because he has only committed himself and no one else. He cannot speak across the barriers of class nor years . . . Things are much changed between the film

and the original novel based on the same story; fourteen
years have seen to that in me. But one thing has not
changed. Bumbo is still broken by the powers that be.
Their hands hold the ultimate banana-skin.

There were scenes in the film which succeeded and still have the
capacity to wound, particularly the night when the chic revolutionaries led by the radical university professor break into
Madame Tussaud's, and he holds a blow-torch to the waxwork
face of Winston Churchill until the glass eyes pop, and he says,
'So much for Dresden.' Filming this shot made some of the
technicians walk out, until I explained to them that Churchill
had killed more civilians and refugees in the one mighty fire-
raid on Dresden as a burnt offering to Stalin or in revenge for
the Blitz, than had been killed in the two nuclear attacks on
Hiroshima and Nagasaki. They did not know that, they came
back to work particularly for the naked love scene with a discarded scarlet tunic and black bearskin and Joanna Lumley in
her first screen role, playing herself as admirably as always with
her swagger and her beauty and her style.

And so my first statement became my latter one, coloured by
way of experience in the 'sixties. Carrie went off with my composer and his musical friends, sometimes returning to me
between flights and cadenzas. And Timon was brought up in
Paris, taught to kiss a photograph of me and say 'papa' as his
first word. I sent him a music-box I had made, which showed
Notre-Dame against a night sky bright with the constellations. So
when I went to visit and found him in a street in Montparnasse
with his grandmother, and she put his hand in mine and left us
together, he knew who I was and looked up at the stars in the
sky and said with confidence, '*Boîte à musique à papa.*' He
imagined that I had made the heavens as well as his music box,
when I could not even make much of what to do about him.
Time is not a great healer, but the faith of small children is.
Whatever had happened between the adults, Timon was there
close to me in our tiny universe of trust and love.

ENDPIECE

And I, what was I doing there, and why come? These are the things that we shall try to discover. But there are things we must not take seriously. There is a little of everything, apparently, in nature, and freaks are common.

SAMUEL BECKETT, *Molloy*

If human existence is seen as a form of play, then the lives of young men may often by defined by some sport or game. In *The Great Gatsby*, F. Scott Fitzgerald located the character of Tom Buchanan in the dramatic turbulence of some irrecoverable Yale football match, while John Updike saw Rabbit Angstrom's climax in shooting basketballs through hoops at high school. For me, it was the wall game at Eton. I became the keeper of the wall, and if Humpty Dumpty was correct and the only question was who was the master, I was that briefly in a muddy rite of passage. Calling myself Arthur Griffin, I wrote about the game in the final volume, *King Ludd*, of my trilogy on the mythological history of Britain, that had begun with *Gog* and *Magog*:

> There is only one Wall and Arthur Griffin is First Wall and the Keeper of the Wall. Red bricks rubbed smooth by the downy cheeks of dead Etonians support his flank as he knuckles the Oppidan First Wall, grinding his fist into the pale face of privilege that is paying for this pain. Arthur inches forward along the Wall. At his feet in the bully, his Second Luke is crouched on the thick mud, his body hunched over the small leather cannonball that he is trying to move forward to Bad Calx . . . Arthur struggles on against the wall, pushing sideways into the enemy. The bricks scrape him through his padded helmet and jacket, the heavier Oppidan Walls claw at his exposed nose with the fives gloves on their hands, they grind their thumbs into his eye-sockets until he has to turn face to the friendly Wall to save his sight. Above him, boys in white ties and tail-coats sit, dangling their shoes over the Wall watching the steam rise from the game below. The minutes pass. The bully does not budge. Arthur is treading on something harder than earth, softer than mud. It does not move. No humpback of the

Second supports his knees. Luke is down. He has been
down a long time. His body is their playing ground.

'Air,' Arthur says to the Wall, then swings his face round
into the knuckles of the Oppidan Wall. 'Air! Air!'

At the shout, the bully slowly breaks up. The lurking
Thirds move back, the four-legged Seconds rise to reveal
their front two legs are arms, the three Walls on either
side shamble apart. Luke is lying spread-eagled on his
face, the ball between his thighs. He does not stir. Arthur
kneels down and puts his gloves under Luke's right arm
and heaves him on to his back away from the Wall. In the
mud, a death-mask is cast, an impression in wet clay of
Luke's forehead and eye-sockets and nose and mouth and
chin.

Luke coughs and then he begins to whimper. Dry sobs
rack him. He sits up and puts his face in his soiled
gloves, but the touch of the mud makes him gag and
drop his hands. He is weeping now, the tears making
furrows through the grime on his cheeks. The other
players, the Oppidan and the Tugs, stand round
embarrassed. Nobody cries at games, certainly not on St.
Andrew's Day, when the best of the seventy poor scholars
meet the best of the eleven hundred fee-paying Oppidans,
and mean intelligence confronts the arrogant weight of
wealth . . .

Nought–nought. That is always the result on St.
Andrew's Day. Once upon a time, goals were scored,
thrown against the green door of Good Calx and the
rectangle outlined on the elm tree of Bad Calx. But that
was a time before mind. Arthur must endure for a draw.
The dozen minutes that he spends squatting on the ball,
taking the knuckles and the elbows and the knees, the
studs and the toecaps and the heels, the bodyweight that
puts a vice and a tourniquet on his arms and legs, they
are to become second only to J. K. Stephens, who sat
on the ball even longer, and whose health is drunk from
a silver cup every St. Andrew's night, *In piam memoriam
J. K. S.* But as he suffers and resists and will not go down,
Arthur knows the battle of Waterloo was not won on the
playing-fields of Eton. Passchendaele, Ypres, the Somme,
these battles were *not lost* in the glutinous trenches, in
the swarm of no-man's-land, during the months of survival

or slow dying in soaking burrow and drenched hole.
However hellish, never go down. Taking it is all. So Arthur
takes it as the Tommies did for twelve minutes against their
four years of war, and he learns the first lesson of the
class he will oppose: Endure.'

The young man I called Luke never played the wall game again
and was to fall to his death mysteriously from a window in
Moscow. I learned from my determining game not to show pain
or fear to the powerful and to outlast them. And I experienced
the pointlessness of applied violence especially in the name of
amusement. That disturbing forecast of the urban jungle of the
future, *A Clockwork Orange*, was turned into the most sickening
portrayal of brutality as entertainment by the genius of the film-
maker Stanley Kubrick in 1971, and its vision of the dispossessed
young on English council estates living a life of aimless horror
and pleasure was so frightening in its indictment of chic terrorism and random revolution that Kubrick himself withdrew the
film from circulation because of the social damage its showing
appeared to cause. The psychopathic gang of droogs, as *Ink*
declared, was the 'logical conclusion of the ideologies currently
peddled by the Underground and the left: the one glorifying
indiscriminate violence ... the other ignoring subcultures as
irrelevant or trying to "politicise" them into its own tired image'.
It reduced the fissiparous actions of the 'sixties to sick jokes.

If *A Clockwork Orange* was the pessimistic denunciation of the
previous decade, *The Greening of America* was its rosy-fingered
embrace. In the survey, the Yale law professor Charles Reich took
the theory of the inclusion of the radical challenges of recent
years to its ultimate degree. The counter-culture could be
absorbed by the middle classes and used to recover a consciousness of self. There was no sacrifice involved or uncomfortable
reversion to the commune in the wilderness or a savage rejection
of modern times. As Voltaire had suggested in *Candide*, to cultivate one's own back garden was good enough – or to bake bread
or play Bach on the recorder or return to family values. Anyone

might go on working in business or the stock market, as long as he or she were not taken in by the falsity of the Corporate State. Anger and protest alienated the authorities, which would fade out voluntarily when the real self was rediscovered by the citizens of the land. This utopian dream was the same as that of the anarchists of eighty years before, stolen by Marx and Lenin to promise the withering away of the state after the dictatorship of the proletariat.

Future history would prove Reich wrong. Although capitalism could commercialize the counter-culture and absorb its organized protest, it could not contain the savage in human nature. With the growth of violent techniques in civilized governments, with the rising rate of crime in most cities that were surrounded or infiltrated by a brick jungle of slums, savagery had become almost acceptable to urban man, a part of his existence and character to be recognized, if not always praised. As the personal terror of the scale of government grew, as the feeling of helplessness of the individual before the computer and the state increased, so the admiration for the savage augmented. From Hemingway through the Second World War writers to Norman Mailer, the exaltation of the simple barbarian who could slough off civilization and let his passion run wild had found a wide and vicarious audience. In *An American Dream*, Mailer's hero Rojack gave way to every impulse of lust and aggression before leaving towards the jungles of Yucatan, back to the beast. Scorn of civilization was now a literary virtue which would have seemed intolerable to any actual pioneer on the frontier, just as the cult of cruelty in modern drama would have seemed devilish to settlers in Indian territory, longing only for peace in the daily insecurity of their lives. As an American historian, the frontier had long pre-occupied me, the shifting line between the wilderness and the city. Now the barbarian appeared to become urban, and the savage was welcomed within the gate and within us all.

Because of the revolution in technology and modern life, the fear of the savage in western societies was replaced largely by the obsession to recapture him. White men's peyote churches

were founded to join in tribal communion, self-expressive dancing imitated the tribal ceremonies and release mechanisms of
pre-literate peoples. The computer in the skyscraper had begun
to conjure up the same terror of soulless destruction that the
Celts once felt, living on the plains under the daily horror that
the sky would break apart one day and fall on their heads. To
cater for such fears in democracies, the supermarkets began to
stock 'organic' foods and 'natural' cosmetics for the suburban
masses, afraid of chemical poisoning. The ecological balance
became a factor in the political process, although governments
– as Magog noticed – were far happier to talk than to do much.
Toxic wastes were still dumped at sea, nitrates fouled the furrows,
acid rain ate the forests, dolphins died in the long killing nets
with the tuna – and yet prevention lagged far behind prolifer-
ation. It was the same tragedy with the spread of nuclear and
biological weapons. Ecology and the conservation of energy
and of the earth were the sops to the green dream within the
counter-culture, but they were swallowed when economics and
strategy dictated that food and heat and goods and defence must
come before ancient nostalgias.

Long ago, the melting-pot of the immigrants had appeared
the solution for the conflicts in American life. The suburb was the
compromise between city and country, the naturalized American
and intermarriage was the solution between native and immi-
grant, mass education was the meeting-point between a barbaric
and an élite culture. Yet when one side picks up arms, so will the
other; when one side commits atrocities, so will the other. The
advocates of Black Power, for instance, stated that the blacks
should arm themselves against all whites because some whites
acted like savages towards blacks. It had been the solution of the
western whites such as Hugh Henry Brackenridge, who used to
advocate harsh treatment for 'the animals, vulgarly called Indians'; it is still the solution of the men who classify many sheep
with a few goats in order to shear the whole herd to their own
advantage. It is also a solution which runs counter to the full
course of American history, which, although often bloody and

racist, has moved inexorably towards the absorption of the classes and the immigrants in one bourgeois whole, as was the hope of *The Greening of America.*

American man was now an urban man and he had recently been a rural man. It would be strange if the psychological shock of trying to find streets as natural as fields or woods had not provoked savage explosions in the cities. Claude Brown's brilliant examination of Harlem, *Manchild in the Promised Land,* showed just how much of the black ghetto's barbarism came from the sudden transplantation of sharecroppers from shacks to tenements. Robert Kennedy was using more than a politician's rhetoric when he stated before his murder: 'We confront an urban wilderness more formidable and resistant and in some ways more frightening than the wilderness faced by the Pilgrims or the pioneers.' Oscar Lewis was showing more than an anthropologist's concern when he demonstrated how the two cultures of riches and poverty, suburb and slum, privilege and *barrio* in the large cities of the Americas were doomed to misunderstanding, friction and violence in the crooked streets of their encounters.

In most of the northern hemisphere, the frontier was moving from the wild to the slums. With more than half of the population of the industrial nations now living in the cities, with the villages of the under-developed world emptying for the doubtful opportunities of the shanty-town, fear of attack had shifted to the corridors from the forests, to the elevator shafts from the trees. *A Clockwork Orange* was the expression of the current nightmare of urban violence, but the governments of the western world appeared to have contained that assault through appeasing mass outbreaks by entertainment and social services, in the same way that circuses and bread had been fed to the Roman mob. In my Nash terrace in Regent's Park, I wrote about these tactics which I now understood: I made my house Magog's home. From the royal park where they were sleeping rough, I invited some of the surviving hippies to live in my basement, and one of them called Nigel remained with me after the rest had left with most of my sheets and money. He finally told me what the working class really thought, after he put down Ken Tynan at a dinner that I was giving for William Golding. In one of his apocalyptic moods, the dandy Tynan was upholding the vision of Chairman Mao and claiming that in the rotten British state, all the workers would rather be Chinese peasants. It was too much for Nigel, who rose and said that he was the only worker among us all, and that all his mates wanted to be middle class like us. Tynan was fazed and left asking why I was living with a skinhead.

Actually, Nigel was living in my house and looking after me while I was making my only good film, *Under Milk Wood*. That was a utopian version of village life, indeed, that satisfied the nostalgia of the hippies and *The Greening of America* for the rich and simple life. The making of it was unlikely, if not incredible. I had done the play version of Dylan Thomas's novel *Adventures in the Skin Trade*, I had the money to put down for the film option on the Welsh poet's great work, and still I believed in Murphy's Law, that if the impossible always happened, at least it might on this project which mattered so much to me.

At times, the luck of setting up the film exceeded incredulity and vanished into Celtic mist. Like a necromancer juggling the elements, any Merlin of the screen has to mix the gold of the backers with the stars in their courses and come up with a horoscope that guarantees fair heavens and a safe return. To go at all, *Under Milk Wood* had to find a time when Richard Burton, Elizabeth Taylor and Peter O'Toole were all available to work and in this island, which was rather like fixing a weekend between Howard Hughes, Elizabeth the Second and Puck. Then the gold had to be conjured in double-quick time from the state and a merchant bank, both of whom were foolish enough to buck the wisdom of Wardour Street and think there could be profit as well as art in the wild warm words of that people's poet, Dylan Thomas. Then there had to be hayfield sun in March in Fishguard, which would be a blessing not seen in thirty years. ('Wales in winter!' said the drenched warriors streaming home from Polanski's protracted *Macbeth*. 'Jesus! Not only did Banquo blow off his horse, but the bloody horse blew away too.') Then we had

a forty days' budget about as fat as Our Lord's when he had the
same schedule in the wilderness. What with sixty sets and seventy
actors, we had to spend a quarter of our time just shifting from
scene to scene; we shot on the run, with the mighty heroes of
Lee Electrics humping the hundredweight brute lights as casually
as kittens on their shoulders. Everything and everyone had to
work too well, beyond normal and half-way to dream. The technicians would mutter about 'Andrew the Luck.' And I would
answer, 'Miracles happen daily.' Frankly they had to, so they did.

Under Milk Wood was selected in 1971 to open the Venice Film
Festival. It was a compromise between the Left and the Right. It
was about peasant life, but it displayed three of the greater stars
in the world, Burton and O'Toole and Taylor. With the publication of the novel of *Magog* that year, it was to be the apparent
apogee of my creative career. The tide and the breaker had come
in for me. And yet what I was achieving was a rock pool compared
to the seas of work of the four British writers and artists whom I
knew and revered for their descriptions of life in our and all time
– illuminations which proved that the experience of a decade or
the analysis of a period were shallows beside the surge of the
artist.

Harold Pinter was my neighbour in Hanover Terrace, and I had
put his wife Vivien Merchant in my film, where she played Mrs.
Pugh to the harsh housewife made. At the time, he was writing
No Man's Land which, I realized much later, when I saw him
playing the lead in it, was about the isolation of fame. The hero,
indeed, lives in a park attended by a strange duo, very like my
friend Nigel and the duenna, here translated to a butler, who
looked after me. Pinter solved the problem which I had always
had of acknowledging the words which he had once written and
were now almost forgotten. I visited him with a horror picture
producer, who had also produced the film of Pinter's *The Birthday
Party* in earlier days, when art meant as much as blood. It was an
uneasy meeting, at which, in the producer's words, Pinter was
like 'a flung knife, quivering in the wood of the door'. But he,

acting his words and pauses, recalled a time when the producer had seen the rushes of *The Birthday Party* and had begun to ask, 'Isn't that the scene when . . .?' And Pinter had interrupted. 'I said – or rather – I was heard to say – I know – I wrote it.'

I know, I wrote it. Neither Descartes nor Beckett ever made more conclusive a statement. For me, the pictures of Francis Bacon were as definitive of the century as any prose. His first retrospective exhibition at the Tate Gallery, in 1962, was to me what he also described it as – a history of the past thirty years. His language formed our way of seeing, as the director of the Tate, John Rothenstein, observed in his introduction to the catalogue: 'Bacon's contemporaries belong to generations that have seen the destruction of cities by bomb, the flight of whole peoples under the lash of fear, the concentration camps, the death camps and the rest. His power of making human anguish dramatically significant to our generation is due in part to the dignity and the sobriety of his treatment of all his subjects, however horrible . . . However extraordinary the image of Bacon, it speaks to us intimately because it speaks a language familiar to us all; a language which, more than any other factor, has formed our way of seeing.' I agreed absolutely at that exhibition. And although I had only met Bacon sporadically in Soho and Limehouse, where he was to buy a studio built from the bombed houses on the river in Narrow Street, his vision in his art in the 'sixties and later his view of life was to confirm my own: a certain exhilarated despair, the wish to live life intensely as if each day were the last. When we talked more later, we found we shared the same interest in Greek drama and in one particular line of Aeschylus, 'The reek of blood smiles out of him.'

During the 'seventies, William Golding had largely stopped writing, until he recovered that inspiration which led to his later superb works and the Nobel Prize. He would stay with me almost every year, and I would give a dinner for him, always believing that he was the greatest novelist of our age. After one of these dinners, he saw the devil in the middle of the night and tore apart a foam dummy of the singer Bob Dylan, which I had bought as an ikon of the times, and which he condemned as an idol out of hell. His matter was always the struggle between the divine and the base, original sin and free will, the glory and the mud, the spirit and nature. It was also the matter of Ted Hughes, who retired to isolation on a sheep farm in north Devon, misjudged for the suicide of his two wives merely from the intensity of his passion for them. Seeing him rarely, I could only watch a Heathcliff come again, a demonic and compelling figure doomed forever to be at odds with the judgement of this world.

The genius of these four creators with their great influence upon me denied the temper of the age. Their work was both contemporary and timeless, and it made historical analysis useless. They suggested that the personal lives of artists were more important than public affairs because the detritus of the past would salvage their works and not those of the rulers and the statesmen, who were held to be significant. What was admirable in that disparate quartet was their fierce retirement from cliques of opinion, their original opinion in defiance of current trend, the incandescence of their inner vision which they imposed upon millions of readers and seers as an insight into the human condition. These were the very few in our time who stated: I AM AN ARTIST. THIS IS WHAT I THINK AND SEE. I DO, THEREFORE WE ARE. As this book goes to press, the death of William Golding from natural causes afflicts us all. We both loved the classics, and this is an epitaph. *Sic transit Golding mundi.* Ted Hughes read from *The Inheritors* at his memorial service at Salisbury Cathedral, as if Golding had in that novel and in *The Spire* discovered in truth the secret of the fall of man.

As a lesser artist myself, who happened to be a social historian, I suppose the times taught me how impossible it was to describe them, and except for the admirable Thucydides, all historical writing was a form of autobiography, at least a revelation of the current prejudices which informed the writer. I have tried to express this thinking by interweaving social history with my life in these years. Occasionally, and often unwillingly, we do find ourselves briefly a part of what has gone by. And at the end of these thousands of days, what was the result of my incoherent performance? Growing, because I could not avoid it. Feeling more, which was equally inevitable. Becoming a flash of the past in William Blake's terms, when he claimed that eternity was in a grain of sand – and so suggested that the doings of each of us might contribute to some moments which might endure in the smallest of ways. Taking some responsibility, because of the needs of the few I loved. And above all, surviving the cruel disillusion of fifteen years into a surmise that if most actions were useless, some printed words and graven images might cause many people to consider and to do – to make a difference.

We can only be a shallow inlet in the ocean of history, but we are accountable to it. Few of us wish to be. But when history impinges on us – a threatened invasion of our land, the moral choice of betraying a country or a friend – we cannot avoid what to do. We have coasted through the past most of our lives, but sometimes we have been in the rapids. We discuss our times, but then we are plunged into them. Social history is a million million biographies of different lives. What happened to each one of us individually may have affected some or many of us. In the little may lie the large.

Notes

1 Philip Larkin wrote his letter to Judy Egerton on 28 November 1959 (see the *Selected Letters of Philip Larkin, 1940–1985*, ed. Anthony Thwaite, London, 1992). Blake Morrison stressed the coherence and importance of *The Movement: English Poetry and Fiction of the 1950s* (Oxford, 1980). *My Oxford, My Cambridge: Memories of University Life by Twenty-four Distinguished Graduates* (ed. and introd. Ann Thwaite and Ronald Hayman) was published in London in 1977. *Declaration*, edited by Tom Maschler, was published in London in 1957. The *London Magazine* asked its questions on Commitment and published the answers in May 1957. *Conviction*, edited by Norman Mackenzie, was published in London in 1958.

2 Donald Davie wrote on F. R. Leavis in *My Oxford, My Cambridge*, work cited; Karl Miller and John Vaizey were also contributors. Trevor Nunn talked to Janet Watts in the *Observer Magazine*, 20 October 1982. I have written previously about the Apostles and the physicists at Cambridge in *The Red and the Blue: Intelligence, Treason and the Universities* (London, 1986). Bamber Gascoigne's comments on the Cambridge satirists come from the preface to Roger Wilmut's *From Fringe to Flying Circus* (London, 1980). Harold Macmillan's words on *That Was The Week That Was* were reported in *The Sunday Times*, 17 January 1993. *All Bull: The National Servicemen* (ed. B. S. Johnson) was published in London in 1973. Richard Hamilton is quoted from the catalogue to his retrospective exhibition at the Tate Gallery in 1970.

3   I bought Lawrence Ferlinghetti's undated pamphlet *Tentative Description of a Dinner Given to Promote the Impeachment of President Eisenhower* at his City Lights Bookshop in the summer of 1960 as I did Bob Kaufman's poem on HOLLYWOOD 59 from the ephemeral *San Francisco Supplement.* Norman Podhoretz's article 'The Know-Nothing Bohemians' was printed in the *Partisan Review,* Spring 1958. My novel *The Hallelujah Bum* was published in London in 1963. I also wrote on Pop Art in *The Need to Give: The Patrons And The Arts* (Sinclair-Stevenson, London, 1990); John McHale wrote the comment on art as a lifestyle in *The Machine, As Seen At The End Of The Mechanical Age* (New York, 1968). George Melly's *Revolt into Style: The Pop Arts in Britain* was published in London in 1970. Allen Ginsberg's poem 'Howl' was published with other poems of his in San Francisco in 1959. I wrote 'A Head for Monsieur Dimanche' for the *Atlantic Monthly,* September 1962.

4   John Osborne's 'Letter To My Fellow Countrymen' was printed in *Tribune,* 18 August 1961. The second volume of his memoirs, *Almost a Gentleman,* was published in London in 1951. C. P. Snow wrote on 'The Moral Un-Neutrality of Science' in 1960, reprinted in *Public Affairs* (London, 1971). Michael Yudkin's criticism of Snow's 'Two Cultures' appeared in F. R. Leavis and Michael Yudkin, *Two Cultures? The Significance of C. P. Snow* (London, 1962). C. P. Snow's *The Two Cultures: and a Second Look* was published in Cambridge in 1964. James D. Watson wrote on *The Double Helix* (London, 1968). Peter Medawar wrote on *The Limits of Science* (Oxford, 1985). T. S. Eliot's *Notes towards a Definition of Culture* was published in London in 1948.

5   Margaret Drabble talked to me personally about her feelings over Suez and Hungary. *Timothy: The Drawings and Cartoons of Timothy Birdsall,* edited by Michael Frayn and Bamber Gascoigne, was published in London in 1964. Bryan Appleyard wrote on 'What Were You Doing When The World Nearly Ended?' in *The Times Saturday Review*, 10 October 1992. Jeff Nuttall, *Bomb Culture*, was published in London in 1968. Bernard Levin's eulogy of Hugh Gaitskell was printed in *That Was The Week That Was* (ed. David Frost and Ned Sherrin, London, 1963). I have already written on the death of literary Soho in *War Like a Wasp: The Lost Decade of the 'Forties'* (London, 1989). Robert Harrison, *In Anger: Culture in the Cold War 1945–1960* (London, 1981), refers to George Barker's comments on the bad prospects of young poets. George Melly told me about Lucian Freud.

The connection between American folk and protest music and early jazz and pop music in Britain is brought out well in Robin Denselow's *When The Music's Over: The Story of Political Pop* (London, 1989). George Melly's *Revolt into Style*, work cited, and introduction to Daniel Farson, *Soho in the 'Fifties* (London, 1989), tell of the early jazz scene from his own experience. John Platt, *London's Rock Routes* (London, 1985), reminded me of where I had been, while the quotation from Andrew Oldham was taken from A. E. Hotchner, *Blown Away: The Rolling Stones and the Death of the 'Sixties* (London, 1990). Philip Larkin, *All What Jazz: A Record Diary 1961–1971* (rev. ed., London, 1985), contains his introduction on jazz.

The Dickinson poem is taken from *The Complete Poems of Emily Dickinson* (Boston, 1951). Angela Carter wrote in *Very Heaven: Looking Back at the 1960s* (Sara Maitland ed., London, 1988). The issue of the *Situationist International* was undated, circa 1963. George Steiner wrote on the Situationists in the *Sunday Times* in 1967. Ferlinghetti's poem 'Adieu à Charlot (Second Populist Manifesto)' was published in *Endless Life: Selected Poems* (New Directions, New York, 1981). T. R. Fyvel's *Intellectuals Today: Problems in a Changing Society* was published in 1968 in London.

6   *A Tribute to John F. Kennedy* (Pierre Salinger and Sander Vanocur eds., Chicago, 1964) was a testament to the true feeling of its time. Michael McClure's *Scratching the Beat Surface* was published in San Francisco in 1982. Kenneth Rexroth's essay on 'The New American Poets' was printed twice, in his *The Alternative Society* (New York, 1965) and in the *Rexroth Reader* (Eric Mottram ed., London, 1972). Timothy Leary made his speech on his League for Spiritual Discovery in Los Angeles, where it was reported by the *Free Press*, 13 January 1967.

7   A. Alvarez wrote in his letter from New York, 'American After-thoughts', in *Encounter*, June 1965. *Wholly Communion*, in which the poems of Ferlinghetti and Mitchell appeared, was published by Peter Whitehead in London in 1965. Jeff Nuttall's novel, *Snipe's Spinster*, was published by John Calder and Marion Boyars in London in 1975. Lord Goodman's speech at the Guildhall was reported by the Institute of Municipal Entertainment in March 1969, while his pessimism about the young in art was recorded in his *Not for the Record: Selected Speeches and Writings* (London, 1972). Clive James wrote a letter to *Oz* 15, which was published approximately monthly in 1968. Richard Neville's important *Play Power* was published in London in 1970. Jim Haynes, *Thanks for Coming!*, was published in London in 1984. Tom Wolfe reported on Ken Kesey's Merry Pranksters in *The Electric Kool-Aid Acid Test*, work already cited, as is Robin Denselow, *When the Music's Over*, who is excellent on the change of Bob Dylan from political protest to inner movement. George Melly wrote on pop music in 1967 in his superlative *Revolt into Style* (London, 1970). Thom Gunn and Norman Mailer appeared in the special issue on 'Violence' in *20th Century*, Winter 1964–5. Robert Hewison, *Too Much: Art and Society in the Sixties 1960–75* (London, 1986), remains a superb chronicler of those times. My novel *Magog* was published in London in 1972, while Brian Patten's poem 'Party-goers' was printed in the remarkable anthology number of *New Departures* 7/8 and 10/11 (Michael Horowitz ed., London, 1975).

8   My version of *Adventures in the Skin Trade* was published in London and New York in 1969. Lorrimer Publishing printed *Blow-Up* with an introduction by Michelangelo Antonioni in 1969. Timothy Leary wrote in *Open City*, Number Seven, 16–22 June 1967, which also printed a version of the lyric 'Heroin', performed by Velvet Underground and Nico, and the call to action on V.D. in Los Angeles. The S.D.S. Convention was reported by the correspondent for *Indian Head*, Vol. 1, No. 2, 21 July 1967; in the same issue, Dave Goggin saw the decline of a trend in 'Hippies: Free Way or Freeway'. The issue of *Avatar* with the interview with Robert Kennedy and the 'Haight-Hate' piece was published in Boston, 18–31 August 1967.

William Golding's essay on 'The English Channel' was printed in *The Hot Gates and Other Occasional Pieces* (London, 1965). I wrote on 'William Golding's *The Sea, The Sea*' in *Twentieth Century Literature*, Vol. 28, No. 2, Summer 1982, published by Hofstra University Press, New York. As a general and sympathetic but impartial summary, David Caute's *Sixty-Eight: The Year of the Barricades* (London, 1988) cannot be bettered, and I am indebted to its insights into a swirling and hysterical situation. Drusilla Beyfus, *The English Marriage*, was published in 1968 in London.

9   I have mentioned Jeff Nuttall's important contemporary work, *Bomb Culture*. Pete Brown wrote 'Pop and the Big Reaction' in *Albion*, No. 1, May 1968. Herbert Marcuse, *An Essay on Liberation*, was published in New York in 1969. David Caute's work on *Sixty-Eight* remains significant, while Alexander Trocchi's 'Invisible insurrection of a million minds' was published in the *Situationist International* in 1962 in Britain. The screenplay of Lindsay Anderson and David Sherwin, *If*, was published in London in 1969. Robert Jay Lifton's article 'Assassination: The Ultimate Public Theater' was printed in the *New York Times* in 1990 and reprinted in the programme of Stephen Sondheim's

Assassins, which opened at the Donmar Warehouse in London on 22 October 1992.

10   Stephen Spender wrote about his experiences at Columbia University and in Paris in *The Year of the Young Rebels* (London, 1969). Peter Whitehead wrote to me from New York on 2 May 1968. Of the many works I have used to supplement my memories of Paris in May 1968, I have found the most invaluable: *L'Imagination au Pouvoir* (Paris, 1968) by Walter Lewino and Jo Schnapp; *L'Événement,* July-August 1968; *Combats étudiants dans le monde* (Paris, 1968); *Edition Spécial, 'Ce N'est Qu'un Début'* (Paris, 1968) by Philippe Labro and collaborators; *Mai 1968: La Brèche* (Paris, 1968) by Edgar Morin, Claude Lefort and Jean-Marc Coudray; *La Révolte Étudiante: Les Animateurs Parlent* (Paris, 1968) featuring J. Sauvageot, A. Geismar, D. Cohn-Bendit and J.-P. Duteuil; *Un Mois de Mai Orageux: 113 Étudiants Parlent* (Paris, 1968); *1968, A Personal Report* (London, 1988) by Hans König; and the generally excellent *Sixty-Eight* by David Caute, work cited.
    John Osborne spoke to Kenneth Tynan on 7 July 1968; the interview was printed in the *Observer.* Useful commentaries on Régis Debray, *Revolution in the Revolution?* (Paris, 1967), can be found in the essays in *Régis Debray and the Latin American Revolution* (L. Huberman and P. M. Sweezy eds., New York, 1968). Peter Buckman wrote his article, 'The State of American Protest' for *Oz* 15, Autumn 1968; this issue also printed an approximate version of the Jagger lyrics for 'Street Fighting Man'. *The Times* lost its nerve about the Vietnam demonstration on 27 October 1968. Tariq Ali, *Street Fighting Years: An Autobiography of the 'Sixties,* was published in 1987 in London.

11   Jim Haynes wrote about the end of the 'sixties in *Thanks for Coming!,* work cited. Huey Newton was widely reported on the demise of the Black Panthers in 1971. *Oz* 17, Winter

1968, published 'Ho! Ho! Ho Chi Mall' and David
Widgery's view of the radical future, quoting Peter
Sedgwick on the necessity of anarchism as the forerunner
of the Marxist revolution. Lorrimer Publishing printed *Viva
Che* in London in 1969 with all the quoted pieces by John
Berger and Nicolas Guillen and Adrian Mitchell. My
Modern Masters book with Marianne Alexandre Sinclair
on *Che Guevara* was published in London and world-wide
in 1970, and *Bolivian Diary* by Che Guevara by Lorrimer
Publishing in 1968. *Twentieth Century*, Vol. CLXXVII, No.
1038, Third/1968, published my piece on *Bolivian Diary*.
Robert Nisbet wrote on the self-love of the young in the
'fifties and 'sixties in *Encounter* in 1972. Nigel Young, *An
Infantile Disorder?: The Crisis and Decline of the New Left*, was
published in London in 1977.

12   Marcia Williams, Lady Falkender, wrote her reminiscences
of the Harold Wilson administration in *Inside Number 10*
(London, 1972). *The Wilson Plot: The Intelligence Services and
the Discrediting of a Prime Minister* by David Leigh, published
in London in 1988, covers the attack of various security
services on Harold Wilson. C. P. Snow's lectures for the
John Findley Green Foundation were printed on a
pamphlet under the title of 'The State of Siege' in Oxford
in 1970. *Timon of Athens* was written by William
Shakespeare, as always the scalpel into the soft gut of our
times. Of course, he wrote *Hamlet*, too, which ended with
obtuse Fortinbras. Christopher Booker's stringent series
of pieces, *The Seventies: Portrait of a Decade* (London, 1980),
remains compelling reading, while Malcolm Bradbury's
collection of articles *All Dressed Up and Nowhere To Go*
(London, 1962) shows what an ironic prophet he was.

14   My novel *Magog* was published in London and New York
in 1972. Noel Annan, *Our Age: Portrait of a Generation*, was
published in London in 1990. Christie Davies' work on
Permissive Britain: Social Change in the Sixties and Seventies

was published in London in 1975. Roger Hutchinson, *High Sixties: The Summers of Riot and Love* (London, 1992), gives a shrewd insider's picture of the underground press, as does Nigel Fountain, *Underground: The London Alternative Press 1966–74* (London and New York, 1988). Peter York's brilliant and patchy *Style Wars* dates from London, 1980, while Richard Neville's important *Play Power* has already been cited.

15   Pete Townshend of The Who is quoted in Robin Denselow's *When the Music's Over: The Story of Political Pop*, work already cited. Charles Osborne published *Giving It Away: The Memoirs of an Uncivil Servant* in London in 1986. George Melly, *Revolt into Style*, has already been mentioned. David Mellor published *The Sixties Art Scene in London* to coincide with an exhibition held at the Barbican Art Gallery in that city from 11 March–13 June 1993, and his commentary is quoted. The film of *The Breaking of Bumbo* and my new introduction to the novel were made in 1970.

End- *King Ludd* was printed in London in 1988 and in New York
piece in 1993. *A Clockwork Orange* was released in England in January 1972, when the anonymous review of the film in *Ink* appeared. Charles Reich, *The Greening of America*, was published in New York in 1970. The film of *Under Milk Wood* opened the Venice Film Festival in July 1971. John Rothenstein's introduction to the catalogue of Francis Bacon's retrospective at the Tate Gallery was printed in May 1962.